SOCIAL & BEHAVIORAL SCIENCES   *Sociology*

30-1806   HT687   91-12907 CIP

Hidden technocrats: the new class and new capitalism, [ed.] by Hansfried Kellner
and Frank W. Heuberger. Transaction, 1992. 246p bibl index   ISBN 0-88738-443-9,
$29.95

These seven integrated essays by American and European sociologists, resulting from a three-year
research project, develop the political and cultural differences between the old middle class based on
traditional professions (engineering, law, medicine, management), having narrowly and clearly defined
expertise and a Cartesian faith in scientific rationality, and a new "floating" middle class of wider skills,
based on the "softer" knowledge industries. This new class is embodied in therapy, human resource
skills, planning, and life-style engineering, where competing and often conflicting theories and
approaches characterize a broadly defined area of interest that lacks precise methodologies and tends to
manipulate images and identities. Modern capitalism has proved resilient because it recognized the
need for this new intellectual service sector, a chief function of which is to facilitate the acceptance by
society of massive technological change. The process by which this occurs and the nature of this sector
as a truly new class, or a power elite, or simply another professional category, remain for time and
research to determine. More analytical and cohesive than *The New Class?* by Robert L. Bartley et al.
(CH, Sep'79). Bibliography and index are useful; style is occasionally pedantic. Advanced undergradu-
ate; graduate; faculty.—*R. E. Will, Carleton College*

HIDDEN TECHNOCRATS

HIDDEN TECHNOCRATS

The New Class and New Capitalism

Hansfried Kellner
Frank W. Heuberger

with a foreword by
Peter L. Berger

Transaction Publishers
New Brunswick (U.S.A.) and London (U.K.)

Library of Congress Catalog Number: 91-12907
ISBN: 0-88738-443-9
Printed in the United States of America

Library of Congress Cataloging-in-Publication Data

Hidden technocrats : the new class and new capitalism / [edited by]
    Hansfried Kellner and Frank W. Heuberger
      p.   cm.
    Includes bibliographical references and index.
    ISBN 0-898738-443-9
    1. Middle classes. 2. Technocracy. 3. Professions.
    4. Capitalism. I. Kellner, Hansfried. II. Heuberger, Frank W.
    HT687.H5 1991
    305.5'5--dc20   91-12907
                                                             CIP

A Book from the Institute for the Study of Economic Culture at
Boston University

Contents

v

Foreword

The present volume contains the results of a research project conducted under the auspices of the Institute for the Study of Economic Culture at Boston University, under the direction of Hansfried Kellner and Frank W. Heuberger of the Johann Wolfgang Goethe University of Frankfurt. The project brought together an unusually competent and lively group. Over the period of the project, from 1987 through 1989, the whole group met for face-to-face workshops three times, but there was a lot of informal communication between the members throughout. It would be an exaggeration to say that a common viewpoint was arrived at within the group, but there was an increasing agreement on what questions were to be addressed and how the emerging evidence related to these questions. Perhaps the most interesting observation to be made about the project is that its results surprised all of us. To the extent that science (social or otherwise) manifests itself by a propensity to disappoint the expectations of its practitioners, the present project can confidently be proclaimed to have been a scientific enterprise.

The project was first conceived in terms of the so-called New Class *problematique* as it has originally been formulated in the United States in the 1970s and intermittently since then. The vision here was a new middle class, based on the "knowledge industry," pitted against the old business-based middle class both politically and culturally.

What was intriguing about the early American discussion of this matter was that the idea of a New Class had both right-of-center and left-of-center proponents (such as, respectively, Irvin Kristol and Alvin Gouldner). They differed sharply in their *evaluation* of the alleged phenomenon (what for Kristol was very bad news was for Gouldner the last best hope of the long-awaited revolution), but they agreed in their *empirical assumptions,* to wit, that there existed in fact such a new stratum and that it had specific characteristics that put it in opposition to the middle class. Unfortunately this very interesting discussion petered out fairly quickly, and there has been a dearth of empirical data to test the assumptions about the putative phenomenon.

The institute, in one of it's first projects, sponsored a reanalysis of American survey data with a bearing on the New Class hypothesis.

This analysis, undertaken by John McAdams, a political scientist at Marquette University, did indeed provide support for the hypothesis. Unfortunately, for a number of intellectually irrelevant reasons, this material has not as yet been published. We then thought of doing a similar analysis of survey data from Western Europe, decided against it in the expectation that the findings would not differ significantly from the American ones and, consequently, came up with the idea of moving into a more qualitative analysis. The result was this project, which was to explore major themes in the assumed New Class culture in five countries—the United States, Britain, Holland, West Germany, and Italy; in the case of the last of these, we focused on an area in the south of the country, to see how the phenomenon manifested itself in what is still an economically underdeveloped region. On one level it may be said that the project did indeed realize the original intentions. But, on a more interesting level, it brought to the surface completely unanticipated results, first perceived by Kellner, and then (after much discussion and some resistance) by the whole group.

These unforeseen results do not exactly contradict the earlier conceptualization of two middle classes arrayed against each other in advanced industrial capitalism. There are indeed both political and cultural conflicts between these two strata. The perspective emerging from the present project, however, differs from the earlier view of the phenomenon in that it shows, over and beyond the continuing conflicts, a *symbiosis in the making*—a new constellation of values and behavior pattern that combine *both* traits of the old bourgeois culture *and* new culture themes clearly identified with the New Class. In other words, we came, unexpectedly, upon what looks like a "historic compromise" between significant sectors of the two classes. It is thus at least possible that there may be not just a New Class but a New Capitalism. It could be described in different ways—"kinder," "gentler," "sensitized," even "feminized"—and these characteristics could have either an approving or a pejorative undertone (a more humanitarian capitalism, or a capitalism gone soft in the head). We do not for a moment claim that this project has conclusively demonstrated this symbiosis. It is very possible that our choice of groups to be investigated biased the findings and that we have in consequence exaggerated the importance of some fairly marginal phenomena (that was McAdam's criticism). It is also possible, though, that we have stumbled on a strategically important change in the ideology and the social psychology of contemporary capitalism in the "North Atlantic" area. Much remains to be done, both in that geographical area and beyond (notably in East Asia).

One of the most important questions to be addressed is whether, if such a new capitalism does indeed exist in the West, will it favor or diminish the international competitiveness of the economies in which it has come to the fore.

The Institute for the Study of Economic Culture at Boston University is a research center, founded in 1985, for the study of relations between culture and economic processes. The present project was supported by grants from the Lynde and Harry Bradley Foundation, the John M. Olin Foundation, and the Sarah Scaife Foundation.

I would like to take this occasion to express my gratitude for their generous support of the work of the Institute and for the personal interest shown from the beginning, notably by Michael Joyce and Hillel Fradkin (Bradley), James Piereson (Olin), and Richard Larry (Scaife).

With the exception of Tracy Fessenden all the authors are sociologists, a fact that undoubtedly helped in establishing a common universe of discourse. Their academic affiliations are as follows: Hansfried Kellner, Goethe University of Frankfurt; Frank Heuberger, formerly of the Goethe University of Frankfurt, currently at Boston University; Anton Bevers, University of Tilburg; Anton Zijderveld,

Erasmus University (Rotterdam); Bernice Martin, University of London; James Hunter, University of Virginia; Paolo Jedlowski, University of Calabria. Tracy Fessenden is a graduate student in religion and literature at the University of Virginia; in addition to coauthoring the paper with James Hunter, she provided invaluable editorial services in preparing the paper for publication. Cara Lea Shockley, administrator at the Institute, also provided important help in the editing and production of the manuscript.

The structure of this volume is of an elegant simplicity. In an opening chapter, Heuberger discusses the course and the antecedent of what (somewhat grandiloquently) has been called "New Class Theory" (it hasn't really been that much of a theory); he also points to the dimensions that has been mostly neglected in the literature, namely the cognitive dimension or, if one prefers, the dimension of consciousness. Most of the rest of this book contains reports on and the discussions of the original findings of the research project. Kellner and Heuberger, in West Germany, studied business consultants in the "soft" areas of management—corporate image, interpersonal relations, and the like. It is this particular study that first adumbrated the main surprise of the project, the curious symbiosis between an older business culture and themes derived from the cultural transformation that began in the 1960s. The following three papers, again surprisingly, generally support this new angle on the phenomenon. Bevers and Zijderveld, in Holland, studied art managers (an ominous oxymoron is already contained in that phrase). Martin, in Britain, studied qualitative market researchers. And Hunter and Fessenden, in the American segment of the project, studied various activists whom they subsume (perhaps with a slightly ironic twist) under the category of "moral entrepreneurs." The Italian study, by Jedlowski, dealt with New Class professionals in a situation in which the *old* middle class, at least in a modern sense, barely exists. The situation might be compared to, say, Third World regions where the favored mode of transportation jumps from animal drawn vehicles to airplanes, skipping the in-between of railways that played such an important role in an earlier period of modernization. In the first chapter, Kellner and I tried to engage in some broader theoretical reflections about these new professions of "life-style engineering." In no way was it our intention here to summarize the group's findings or to say the last world about their implications. As happens so often in the field of social sciences, whatever answers we stumbled on raise new questions. Very much remains to be done.

PETER L. BERGER,
Director Institute for the Study of Economic Culture,
Boston University

1

Life-style Engineering: Some Theoretical Reflections

Hansfried Kellner and Peter L. Berger

This volume focuses on a curiously ambiguous group of occupations. On the one hand, these are considered, or are trying hard to be considered, "professions"—a term that has a fairly hoary history in Western culture, still carrying with it (despite some recent debunking) the aura of privileged knowledge and status of priest, jurist, and physician. On the other hand, these are new occupations, their bodies of knowledge often undefined and their claims to authority disputed. They are the occupations that have been variously defined as consisting of people in the "knowledge industry," as technocrats dealing with the production and distribution of nonmaterial goods or services, as the "new clerisy," or even as, *tout court*, the new intelligentsia (or pseudo-intelligentsia, by those who disliked them). Helmut Schelsky, who still called these people "intellectuals," described them as occupied with *Belehrung, Betreuung, Beplanung* (the German alliteration is untranslatable)—

that is, engaged in education and communication, in various forms of therapy, and in "planification." One of the characteristics of these new occupations is that they claim expertise in areas of life that were previously outside the jurisdiction of any profession, areas that may loosely be described as pertaining to the "life-styles" of individuals. The new occupations, or would-be professions, apply an essentially technocratic mentality to aspects of human life that are intrinsically resistant to this type of rationalization. This is why we use here the shorthand (and, admittedly, imperfect) term "life-style engineering" to describe their activity.

It is important to understand the deeply grounded differences between the old and the new professions. The expertise of the long established professions was rooted in the mastery and management of a clearly defined body of knowledge, with an intrinsic logic applied to each situation in which the professional's services were called upon. For example, a physician can relate his work to a long tradition of validated knowledge, with its own logic (an expression of modern scientific rationality) putatively grounded in the inherent logic of the human body. Similarly, a lawyer or an (old type) engineer can call upon a clearly formalized and codified body of knowledge, in each case dominated by a logic of its own. The individuals exercising these professions can apply the respective bodies of knowledge "logically" (that is, by the intrinsic logic of the profession) through an equally formalized and codified body of instrumental procedures—their "bag of professional tricks," if you will (in the case of the old style physician, literally so). These individuals, in their professional capacity, both think and act qua representatives of the respective professions; indeed, as a number of studies in the sociology of professions have shown, a good deal of professional training is concerned with the socialization of the neophyte into the proper professional role ("bedside manner" and all). Now, what must be further stressed is that the old professions in their modern form (that is, leaving aside what their predecessors were and did in premodern times) embodied a rational understanding of the world and the implementation of rational means of dealing with the world. That is, these profession were "carriers" (*Träger* in Max Weber's sense) of modern rationality (Weber would say, "functional rationality"). Thus the modern physician and the modern engineer, each in his own way, have long been representative of scientific rationality (often in conflict with traditional, "irrational" beliefs and folkways); the modern jurists, too, represent a form of rationality, this one not rooted in natural science but, perhaps even more distinctively modern, in a Cartesian urge to impose a rationally comprehensible order on all aspects of human reality.

The new professions under analysis here are quite different. To be sure, they too perceive themselves as standing within the modern paradigm of rationality (indeed, every conceivable body of knowledge, however crazy, presents itself today as being some sort of "science"). Their activities, though, have taken the new professions into uncharted areas of human life that are not so readily subsumed under this or that generally accepted logic. Take the therapist, or the human resources manager, or the planner for this or that social program. How does one achieve "mental health" and how does one determine that it *has* been achieved? Or a satisfactory "work climate"? Or a situation of greater "social justice," or more adequate "quality of life"? Most of the new professionals have been trained in the social sciences and the humanities, disciplines with subject matters difficult to delineate, very much in flux, and with criteria of validity that are notoriously unreliable (and deeply suspect to the general populace outside the various professional subcultures). The social sciences (let alone the humanities) do not possess unified and unequivocally validated bodies of knowledge, as compared with the natural sciences. Competing and conflicting theories, approaches, and methods exist side by side. Inevitably, the representatives of these disciplines and of the professions based on their alleged validity must face the public with a certain nervousness; in a highly competitive market, these people are forced into a certain "conmanship" as they try to peddle their wares to the public (or, if they can, the government or the corporation).

Moreover, the old professional applied his expertise to a narrowly defined, clearly staked out sphere of reality. The physician could deal professionally with his patient's bodily complaints, but he could relate spontaneously, naturally (that is, *un*professionally), as soon as the patient discussed, say, his marital problems. Similarly demarcated zones of relevance were presided over by the engineer or the lawyer. The new professionals are constantly moving across boundaries, expanding into new territory, disputing jurisdiction with others. Take some of the above-cited goals—"mental health," "work climate," "social justice," "quality of life." Where are the boundaries of these presumed areas of human life? How is one to say what is and what is not relevant to the professional's interest here? The result of this fluidity is what one may call a built-in imperialism in these new professions. Each one is a budding, potentially all-embracing empire. By contrast, the old professions were modest, conservative nation-states, contentedly cultivating the rose gardens within their clearly marked borders. This imperialistic propensity of the new professions, however, has a more serious consequence than the self-aggrandizement of this or that occupational group. To repeat: The new professions, like the old, are carriers of modern functional rationality. But the old professions only sought to rationalize (in Weber's sense of the word) *limited* areas of human life; the new life-style engineering is potentially *without limits*. Consequently, it has the capacity to interfere much more massively in the spontaneous, "natural" processes of everyday human life (if you will, in the "life-world"). The penetration of psychoanalytic, sociological, or political-ideological jargons into the everyday language of people adhering to these rationales gives a vivid sense of what this means. Fortunately, because of various profoundly grounded aspects of human nature, ordinary people (and even people who have been converted to these rationalizing imperialisms) instinctively resist the imposition of an abstract logic on everyday life. Put differently, there are anthropologically given limits to the imperialisms of functional rationality. But, even within these limits, there can be and is a far-reaching invasion of ordinary reality by the rationales administered by the new professionals. The effect of this is diminished by the fact that the latter compete with each other, at least in Western capitalist democracies. If any single rationale, and the profession embodying it, would succeed in establishing a monopoly, social reality would be seriously threatened with petrification, and then, in Isaiah Berlin's words, "life would be taken out of social life." Precisely this, of course, is one way of defining and describing a modern totalitarian society: "Grey theory" (Goethe) rules everywhere.

Some of the new professions are, still, very much oriented toward the private lives of individuals, even if they employ public institutions (especially those of the welfare state) to fund and purvey their services. This, for example, continues to be so with many therapeutic activities. But with the development of modern megastructures, both in the economy and the government, the new professions are increasingly called upon to help with the efficient functioning of these institutions of the public sphere. Often they actually design and then help implement rational procedures for these institutions, not just technically in the narrower sense (say, "How can we most efficiently market this product?"), but in the sense of "human capital" ("how can we retain the loyalty of our employees?") and public relations ("What should be our corporate image?"). Here, of course, the old technocracy (of production, distribution, administration, financing, and the like) merge with the new (of the manipulation of the images and identities). The new professionals also function to contain and repair disturbances in the smooth functioning of these highly complex organizations; these are the functions, in Parsonian language, of "system maintenance" and "maintenance repair." Here, of course, the new professionals' alleged expertise in human behavior and motivation is called into play. Finally, the new professionals (especially those coming out of the social sciences) are expected to be alert to changes in the external social, political, and cultural environment of these organizations, in such a way that the latter will be able to adapt to and even profit from these changes. These functions can be fulfilled regardless of whether the professional is directly employed by an organization or serves it as an outside, free-lance consultant.

Again, what is important to note here is the fluid, unbounded character of these professional services. They particularly cross back and forth over the line that used to separate private life from large public institutions. The establishment of this line (or, if you will, the "invention" of the private sphere) was one of the historic achievements of the modern bourgeoisie. Conversely, the free-swinging interventions of the new professionals are antagonistic to traditional bourgeois culture and possibly imbued with a certain certain demodernizing impulse as well.

Where are the new professions to be located in the stratification and power structures of contemporary Western societies? (It should be stated, if only in passing, that their possible location in non-Western societies, fascinating though the question is, must remain outside our purview here.) The professions in general (both these we call old and those we call new here) have presented social theorists with a location problem for some time. They don't fit too readily into various theoretical interpretations of modern society. Thus Marxist theorists have worried for a long time about whether intellectuals and professionals ("culture workers") should be assigned to the capitalist bourgeoisie, to the working class, or to some intermediary position. Antonio Gramsci, for example, has awarded an important role and a degree of autonomy to these people (and, not surprisingly, enjoys great popularity to this day among them). But non-Marxist sociologist too have pondered the question of "where to put" these occupational groups. Are they simply part of the middle class? Or should they be considered a special grouping either within or alongside the middle class? Are these groupings representative of bourgeois culture or do they have an independent mentality of their own? (Ironically, of course, much of this theoretical discussion is directly related to the self-image of the theorists doing the discussing!) Some of these discussions reach back to before World War I. Thus Emil Lederer called these people "settlers on a social frontier," claiming that they descended both from the bourgeoisie and the working class. This phrase adumbrates the most famous description by Karl Mannheim over a decade later, who called them the "free-floating intelligentsia" (that is, freely floating over class boundaries). If the new professionals have a somewhat uncertain social location, then they must carve out their own niche in society. One way of doing this is by instituting procedures of "credentialling": employing mainly meritocratic (and ipso facto rational, even scientific) criteria, the new professions create their own boundaries, then proceed to cajole (and, if possible, to coerce) the public into accepting the territory thus staked out.

This also has important implications for the self-understanding of these individuals. They derive their status and their income from an alleged intellectual superiority, which is validated by means of educational and meritocratic credentials. These individuals, then, consider themselves "intellectuals" in some sense, and certainly identify with a Western tradition of intellectuality, which, going back to at least the beginning of the nineteenth century, stood in a certain tension with bourgeois culture. As certified achievers in an arena of nonmaterial production, these "culture workers" are individualistic in outlook, competing with each other for success and social mobility.

Alienated from traditional bourgeois solidarities, they attempt to construct their own lives in an allegedly individualistic ("creative," "self-realizing") mode, though, of course, upon closer investigation these constructions turn out to be considerably standardized. At the same time, some sort of new solidarity emerges among these people. They frequently share vested interests and, therefore, political inclinations. But there also emerges a new culture (or, if one prefers, subculture) to which people have a sense of allegiance, sometimes intensely so. Consider the intensity of commitment to both political and cultural agendas that are distinctively located in these groups— such as feminism, environmentalism, antimilitarism, and others. Put differently, like members of other social groupings, members of this subculture have no difficulty "sniffing each other out" by clearly defined and understood signals. To make this point graphically, imagine how easily two social workers would find each other in a gathering of police officers, or two anthropologists at a businessmen's luncheon.

Granting that here is a sociologically distinct grouping, how ought one to describe it further? Simply as a professional category? As a new class or power elite? As a subculture or subcultural movement?

One approach to answering these question has been to set them in the context of the theory of "mass society." It is argued here that the middle class, having become ever larger and culturally heterogeneous, can preserve some sort of class solidarity only by diffusing middle-class life-styles and values throughout its burgeoning population, and thus the function of the "culture workers" is to perform this task of socializing this "mass" into middle-class culture. The interpretation can, of course, be put in Marxist terms, but non-Marxists have made such arguments too. Thus as early as 1950s Helmut Schelsky spoke of a "leveled middle-class society," which requires some sort of cultural reconstruction. Many theorists believed around that time and somewhat later that this "mass society," no matter how much influenced by its "culture workers," was not prone to ideology or political mobilization (David Riesman's "lonely crowd" heralding Daniel Bell's "end of ideology"). The late 1960s, with the eruption of radicalism in precisely the milieu of the putatively deideologized, depoliticized middle class, put an effective end to this set of interpretations.

Another approach to the issue emphasizes power and power relations rather than sociocultural dynamics. The group of social scientists employing this approach has been called (somewhat too broadly) "power elite theorists"; Ralf Dahrendorf is usually cited as a prime exponent. Looking at the heterogeneous middle strata of modern society, these analysts first ask which elements within this "middle mass" participate in the exercise of power. Middle-class groups differ in their access to the central (political and economic) institutions exercising power. The largest element within the middle strata clearly has little or no power access. However, some other elements do, and these (which is the relevant point here) are primarily characterized by high professional qualifications. It is important to note that individual professionals rarely possess power directly; rather, whatever power they exercise depends upon their activities within the larger scheme of things—typically, by way of functions they carry out on behalf of the political and economic power centers.

In other words, these professionals are usually "agents of power." The progressive technicization and bureaucratization of modern society increases the demand for these "agents." The professionals do then constitute a sort of power elite, but of a subordinate status; they are, one may say, a petite power elite. But in this they differ significantly from what, earlier, had been called the petit bourgeoisie: while the latter (as part of the general bourgeoisie, the capitalist class) exercised whatever power it had because of its economic clout (property and income), the former held their position by virtue of an alleged competence in terms of knowledge and instrumental ability.

Again, it is not difficult to adapt this approach to Marxist formulations. For example, introducing the term "cultural capital" (as far as we know, this was first done in a Marxist ambience in France) allows an accommodation of these new phenomena within the body of more or less orthodox Marxist theory. At the same time, the approach can and has been employed by non-Marxist analysts (Dahrendorf among them). In either case, for Marxist and non-Marxist alike, the key factor to be dealt with is that in a modernizing society it is science and technology that constitute the major "productive force"—and this force depends crucially upon knowledge, concretely upon those who possess or are believed to possess this knowledge. C. Wright Mills, both in his studies of American white-collar class and of the American power elite, well represents this approach (leaving aside here the disputed question to what extent Mills could be called a Marxist). Important here is the notion that the power interests of the new "agents" and of the old elite (based on capital) are identical: The power of the former depends upon that of the latter. Thus Mills saw the new professional groups as collated with the old capitalist class. In the language of Marxist opprobrium, these professionals served as "lackeys" ("running dogs" in Chinese) of the capitalist power elite.

It is significant that these interpretations (Dahrendorf's as well as Mills') antedated the outbreaks of the late 1960s. Both in America and in Western Europe it seemed plausible, at that time, to view the cultural institutions as "agents" of the power elite—Columbia University, say, as a dependency of Wall Street. As the campus erupted in radical tumult and "culture workers" competed with each other in denouncing "the system" and all it stood for, this view became (to put it mildly) less plausible. Even more disturbing to this earlier interpretation, the adversary stance of the cultural institutions intensified with proximity to the old elite—it was at Columbia (or Harvard, or the Sorbonne), *not* at some provincial university far removed from the national power centers, that the new radicalism was most intense; the aforementioned theory of the power elite would, of course, predict the precise opposite.

In the early 1970s so-called "New Class theory" (somewhat of a euphemism, given the sparseness of the relevant literature) attempted to make sense of the new facts brought to light in the late 1960s. Interestingly, the theory came in both a left and a right version. Both versions agreed that there was a new middle class consisting of credentialed people in the "knowledge industry" (*that* term was coined a decade earlier by the economist Fritz Machlup), and they further agreed that this New Class had both ideas and interests that were antagonistic to the old middle class. Where the two versions differed (Alvin Gouldner and Irving Kristol were the best-known protagonists of, respectively, the left and right version of the theory) was in the evaluation of the agreed-upon empirical situation: not to put too fine a point on it, the left thought that the advent of the New Class was good news, the right looked upon it as bad news. The left version of the "New Class theory" has roots in earlier neo-Marxist writings (Gramsci again, and importantly the theorists of the Frankfurt school) that tried to cope with the inconvenient fact that the working class in Western countries kept on refusing to play the revolutionary role assigned to it by Marxist prophecy: it was here argued that the intelligentsia (read now: the "New Class") would play such a revolutionary role instead. In America around the 1970s, as engagé professors of literature called for violence in the streets and their students complied at least to the extent of defecating on the rug of the dean's office, the idea of the intelligentsia overthrowing "the system" seemed, for one brief moment, less than ludicrous to many. Seen from the right, all this "adversary culture" (Lionel Trilling's term) was an expression of the vested interests of the New Class, who were intent on wresting power and privilege from the old bourgeoisie. The *Kulturkampf* in the contemporary West, as often before, mirrored an underlying *Klassenkampf*. Thus was Marxist theory stood on its head and employed as an antileft rhetoric—to the intense irritation of leftists, one may add. In any case, what everyone involved in this debate agreed upon was that the power interests of the old and the new middle class were far from identical: there was conflict, *not* a coalition, between the two groups.

The two elites are now seen as grappling for power, privilege, and prestige—the old elite centered in the business community and the new elite based on the production, distribution, and administration of symbolic (nonmaterial) knowledge. It was the former who represented the functional reality of modern industrial capitalism; the latter were vulnerable to various forms of irrational ideology—to wit, the much heralded "counterculture," temporarily (it turned out later) in alliance with political radicalism. The alliance was hailed on the left, perceived as a disintegrative force from the right.

It is possible to give these various, more or less recent interpretations greater historical depth, something we can only do here very sketchily. More than 150 years ago, Henri De Saint-Simon and Auguste Comte looked to an educated elite as the vanguard that would take society out of the shackles of its medieval past into an age of reason and humanity. This, of course, was a direct consequence of Enlightenment thought: The enlightened were the only ones who could be trusted to be both reasonable and humane. The problem, of course, has been all along to identify this cognitive and moral elite. To give but a few examples, Lenin invented the party as the "vanguard of the proletariat" (this, as noted above, after the proletariat severely disappointed the theorist who had counted on it), Thorstein Veblen thought that engineers (of all people) would bring the society into an enlightened state, James Burnham (an ex-Marxist prone to look for vanguards) spoke of the "managerial revolution." More recently, and without the utopian expectations, John Kenneth Galbraith and Daniel Bell have looked at the central role of the knowledge elite in modern society.

Very few analysts of modernity would agree with the core proposition that knowledge and education (the process that, supposedly, makes people knowledgeable) occupy a position in contemporary society more important, more central, than in any earlier society. There is further agreement that the scientific and technological understructure of modern society makes this inevitable. Granting these assumptions, it is not difficult to see how modern professionals have a ready-made legitimation for their claims on the public's respect and pocketbook. This was already so with the old professionals. The new professionals have the relatively easy task (easy as compared with the early struggle between modernity and countermodernity—say, between scientists and clergy) of convincing the public that their knowledge too is a valid extension of enlightened rationality and that it is needed as such in whatever area of life it is alleged to apply. That is, the new professions too must wrap themselves in the cloak of guardians of progress and of the legitimate definers of the common good.

The expectation (be it with hope or in fear) that professional experts would take over the productive machinery of modern capitalist society turned out to have been false. No such thing happened. Professionals did indeed remain in the role of "agents," however well-paid or respected. In the West, one could, without thereby becoming a Marxist, describe these people as "agents" of the capitalist class. But socialism seems to bring about no change in this dependent status of professionals, simply making them "agents" of the party bureaucracy that replaces the capitalist under "real-existing" socialism. One can say, then, that the vision of "technocracy," a prototypically Enlightenment vision, has remain unfulfilled.

In a curious way, however, a kind of technocracy has emerged elsewhere—not in the productive sector of modern society, but instead in its expanding welfare sector. The modern welfare state has, of course, been made possible by the immense productivity of industrial capitalism. As it not only grew very rapidly but also became increasingly sophisticated in the range of its services, the welfare state (and beyond it, all other branches of government bureaucracy) provided increasing opportunities for the employment of professionals. Government, needless to say, also conceives of itself as a rational entity; indeed, Weber is probably correct that modern bureaucracy is the most rational form of administration ever conceived (though clients of bureaucracy may occasionally wonder). But this public sector rationality is significantly different from the rationality of the market. It is, as it were, looser. Put differently, the government, especially in its welfare sector (which constitutes by far the largest expenditure in any Western democracy), can allow the unfolding of a *normative rationality* that the market economy cannot afford. Here highly rational modes of analysis and action are deployed in order to achieve normative goals such as social justice, equity, and other national ideals; a business firm using its resources to such ends would soon go bankrupt. Also, the logic of the marketplace imposes constraints on normatively legitimated expenditures—the discipline of the "bottom line." By contrast, moral experiments of all sorts undertaken by government only have to face the milder constraints (at least in the shorter run) of what politicians and bureaucrats can extract from the tax-paying electorate. As a result of this, considerable tension has developed between the normative orders of the market economy and the welfare state, with the latter more readily able to present itself as the guardian of the common good against various "special interests." It is all the more important to see that the welfare state has produced its own "special interests"—not so much of its beneficiaries as of its functionaries. Among these professionals are quite prominent.

Already in the earlier thinking about "technocracy," there was a pessimistic as well as an optimistic streak. In the enlightened view and its successor theories, the technocratic professionals played the very beneficent role of making the world safe for reason and humanity against the dark forces of superstition and tyranny. But there also developed the much more negative view of the technocrats as imposing a new sort of tyranny on society, the tyranny of an abstract rationality that has become separated from moral purpose or human sensitivity. The technocrats are seen as harbingers of alienation (in a Marxist sense) or builders of an "iron cage" (Weber) in which human spontaneity, creativity, indeed life itself is to be imprisoned. The new professionals, the ones we have dubbed "life-style engineers," evoke this negative view of technocracy more easily than did their professional predecessors. After all, they are not just dealing with this or that circumscribed area of life—the building of railroads, or the treatment of liver disease, or the law of inheritance—but, in principle, with *any* area of the individual's existence. Functional rationality now becomes sinister indeed. It permeates the private lives of people just as it dominates the public sphere. It undermines all traditions. It makes ever more precarious the individual's quest for meaning and identity.

The new professions apply an engineering mindset to the searing questions arising from the modern crisis of meaning and identity, a crisis to which modern production with its manifold tensions has significantly contributed. Modern man undoubtedly has benefited enormously from modern rationality; he also suffers from it. The irony is that the very wounds caused by engineers' rationality are now to be cured by other engineers using the same kind of rationality. This may well be a case of driving out the devil with Beelzebub; or as Karl Kraus already put it in the 1920s, when the early form of "life-style engineering" represented by Freud's disciples became *en vogue* in Vienna: "Psychoanalysis is the disease of which it believes itself to be the cure."

All professions regardless of whether they are directly linked to the production process or not, belong to the economy's so-called "service sector." This sector, as is well known, has expanded immensely in the course of modernization, and it continues to expand. The reason for this is essentially simple: due to increasing technological sophistication, fewer and fewer people are needed to man the extractive, manufacturing, and distributive operations of the economy, leaving a vast assemblage of manpower free for services of every conceivable kind. It is this fact that underlies the (misleading) notion that we now live in a "postindustrial society" (misleading, because the necessary foundation of all these proliferating services is a productive industrial economy).

In the final analysis, all services are dependent upon and function to maintain the overall institutional order (this is the valid kernel of

Marxist as well as structural-functional theories of modern society). They keep going and, where necessary, repair the various megainstitutions. At the same time, they must help individuals to perform their appropriate roles within these institutions, a function that increasingly has come to include promoting the social and psychological well-being of individuals. As the welfare state developed, a special set of services was put in place to take care of individuals (from the elderly to discriminated-against groups) unable to function in or marginalized by the megainstitutions. This too (as Bismarck already realized when he, probably before anyone else, conceptualized the modern welfare state) is functional for "system maintenance" (Talcott Parsons). As service professionals developed their own ethos in serving various categories of "society's victims," they could no longer be relied upon to "serve the system"; they became independent as against the functional requirements of "the system," and some of them became adversaries to it. There are limits to this adversary stance, for the simple reason that finally the entire edifice of welfare services (no matter whether publicly or privately funded) depends upon the productivity of the economy. (This, incidentally, is as true in a socialist as in a market economy.)

The relative autonomy of the service professions as against the production process has further implications. The performance of all occupations directly linked to production can be measured, typically in quantitative terms, by input/output quotients—quantity produced, unit cost, time consumed, profit attained, and so on. The service professions that concern us here lack these easily measurable criteria for performance. Typically, their performance is not readily visible in terms of input/output calculi; it can only be evaluated in terms of normative definitions of what is good for the clients of these services and/or for the common well-being of society. This is the fact which (if you will) opens up a vast opportunity for conmanship. On the other hand, because these service professionals have the engineering mentality mentioned previously, they are pressured to make these services calculable too; in publicly funded services, of course, there is the additional pressure to legitimate the expenditure of scarce tax funds. When these services are put on the market for purchase by private clients/consumers, the latter must be propagandized to feel a need for them. As every advertiser know, this is an expensive, endless, and risky business. From the standpoint of the service professional, funding by the public sector is the much more desirable option. Here the assessment of needs depends upon the outcome of political campaigns and negotiations, and normative legitimations ("the common good" and various ideals of social justice or equality) are crucial. While here too economic considerations obtain (to repeat, the tax coffers of the state are limited), the immediate economic discipline endemic to the market sector is lacking. Still, as the welfare state expands (the category of "victims of society" has shown itself to be energetically inflationary), more and more frequent tensions arise between normative legitimations and economic constraints. This conflict has become a major factor in the politics of Western democracies; indeed, this conflict broadly separates left-of-center and right-of-center parties in these societies.

The providers of "human services," insofar as they deal with individual clients (most of them do), enter into face-to-face relationships that embroil them in the dynamics of reciprocal expectations that psychologists and social scientists have studied for a long time. The client, for whom these services are allegedly put in place, cannot simply be administered; his cooperation is almost always necessary, and thus his expectations must be mindset coordinated with those of the service professional. In one form or another, this coordination must be institutionalized—that is, regularized, organized by readily applicable rules, made predictable. Sometimes this can be achieved spontaneously in face-to-face interaction (for instance, in therapeutic settings). More often, though, individual professionals and clients cannot be counted upon to produce such an order; rather, it must be defined and administered "from above." This brings about a new set of tensions.

Every individual case is screened in terms of politically defined rules of entitlements. Thus highly individual needs are subsumed under general, abstract criteria. This, of course, is what happens whenever concrete human realities are converted into "cases" that can be dealt with in a bureaucratic manner. Almost inevitably it leads to resentments and frustrations on the part of the client population, no matter whether the problem at issue is major (say, obtaining the license to operate a business) or minor (say, trying to correct an error in one's phone bill). In the area of "human services," however, these typical bureaucracy-engendered tensions are particularly serious because they directly interfere with what is or is intended to be an emotionally positive human relationship, and also because they contradict the elevated legitimations by which these professionals define themselves. Most of them were the kind of students who, when asked in college what they wanted to do later in life, answered "I want to work with people!"

As human services expand, especially within the public sector, different professional groups struggle among themselves over the jurisdiction over groups of clients, and of course over the funds that go with these clients' alleged needs. Psychiatrists and psychologists, social workers and educators, experts on crime and experts on crime prevention, and many others find themselves pitted against one another in various areas of the immense welfare system. Yet that system as a whole has a built-in expansionist tendency: new categories of "victims" are discovered, new entitlements are legislated, and new regiments of professionals array themselves to occupy the territory thus opened up for their activities. This professionalized welfare system obtrudes unceasingly upon the means by which human problems were traditionally dealt with—in the family, the church, the village or neighborhood, the voluntary group. These "unprofessional" institutions are shunted aside, defunded, sometimes legally prohibited from engaging in their traditional helping activities, and on occasion (perhaps the worst fate of all) themselves professionalized. They do not take this fate lightly; there are resistances, and at least in democracies these can become politically significant. Thus the new professionals who function as "human services providers" frequently find themselves marching through one political minefield after another, some of the mines laid by angry clients (especially those who have managed to organize—"victims against victimologists"—the sort of pithy situation as when the employees of a labor union go on strike), other mines laid by cost-conscious politicians and administrators, and yet others put there by competing fellow professionals. Needless to say, the grubby politics and economics associated with these conflicts do not go terribly well with the rhetoric of compassion and service by which these professionals legitimate their activities.

The importance of the new professionals in the public life of Western industrial societies ensures that political debate is heavily charged with moral content. Here is a population of inveterate moralizers by virtue of their very social existence. In consequence the political life of these societies has been marked by a shift away from some of the traditional left-versus-right issues, most of them concerned with distribution and redistribution of material resources, or with the inclusion and participation in society of previously marginalized groups. These issues, of course, continue to be politically relevant. But now there are new issues over which it is not so easy to see a clear division between haves and have-nots, ins and outs— normatively charged issues like abortion, the gamut of feminist issues, gay rights, ecological balance, global peace, and communal identities. New professionals have been very busy in defining and propagating these morally elevated issues—as producers and propagators of the relevant theories (often from within academia), as political activists, as consultants to government and to private sector organizations, and (last but not least) as employees of organizations (again, both within and outside government) that embody these agendas. In all of this, skills of both political infighting and sometimes exuberant entrepreneurship can find high rewards.

But the major skill required here is intellectual—in the construction and propagation of values, theories, and practical blueprints legitimating the new professional enterprises. Since the new professionals (unlike many of the old ones) are trained in disciplines that place a high value upon rhetorical ("communicative") skills— some of their detractors claim that this is *all* they are—these people are usually very good indeed at pushing their agendas in the public arena. Most of the time, they—wielders of words, "wordsmiths," lovers of *les mots*—beat business people hands down. And since they run the institutions by which societal symbols are fabricated and disseminated—universities, schools, communication media, large portions of the legal system, in addition to the vast structures of organized compassion—it is a foregone conclusion that the morality, the worldview and the specific opinions of the new professionals will spread beyond their own ranks. The question is how far they have spread and what resistances they have encountered.

The most obvious resistance, one would expect, will come from the old bourgeois culture, from the "Protestant ethic" with its values of achievement, discipline, and self-denial. And indeed, new professionals have been prominent among those who have explicitly opposed these bourgeois virtues in the name of this or that "liberation." This opposition, as noted above, led to the formation of the "New Class theory," which posited an adversarial relationship between the old bourgeois culture and that of the new professionals. And there can be little doubt that at least some of this opposition continues to exist, especially (but not exclusively) in the area of politics: How many new professionals vote for the parties of the right? How many oppose abortion or gay rights? How many (especially in Europe) go to church? Conversely, business executives, corporation lawyers, oral surgeons, and aerospace engineers are likely to be both politically and culturally more conservative. There is strong empirical evidence to that effect for the United States, and there is no reason to think that the situation in Western Europe is very different. This, though, is not the whole story, we think, and to that extent we would want to modify "New Class theory" on a few points.

If the market economy is to maintain its productivity, it must somehow accommodate the aspirations of these groups that it needs for its functioning—including the aspirations of at least some of the new professionals and (more important) of a larger group of the population that has been influenced by the new culture. To be sure, the economy cannot absorb all these aspirations, especially those of the more utopian or messianic sort. Thus one cannot expect the market economy to absorb the revolutionary socialist or anarchist impulses of the late 1960s. But the market economy can, and to a large extent already has, absorbed, adapted, or (if you will) co-opted many other impulses of that era, notably those emanating from feminism, environmentalism, and the overall ideology of personal self-realization. If one envisages the old and the new bourgeoisie as two distinct groups who have entered into a negotiation process with each other (a heuristic depiction that, obviously, is something of an oversimplification), then we can see here at work what in the sociology of knowledge we would call a process of "cognitive bargaining"—"you give me that; I'll give you this." We would content that a kind of "historic compromise" (*compromesso storcio!*) is in the making here. If we were pressed to describe the nature of this compromise, we would say (tentatively, hypothetically) that the old bourgeoisie is winning out on the key economic and political points of contention (notably, in the mutual agreement on the basic structure of democratic capitalism), but that the new bourgeoisie in turn is getting the bulk of its cultural demands (which in America were subsumed under the category: "social issues"—the "soft" issues, so to speak).

It would then appear that the "New Class theory" was quite correct in perceiving the basic culture clash and its political manifestations. But it was less correct in visualizing this contestation in terms of a classical, quasi-Marxian class struggle. To be sure, there have been victories and defeats on both sides. But what is shaping up is not a sharpening class war but rather a mutual cultural exchange. The old industrial order is being modified, to some extent "softened" by the cultural trends of which the new professionals are the principle carriers. The latter, however, are themselves being changed as they enter into this bargain. At the end of the day, it is not clear *who* is co-opting *whom* in this somewhat surprising symbiosis!

Important to this development is the vulgar fact that the new cultural trends have opened up new markets for the economy. It may be impossible, or at least difficult, to cash in on revolution (though some writers, academics, and publishers have successfully done so). It is certainly possible to make big bucks on other aspects of the "counterculture." Just think here of the burgeoning markets created by feminism, for example, or environmentalism. A better "quality of life" may be defined in very philosophical terms; economically speaking, it requires sundry goods and services, some of them very much upmarket. The phenomenon of the so-called "yuppies," though the term is sociologically imprecise, is real enough and nicely illustrates this marriage of "soft" values and hard cash. In terms of goods, think of the markets for self-expressive clothing and home furnishing, for health foods and equipment for what purports to be a healthy life-style, not to mention the plethora of enormously expensive tools employed to protect the environment. As to services, there are the markets for a multiplicity of counselors (from karate teacher for women to geriatric sex advisors), agitators and lobbyists for the various New Class causes, environmental experts, affirmative action officers, consultants to industry on antismoking regulation, "humanizing the workplace," or catching the flak of single-minded pressure groups, and so on and so forth. Thus, ironically, some of the very people who twenty years ago were perceived and perceived themselves as enemies of "the system" have become sources for expanding, revitalizing, and indeed enriching the same "system."

The new professionals occupy a strategic position in this creation of a (so to speak) liberation market. As in other markets that cater mainly to upper-income groups, designers play an important role. We have designer jeans and polo shirts. We now also have putatively liberating designer life-styles, of which new professionals serve as the Yves St. Laurents. As with other up-market products and services, mass production is always lurking in the bushes just a few steps behind the pioneer designers. In this way the new culture too must tolerate downmarket imitations. Lower-middle-class individuals now munch health foods and working-class individuals participate in feminist support groups. But here too the new professionals have a role, one that has been a traditional upper-middle-class role for at a least 150 years—uplifting the great unwashed. Just as, say, pedagogues, social workers, and Salvation Army officers taught the proletarians of yesteryear to behave properly at table, to give up drinking, and to eschew profanity, so their contemporary successors (teachers and social workers once more, but a host of more novel professionals as well) instruct the lower classes in the proper way to relax, to give up smoking, or to use "inclusive language." Major Barbara reemerges as Ms. Barbara, M.S.W. The new embourgeoisement looks rather a lot like the old one, not least in the parts played by schools, churches, and large numbers of high-minded, upper-income women with a burning sense of mission.

All of this has a significant, and (we would think) invigorating, impact upon the industrial system. Mass production, with its guiding principles of standardization and marginal differentiation, remains in place. But it is now modified by a perpetual search for new market niches, for specialized and individualized ("personalized," in the inimitable American term) goods and services. It would seem to follow that at least a segment of the managerial and entrepreneurial groups must themselves develop, if not a new life-style, then a new mindset that is sensitive to all cultural changes. This hypothesis is apparently supported by new managerial ideologies and practices in evidence both in the United States and in Western Europe. There are also organizational consequences. At least some companies move away from the streamlined and hierarchical patterns of the past and toward more flexible, variegated structures. Companies develop horizontal clusters of teams organized around a particular product from its initial design to its final manufacture. These teams, even while part of a large organization, are encouraged to operate in an entrepreneurial fashion (the not very attractive term "intrapreneurship" has been coined to describe this phenomenon), to innovate, experiment, and to encourage individual initiatives. While such modifications of corporate structures are functional in facilitating adaptation to a complex, highly competitive, and always rapidly changing market, they also correspond to New Class cultural demands for self-expression and community. Decision-making too becomes less hierarchical, more flexible and in a way more "democratic"—again combining economic functionality with new cultural expectations. One of the problems that arises from this is how to keep all these bubbling initiatives under one roof in a manageable way. This used to be the problems of university deans; to the extent that the new professional culture has important academic roots, it should not surprise that top corporate executives now have similar problems.

In this way New Class culture not only finds a haven within the (old class) business world, but even within the hearts and minds of business executives. We cannot say at this point how far this "cognitive contamination" has spread or how far up the corporate ladder it reaches. But there can be no doubt that there now exist executives who not only dress and behave in a way that make them resemble New Class academics, but who appear to have internalized important elements of New Class ideology. These people are very different from the old, "Protestant" type of businessman—sober, conformist, hierarchy-conscious. They exhibit (with whatever degree of genuineness) an exuberant *joie de vivre*, a sense of personal autonomy and sometimes even eccentricity, and a degree of irreverence toward any and all traditions. They view themselves and succeed in projecting an image of *condottieri* of industry, freewheeling and lusty, in sharp contrast to the "officer corps" of previous industrial organizations. This gives the workplace a much more "humanized" look. At least on the surface, there is less alienation from the job. Instead there are new forms of identification with the job, with the firm, and (at least implicitly) with the entire economic system. In some aspects (by no means all) there are features here of

Western industrial order that are strangely reminiscent of Japan. Clearly, these people must remain "organization men." They must become part of the corporate culture, identify with the corporate identity, and be given a corporate philosophy. Needless to say, there are new professionals, on the market now as business consultants, who claim to be ready to teach management how to accomplish these tasks. One could say that they teach Westerners the idea and techniques that come naturally to the Japanese!

What one perceives here is a convergence of cultural themes as the business community and the general society come to be preoccupied with questions first raised by the "counterculture"—pertaining to meaning, moral worth, quality of life, identity, participation, and self-expression. Of course, these themes change significantly in substance as well as form as they pass on the "long march through the institutions" from their original social locations (say, Berkeley or the Left Bank) to the upper reaches of corporate capitalism. So do the people who "carry" these themes. But the capitalist order and the business community are equally changed in this process of interpenetration. The "cognitive contamination" is mutual. In this process it becomes more difficult to think in terms of "adversary culture" or of class struggle. Instead there is the aforementioned negotiating process, with compromises and coalescences. At the center of it stand the new professions that have been our concern here.

Another way of looking at this, especially if one compares the present situation with the doomsday predictions not only of Marxists but of analysts like Joseph Schumpeter, is to see it as showing the extraordinary resilience of modern capitalism. Whatever its inner problems and malfunctions, the capitalist system remains immensely vital, retaining an astonishing capacity to deflect, absorb, modify, and even profit from every conceivable challenge to it. Whether one regards this as good news or bad will obviously depend on how one evaluates the moral and human worth of this system as against the empirically available alternatives. There can be no doubt about the importance of the fact.

2

The New Class:
On the Theory of a No Longer
Entirely New Phenomenon

Frank W. Heuberger

In the early seventies, discussion of a New Class became political as well as intellectually charged. Neoconservative American critics, in particular Irving Kristol, were especially significant in drawing attention to what they conceived of as the penetration of a dangerous new elite into vital spheres of the so-called postindustrial societies. Because of its growing political influence and its pursuit, under the guise of altruism, of its own special interests, this "intelligentsia" is alleged to have contributed greatly to the fiscal and moral crises of the contemporary welfare state. In continuously promoting its own ideas and values as cures for the ills it helped to create, the New Class has forged its own political and cultural identity. It is also said that the New Class in its opposition to old middle-class values and to the rationality of the global capitalist economy as a whole, has gained more and more influence on the public through education and journalism. Through the control of these two principal agents of socialization, the New Class has become increasingly the center and symbol of new social movements (ecology, feminism, gay rights, disarmament, etc.) and the promulgators of a new concept of society.

To assess such claims requires that we step away from the overheated rhetoric that commonly pervades discussion of this topic, and do two things. First, it is imperative to forge ahead with empirical analyses of the New Class phenomenon. Second, and simultaneously, it is essential to analyze the theoretical underpinnings, both implicit and explicit, of this ongoing effort. My purpose here is to contribute to the latter by addressing two theoretical questions. The first, which will detain us only briefly, relates to the problem of whether the phenomenon in question is really one of "class" at all (Pryor 1981). Second, the theorized location of the New Class within the wider social structure must be considered.

Interestingly enough, the term "class" is used not only by the neoconservatives who first brought it into the discussion, but also by neo-Marxists, who in no way deny the existence of a New Class. The latter, however, have difficulties deriving a New Class theory, due mainly to their stubborn entanglement in the undergrowth of classical Marxist theory. According to classical Marxist theory, to begin with, that the broad middle class might contain within it a stratum of anticapitalist professional workers is almost unthinkable. It is similarly assumed that the fount of political power is control of economic processes, and that the ideological superstructure reflects nothing but this economic base, relegating the forms of intellectual work to capitalist ownership. All theory, of course, rests upon certain axioms. The problem with classical Marxist theory is that it chooses as axioms statements which must be taken as hypotheses if the existence of a New Class is to be opened to empirical investigations. Furthermore, even the more sophisticated neo-Marxists have not adequately updated their theory to grasp the growing significance in modern society of abstract knowledge and higher education. The enormous productive power of science as a variable that is partially independent from the economic structure and that exerts its own influences on political decision making is not taken into account by neo-Marxists. There is growing awareness that economic interests and policymaking in contemporary societies often diverge to an astonishing extent. Neo-Marxists also have difficulty coping with new social movements that arise as the boundaries of class are stretched in the maturation of industrial societies.

The neoconservatives, for their part, take a different path to the same mistaken assumption. The neoconservatives, while paying more attention than do the neo-Marxists to the empirical reality of the New Class phenomenon, nevertheless pass too quickly to its theoretical definition. Though with quite different implications, the neoconservatives end up articulating a class concept not too dissimilar from the Marxist perspective. Yet, with their class theory they do not wish so much to identify the private owners of the means of production and the workers as two antagonistic classes, as to identify a stratum of intellectuals and professions that, in the view of Schumpeter, enacts a permanent criticism of capitalist social and political order and of capitalist modernization processes. The neoconservative evaluation of the New Class therefore is almost by definition negative in the sense that the New Class, through its forms of criticism, endangers the existing order of free modern society. In this way the neoconservatives fall into the same pattern of misleading generalization. One scholar who is commonly cited as a neoconservative deserves to be singled out, however, for his efforts to avoid this common trap.

In his book *The Coming of Post-Industrial Society* (1973), and more elaborated in *The Cultural Contradictions of Capitalism* (1976), Daniel Bell presents a clearly defined conceptual model of postindustrial societies and repudiates the validity claimed by Marxist-oriented models for a holistically structured society. According to Bell, "contemporary societies" (including socialist ones) are made up of three clearly defined areas, each of which follows its own "axial principle." For Bell there exists a "techno-economic sphere" (equated with "social structure") that consists of the economy, technology, and the professions. This sphere follows the axial principle of "functional rationality" and is controlled by "economizing." The second sphere, called the "polity," is structured according to the axial principle of "legitimacy" and the possibility of "representation and participation." The third sphere is that of "culture"—unfortunately reduced by Bell to the production and presentation of art—and is grouped around the axial principle of the "self." (A self, however, that in its hedonistic striving for self-realization has, at least in art, ended up in the desolate self-admiration of its own way of life.) Initially the term postindustrial society is used by Bell to signify fundamental changes taking place in the social structure. Yet because of the relative autonomy of the social spheres, changes in one sphere do not necessarily bring about changes in the other ones. Therefore, a monocausal determination for all changes cannot be formulated. The central dimension of postindustrial society is seen by him as a transition from a goods-producing economy to a service economy, and in this situation technology and theoretically codified knowledge are becoming accordingly the primary "productive power." While private ownership of the means of production was regarded as the central axial institution of past capitalist societies, in postindustrial society it is replaced by the principle of theoretical knowledge. The productive power of theoretical knowledge is becoming the dynamo of technological innovation and the basis for economic decision making. It is also the decisive variable responsible for changes in the stratification system of societies. The "game against fabricated nature," characteristically predominant in the industrial society, has turned into the "game between people," dominated by an "intellectual technology."

One of the major problems of the postindustrial society, thus, is the organization of science in the institutions of higher learning and research. A second major problem comes with the emergence of a New Class of academically-trained experts, who are displaying growing political and cultural influence, and who are fostering a new kind of politics that depends upon the availability of scientific prognoses. Bell emphasizes that neither the "tertiary sector" (transportation, utilities) nor the "quaternary sector" (banks, insurance companies, trade, and finance) but the so-called "quinory sector" (health, education, research, government, recreation) has attained functional dominance over the industrial "secondary sector" of goods production (Bell 1973, 116f). However, Bell regards the possibility that the academically trained professionals in the quinory sector are raising themselves to the level of a ruling class with skepticism. Nor does he consider it likely that health experts, technicians, scientists, administrative specialists, and artists will be able to find a common identity. Their wide dispersal throughout private and public sectors (profit and nonprofit) provides little opportunity for the development of a collective consciousness as a class by itself. This "knowledge class" is further likely to remain politically weak, simply because the political system would continue to recruit its partisan followers by their membership in political organizations (with their own internally organized forms of promotion) and not on the basis of formal educational and scientific qualifications.

Moreover, Bell argues that because of the relative autonomy of the three spheres there should be no fear that any of these will ever completely be able to take the whole of society under its particular axial principle. For this reason, it is also not to be feared that the influence of New Class professionals (who are carriers both of the axial principle of participation and functional rationality) on political decision makers will cause a complete takeover of society either in the direction of participation or of functional rationality. According to Bell, the picture becomes even more complicated if we realize that the concept of rationality, as held by New Class representatives, is changing. This assessment is provided by the notion of a shift of the class struggle from the distribution of productive goods to that of a cultural conflict with the state in a postindustrial situation. What the content of the new rationality is, Bell unfortunately does not specify. What is needed therefore, is a theoretical frame which builds upon Bell's insight, but gives us access, as his work does not, to both the rationality and logic of interaction taking place in this cultural conflict and a way of evaluating the impact of a burgeoning knowledge elite across all spheres of postindustrial society.

Theorizing the New Class

To approach the New Class phenomenon in adequate class theoretical terms, then, we would be well advised to avoid the pitfalls of the Marxist approach and the enflamed usage of "class" by the neoconservatives, even that propounded by Bell. It would be better to take up Max Weber's theoretical perspective on social stratification (Weber 1968; Giddens 1973). Weber approaches social stratification in a more multilayered fashion than do the rather one-dimensional Marxists. Though he also differentiates groups and strata of society in terms of their economic location and their placement in political power formations, he uses these two dimensions in such a way that they function both as dependent and independent variables. Even more than this, he grasps economic locations and power affiliations not only in structural, that is objective, terms, but also attempts to take the subjective self-evaluations of members of groups and strata into account. Accordingly, people do not find themselves solely by chance in their class or power relationship but place themselves by their perspectives and interests in distinct social groupings and strata. In this sense, class positions can be derived both in terms of objective "life chances" in the economic market and subjective attempts to meet and alter existing conditions. The same applies to power relationships. Life aspirations and styles, Weber argues, may also operate as independent differentiating and stratifying principles. Though empirically, of course, objective and subjective interests regularly do interpenetrate, they are not necessarily bound to each other absolutely. On the whole, Weber's perspective and conceptions leave open possibilities to cope with empirical phenomena and do not force the researcher into a one-dimensional class theory. This makes it possible to identify any particular group of people with regard to the objective and subjective determinants of its members' class positions, power relations, life-styles, and world views, without assigning them a particular class (or, for that matter, estate or a subculture).

The multilayered Weberian framework corresponds well with the multidimensional New Class phenomenon. The label "class," if not understood in the Weberian spirit, either grasps too little, or one-dimensionally emphasizes too much. In any case, the phenomenon is forced into a too narrow theoretical matrix that is more suggestive than analytically helpful. Since the label "class" has become customary, however, we are forced to stay with it. No particular damage is done, if we remain aware of the problems involved.

Responding to the extraordinary postwar boom, C. Wright Mills, writing in the 1950s, painted a gloomy picture of a broad middle-class "mass society," within which emerges a type of employee that is politically apathetic and can be easily manipulated. This new type of employee largely replaced the production of goods by manual labor with "impersonal" management of people and symbols. The media of these workers are money, paper, and people. What they are doing is to "steer, administrate, register, and distribute" (Mills 1951). Even though they, like the old working class, do not possess the means of production, they nevertheless, by means of their technical knowledge and qualifications, are involved (if only indirectly) in the maintenance of capitalist conditions. Their technical and symbolic qualifications put them not only on good terms with the ruling class but make them indispensable to it. The same qualifications serve also to decisively demarcate the New Class from the classical proletariat. For all of these reasons the educational system has become extremely important for this new middle class. For similar reasons they have become quite susceptible to behavioral attitudes such as individualism, career orientation, and prestige consciousness.[1] Their political apathy and passivity in public affairs can be subsumed under the rubric of "other-directedness" in David Riesman's sense (1950). Against this apathetic and passive middle class, C. Wright Mills longed for the emergence of a politically engaged vanguard who would alter this situation.

The class of industrial managers, productive engineers, and technical experts, which Mills recognized as gaining importance in the 1950s, had actually been the subject of critiques decades before. Already in 1921, Thorstein Veblen warned against the highly qualified production engineers, the "soviets of technicians" in his understanding. In his opinion, they would apply the logic of optimal use of technocratic capacities of production to all spheres of society. Politically speaking, that would establish the technocratic rule of the law of necessity globally, which would barely camouflage technocracy's undemocratic face with promises of material affluence (Veblen 1921; 1965). Years later James Burnham warned against an emerging manager state in which planning specialists in production and politics would merge to form a new ruling class (Burnham 1941). Still later John Kenneth Galbraith saw in the rise of scientifically oriented production the emergence of a widespread "technostructure." To him planners and technicians, but also the professional group of educators, would take over political power, yet also assume political responsibility to limit the monopoly of the industrial system in the name of "just" social aims (Galbraith 1967).

Galbraith's rather hopeful assessment of the potential for New Class members to exert a liberal "countervailing" power stands in opposition to Lionel Trilling's equally famous argument about an "adversary culture" and its quasi-socialist political stance. The political orientation of this adversarial cultural group was concerned with a critique of the educational system and social politics as well as the weaknesses of the European parliamentary systems, the immorality of foreign policy, and the puritanism of the cultural establishment. This group, mainly made up of students, college graduates, and members of the middle to high income strata, became the source of what was called then the paradox of upper white collar liberalism and dissent (Brint 1984). The immense explosion of the educational system in the sixties and the ongoing scientization of production, politics, and administration broadened the base of this group and provided them with increased political influence. This lead to passionate theoretical discussions about a sensible course of democratic education policy and about the social function of intellectuals. These questions of morality and democracy provide the starting point for a considerable number of New Class theories. Almost without exception they are concerned with a criticism and/or self-criticism of the New Class as a part of an allegedly adversary culture.

Michael Harrington has attempted to develop a scheme by which a negative and positive assessment of New Class intellectuals with reference to their various socialist or conservative theoretical traditions becomes possible (Harrington 1979).[2] Even though he has some difficulties in coming up with clear-cut definitions, he identifies two major elite theories. The first is the socialist elite theory in the tradition of Saint-Simon and Kautsky that on the whole reclaims a vicarious role for the intelligentsia in the general welfare of society. This presupposition was questioned, following the tradition of Bakunin, in terms of a critique of power and bureaucracy in an anarchist perspective. More recently a similar critique has been advanced by Milovan Djilas (1957) and Gyorgy Konrád and Iván Szelényi (1978) on the New Class in socialist countries. The other tradition Harrington identifies follows Pareto's theory of the "circulation of the elites." It openly affirms the demands for power and domination by particular interest groups as necessary for the vitality of society.

In the moderate conservative and neoconservative camp we find a not too dissimilar critique of intellectuals as in the anarchist inspired criticisms of socialist elites. Joseph Schumpeter's[3] chapter on "Sociology of Intellectuals" in his classic work *Capitalism, Socialism and Democracy*, provides a major theoretical basis for attempts to systematize the phenomenon of the New Class.[4] Schumpeter shows— and this thesis is taken up repeatedly by Bell—that the capitalist production process fosters a social atmosphere of hostility that appropriates a rationalistic criticism and moral authority, formerly directed against feudalism, and slowly channels them into an attack against private property and the whole of bourgeois value patterns. The intellectuals, even more than other classes, react sensitively to the destruction of the emotional attachments to the social order caused by industrialization and modernization and develop an attitude of permanent criticism toward the existing social and political order. Schumpeter's sociology of knowledge and class-theoretical evaluation of intellectuals, including his critical assessment of the expansion of the educational system and the growth of the service industries, left a lasting imprint on the New Class debate.

> Intellectuals are in fact people who wield the power of the spoken and the written word, and one of the touches that distinguish them from other people who do the same is the absence of direct responsibility for practical affairs. This touch in general accounts for another—the absence of the first hand knowledge of them which only actual experience can give. (Schumpeter 1943, 147)

> Intellectuals rarely enter professional politics and still more rarely conquer a responsible office. But they staff political bureaus, write party pamphlets and speeches, act as secretaries and advisers, make the individual politicians newspaper reputation which, though it is not everything, few men can afford to neglect. In doing these things they to some extent impress their mentality on almost everything that is being done. (154)

> Intellectuals are not a social class in the sense in which peasants or industrial laborers constitute social classes; they hail from all the corners of the social world, and a great part of their activities consist in fighting each other and in forming the spearheads of class interests not their own. Yet they develop group attitudes and group interests sufficiently strong to make large numbers of them behave in the way that is usually associated with the concept of social classes. (146)

If we keep this characterization in mind and leave at the same time the political yardstick of "right" versus "left" in the evaluation of the New Class behind—since this would always lead us into certain confusions—two key intertwined questions in the assessment of the New Class phenomenon must be problematized. First, what kind of knowledge and what logic of action does the New Class apply in its attempts to solve complex social and technical problems?[5] Second, to which subsections of society do New Class members primarily offer their expertise and services? The "answers" suggested in the relevant literature to these questions are as varied as they are interesting. Recent literature on the New Class unfortunately, has often slighted the former question and has instead emphasized a taxonomy of the service professions. An exploration of the literature is worthwhile nevertheless.

To detect some informative patterns of the kind and knowledge used by the New Class members, I first want to refer descriptively to some contributions contained in the Barry Bruce-Briggs reader, *The New Class?* (1979).

Jeane J. Kirkpatrick, using H. D. Lasswell's term, speaks of the "symbol specialists." She mainly has in mind those journalists, clergy, professors, public relations and advertising specialists, and some upper-level bureaucrats who are active in the area of the "second level political elite," all professions that demand high "verbal and communications skills." Such persons manipulate ideas and words and raise questions of the legitimacy of the political order. Their logic of action is "issue oriented," "rationalistic," "moralistic," and possessed by a "reformist approach to politics." They aim to establish a particular vision of reality. Their growing political influence is leading to an expansion of the public sector and of government's authority. This results in a shift of responsibility for the quality of social life from the individual, the family, and private groups to the government (Kirkpatrick 1979).

Peter Berger, who prefers to use the term "knowledge class" instead of New Class, speaks of widely "divergent sociocultural milieus," that can be found in planning and administration agencies. He perceives a religious dimension to the knowledge of the New Class. Based on the observation that religion in the experience of modern consciousness has become a matter of personal preference, he shows that the implied loss of the old transcendental orientation has led the individual to moral and religious insecurity. Individuals are attempting to fill the hole that has been left by means of scientific or moral discourse, resulting in a new "secular theodicy." The New Class is trying to conceal its striving for power by means of creating and providing meaning for others as the vanguard of a new "secular humanism." It camouflages its class interests with the claim that it "contribute[s] to the welfare of the downtrodden" (Berger 1979, 53). Berger's assessment of the New Class is clearly influenced by Helmut Schelsky who speaks of the emergence of a "hierocracy of intellectuals" (*Priesterherrschaft der Intellektuellen*). Schelsky summarizes his analysis of what he calls the "reflection elite" as follows:

> More and more enlightenment through information, more and more understanding through instruction, more and more social justice through caring, more and more security for the future through planning, that is the illusionary syndrome of the belief in social salvation, the joining together of indoctrination, caring, and planning [*Belehrung, Betreuung, und Beplanung*] into a form of domination over the faithful masses of modern society. (Schelsky 1975, 374f. author's translation)

Nathan Glazer concentrates on public interest lawyers and lawyers who work for the government. To him the main activity of the members of the New Class consists of "defending the rights and interests of minorities" and of "law reform work." In their passion for justice and rights they are inclined to argue that "law itself emphasizes many themes that have become the essence of liberalism" (Glazer 1979, 98). Their knowledge relates to the history of law with its logic of a "system of reasoning by analogy." In Glazer's opinion, even if there exists an increased demand for lawyers in many nongovernmental social sectors, this type of public interest lawyer is undoubtedly interested in the expansion of governmental powers. In their battles against a feared institutionalization of a legal practice curtailing basic individual rights, they call upon the courts continuously to read into vague statutes and constitutional provisions the ideals of their class. The lawyers as part of the New Class are in agreement with other groupings of the New Class furthermore in their rejection of the market as the medium of the distribution of wealth. Thus, Glazer comes to the conclusion that "lawyers are indeed important members of the 'new class' if we consider that its essential character is to call for, to defend, and to benefit from expansion of government" (Glazer 1979, 99f).

Andrew Hacker prefers C. Wright Mills' term "elite" over "class" because the former term permits him to include in his characterization of the New Class dimensions that are independent of occupational and institutional contexts but are constitutive for the New Class.

According to Hacker, one important characteristic of the New Class is that its protagonists are not involved in the production or distribution of goods, "but bring about experiences for others." Together with the ability to explain ideas and to provide interpretations for others, they generate "information" and "explanations." Their work consists of "planning," "programming," and "coordinating." Following Schumpeter, he speaks of a "rationalist attitude" that serves to consolidate their work ideologically: "the use of symbols—verbal, mathematical, etc.—to create and then impose an order that is beyond the capacity of reality to absorb" (Hacker 1979, 164). Their presumptuous attitudes lead them to the conclusion that the quality of life and social justice can only be improved and achieved by their means of interpretation. In Hacker's opinion, this unspecific knowledge operating against the background of the "rationalist attitude" and the ability to interpret—which one also finds in the "current military establishment and significant segments of corporate industry"—does not constitute a new class. The elite itself Hacker does not regard as new, what is new is the structure provided by the logic of the capitalist production within which the knowledge of this elite comes to be applied. Their power is "rather corporate than corporeal." The status he assigns it is the "upper level of our proletariat." Thus Hacker's assessment of the political position of the New Class remains undecided, as does Michael Harrington's who does not see any politically unequivocal left/right alignment. In the political orientation of the New Class, two tendencies come together: a "liberal elitism" and a "democratic politics of alliance with working people and the poor" (Harrington 1979, 134).

A number of other essays worth mentioning contained in Bruce-Briggs' reader, could be added here. They all deal in one way or another with the New Class's relation to politics, class, status, knowledge, and its putative threat to existing social conditions. There is Robert L. Bartley's contribution on the struggle between the business class and the New Class using the example of the new industry of "public interest" advocates; Everett C. Ladd's essay on new forms of class conflict in postindustrialism between the "upper-middle-class-as-intelligentsia" and the "embourgeoised working class"; and Aaron Wildavsky's rather polemic article on the ecology movement. It argues that the ecology movement of the New Class derives from the class struggle against the old wealthy middle class and the New Class's attempt to obtain "pure air" and "clean water" in using public money and restrictive state regulations, goods that the old middle class could easily afford privately.

Paul Weaver and Peter Steinfels, two highly respected authors, offer more balanced analyses of New Class politics. Weaver distinguishes between two kinds of government regulation in America today. To him they represent the social policy of two different classes with very different political philosophies. While the term "Old Regulation" is used to describe the social policy of the class of reformers, professionals, politicians, and businessmen who transformed the traditional, bourgeois political economy into a corporate order at the turn of the century, the term "New Regulation" is used for the social policy of the New Class.

> It is the social policy of the new class—that rapidly growing and increasingly influential part of the upper-middle class that feels itself to be in a more or less adversary posture vis-à-vis American society and that tends to make its vocation in the public and not-for-profit sectors. Over the past decade it has come to be represented by a broad constellation of institutions—the "public interest" movement, the national press, various professions (law, epidemiology), government, bureaucracies, research institutes on and off campus, the "liberal" wing of the Democratic party, and the like. By means of its regulatory policy, the new class is, among other things, bringing about what Murray Weidenbaum has described as the "second managerial revolution." The first managerial revolution, of course, involved the displacement of the old bourgeois class by the corporate managerial class, and a corresponding shift from purely private economic institutions to quasi-public institutions like the corporation. The second managerial revolution is transferring power from the managerial class to the new class, and from quasi-public institutions to fully public ones—i.e., to the government. (Weaver 1978, 59)

Weaver's evaluation of the New Class differs from the neoconservative mainstream. To him it is not their animosity toward big business and technology and an accompanying hidden anticonsumerism, but their rejection of liberal values served by corporate liberalism that is decisive. Thus he understands the ethos of the New Class to be "indifferent to the liberal promises of individual autonomy and social abundance" and "hostile to the achievements and aspirations of so many liberal institutions." Nevertheless, this indifference and hostility can be linked up with a political indeterminateness.

In his wide-ranging and very sharp-sighted study *The Neoconservatives*, Peter Steinfels retraces the metamorphosis of the former liberal self-image of prominent contemporary neoconservatives. Steinfels thus takes up the various criticisms of the New Class and discusses them as self-criticisms of what he calls the "counterintellectuals." This is possible for Steinfels, because he is even more convinced than Harrington that this new segment of the population is neither radical nor adversarial but rather undetermined in its politics. Even though Steinfels disagrees on various points with the neoconservatives in the assessment of the New Class and even though he makes some effort to distance himself from the ideological offensives of this camp, he, in my opinion, arrives at an evaluation that coincides with a wide spectrum of neoconservative criticisms of the New Class:

> Whether due to its training in mental work or its escape from the everyday routines that so reinforce social reality for much of the population, the "new class" quickly registers the incoherencies or inconsistencies of governmental or institutional policy. And ready access to a range of information sources, without the censoring and interpreting screens of inherited beliefs, opens the "new class" to a shower of conflicting images and reports, all of them putting pressure on standing justifications for authority and demanding constant reassessment, revision, reassertion, in that sphere of ideas and symbols that legitimates social institutions. Relative to other segments of society the "new class" is thin-skinned about legitimacy, high-strung, liable to a case of "nerves." (Steinfels 1979, 289)

Like Kirkpatrick, Steinfels, in seeing the increasing need for experts and bureaucrats, academics, and intellectuals in the public sphere, argues that this development gives rise to "new men" in government. Next to government, the second important area is the knowledge industry, that is the universities, think tanks, publishing houses, and journals. The power of the New Class rests on the need for "'expertise'—technical knowledge and skills" and "'position'—posts in large, complex organizations that both depend on the expertise of the 'new class' and provide the necessary conditions for its exercise" (Steinfels 1979, 268). Their general activity, however, is "criticism." The question therefore arises, posed again and again particularly by the neoconservatives, whether this criticism (practiced, according to Steinfels, by the neoconservatives themselves), in its subversiveness toward accepted norms, is used by an ambitious elite only to conceal its lust for power.

Publications on the New Class have increased dramatically in the last few years, making it impossible to review all of them here. Before we can attempt a comprehensive evaluation of New Class literature, we must refer to another group of authors coming from a more radical perspective than either the neoconservatives or their more mainstream critics.

The previously mentioned work by Konrád and Szelényi, *The Intellectuals on the Road to Class Power*, can be seen as a neo-Marxist endeavor, not only to provide a general history and sociology of the intelligentsia, but also as an attempt to delineate the differences between the bureaucratic elites hitherto in power in Eastern Europe and an emerging class of intellectuals that is seeking to establish itself in "state-monopoly capitalism." Though the authors assume an increase in power for the intelligentsia in the West, they nevertheless do not see present in this part of the world the conditions necessary for its formation into a class under state-monopoly capitalism. The authors believe this can be deduced from the structure of a capitalist system, in which the legal claim to control the produced surplus is still bound up to capital ownership: "Under state-monopoly capitalism, then, the intellectual stratum, which typically occupies an intermediate position between capitalists and workers, undergoes a noticeable differentiation. One occupational group of intellectuals emerges with its power substantially enhanced, in many respects coming to share economic power with the owners of capital and political power with politicians chosen on the representative principle" (Konrád and Szelényi 1979, 77). To Konrád and Szelényi this development is accompanied at the same time by a tendency toward the proletarianization of other parts of the intelligentsia. Alvin Gouldner (1979) quite rightly points out in his criticism of Konrád and Szelényi that they do not differentiate clearly enough between the Western intelligentsia and Eastern bureaucratized intellectuals, who have already established themselves in important positions in the state, party, and administration. Whereas the Eastern intelligentsia because of its technocratic and bureaucratic status has extensively pushed out the old party elite and indeed is in power, that part of the Western intelligentsia which can be integrated without any difficulty into the "technocratic-bureaucratic system" is still on a thorny path toward publicly legitimated power positions. For those unwilling to submit to the technocratic logic of state and big business, there only remains the retreat into the ghetto, be it that of the artists, radical political activists, or of bohemian academics. According to Konrád and Szelényi, both those willing and unwilling to live and work in the technocratic-bureaucratic system exist unlinked next to each other, and it is up to the reader to imagine reasons why they belong to one or the other social position. The authors omit a common background, against which the technocratic rationality and the intellectual-artistic adversary culture are no longer mere opposites. Yet they point in the right direction in identifying the essence of intellectual knowledge as being "cross-contextual" in nature. The full analysis of the structure of intellectual knowledge, however, so decisive for understanding the New Class, is lacking. Because of this, they comprehend the danger of the intellectuals striving for power only in terms of mighty "multinational corporations' executives" anticipating themselves as a new "world intellectual." "The multinational technocrats have rebelled against what they consider a petty compromise between national capital and the national government's bureaucracy, and have removed themselves from the control of both" (Konrád and Szelényi 1979, 83). Konrád and Szelényi's analysis of the Western intelligentsia is much too one sided and too tightly squeezed into the orthodox Marxist corset, with the result that even the questions they ask are not suitable for providing appropriate answers for the meaning and future of the New Class.

The most interesting book on the social structure of the intelligentsia and its future that seeks to fill this gap and is written from a somewhat neo-Marxist point of view is Alvin W. Gouldner's *The Future of Intellectuals and the Rise of the New Class.* In order to grasp the common factors and sharp contrasts within the New Class, Gouldner identifies two lines of development of the intelligentsia in the nineteenth and twentieth centuries, pointing to the adherence to the ideals of either the bourgeois or the socialist revolution. In brief, this implies either a commitment to a struggle for individual autonomy and private possession of the means of production or the quest for the equitable distribution of property, the collectivization of private property, and the spreading of state ownership of the means of production. Unified only in as much as they have a high degree of education, called by Gouldner "cultural capital," the New Class is divided into two opposing elites. On the one side is the "intelligentsia whose intellectual interests are fundamentally 'technical,'" and on the other are humanistic "intellectuals whose interests are primarily critical, emancipatory, hermeneutic and hence often political" (Gouldner 1979, 48). In the course of his investigations, however, Gouldner comes to some rather unconvincing conclusions. The revolutionary intellectuals in their avant-garde function appear to him as a "medium of an ancient morality," that solely in the name of liberatory ideals, transgresses the borders of the valid "paradigms" of "normal science" in order to unite the past and the future within the view of an all-embracing morality. In contrast, the technical intelligentsia, which is only interested in "fine-tuning" and in an increase in effectiveness and productivity within the frame of an accepted paradigm, is stamped as a "medium of a new amorality." The paradox of this assessment becomes clear when for the technical intelligentsia negative structural reasons are spelled out. "[I]t is their social mission," Gouldner writes, "to revolutionize technology continually and hence disrupt established social solidarities and cultural values by never contenting themselves with the *status quo*" (Gouldner 1979, 48). For the humanistic intellectuals, by contrast, a positive social function is claimed, namely the visionary task of balancing out "good" and "power," a task which Gouldner judges to be sufficient. Even granted that it were true that the technical intelligentsia is more closely connected to bureaucracy and technocracy than the humanistic intellectuals, and is prepared to accept the destruction of cultural and moral values in a methodical pursuit of technical effectiveness, there remains the fact that the humanistic intellectuals, due to their logic of action and their lack of a valid paradigm are, with their permanent critique of given normative systems, destroying and alienating traditional values just as systematically as the alleged "amoralists." The humanists, it turns out, are at least as "amoral" as the technocrats in asserting their right to judge the normative course of society as a whole.

The magnanimous reader can find within Gouldner's text, however, a way out of this difficulty. Gouldner, to begin with, characterizes the whole New Class as a "flawed universal class" and isolates a common rational type that connects both groups identified above. The basis for this is the amalgamation of an ideology of professionalism with an emphasis on autonomy that is inserted in place of traditional forms of experience, a specialized knowledge based on rules of "cultural capital" comes to dominate. The qualitative difference with the modes of experience of other social classes expresses itself in a "culture of critical discourse" (CCD), that is shared by both the technical and the humanistic intellectuals. The ideology of the CCD is "a grammar of discourse, which (1) is concerned to *justify* its assertions, but (2) *whose* mode of justification does not proceed by invoking authorities, and (3) prefers to elicit the *voluntary* consent to those addressed solely on the basis of arguments adduced. CCD is centered on a specific speech act: justification" (Gouldner 1979, 28). In the framework of the "culture" of this critical discourse implicit, context-limited meanings are thought little of, whereas the relatively context-free argument based on rational reasons is valued as being conclusive and worthy of recognition. When dealing with the justification of claims, this grammar of rationality forbids taking into consideration either circumstances, the person, authority, or social status of a speaker. By means of this ideology the New Class is advancing toward "guild masters of an invisible pedagogy." The areas in which this knowledge is mainly put into practice currently are in the protection of consumer rights, development of scientific management, brain trusts and expertise in public policy development, reform movements seeking "honesty in government," and the international ecology movement. The increasing scientization of important fields of work in the state, administration, and industry allows the New Class to grow more rapidly than any other social class, and there are signs that it is well along the road to becoming a universal class. As a new cultural bourgeoisie, the rationality of its CCD fosters a "'theoretical' attitude toward the world." The question arises, whether the New Class with its ambivalence toward traditional and established values contributes more to the destruction of everyday human solidarity, warmth, and spontaneity than it contributes to the realization of truth by means of its logic of justification and its discourse of rationality. The contradiction between elitist claims to power and nonclass specific emancipatory interests cannot be solved. Thus it seems, all in all, that Gouldner's analysis of the New Class and Schelsky's characterization of the "reflective elite" agree in most important points, despite the great differences in their political positions.

Barbara and John Ehrenreich come to an even more pessimistic view in their more strictly neo-Marxist consideration of the emergence of a kind of solidarity out of the new middle-class stratum, thought to be beneficial to the working class. Based on the classic Marxist premise of an antagonistic contradiction between wage-earning labor and capital, they discover in the center of this spectrum a "professional-managerial class" (PMC), which in its economic and cultural interests as well as in their collective mentality, seems to differ as much from the working class as from the bourgeoisie. While most of the neoconservative New Class theorists quite clearly do not include the industrial managers in their classification of the New Class, this neo-Marxist version does so without hesitation, going further than any neoconservative evaluation. With an overwhelmingly elitist self-orientation and in contrast to the interests of the working class, the PMC not only consists of teachers and social workers, but also of middle-level administrators, managers and engineers, nurses, and corporate, as well as state, bureaucracy managers. Not only do their knowledge and their skills divide them from the working class but in being salary-dependent mental workers, their objective relationship to the reproduction of capitalist culture and capitalist class relations does too: "We define the Professional-Managerial Class as consisting of salaried mental workers who do not own the means of production and whose major function in the social division of labor may be described broadly as the reproduction of capitalist culture and capitalist class relations" (Ehrenreich and Ehrenreich 1977a, 45). Despite the experience of its functional role overseeing the maintenance of both the interests of capitalist reproduction and cultural industry, it is the emergence of a pronounced professionalism—which between 1880 and 1920 took on distinct institutional forms—that unites the PMC, gives it security, and distinguishes it from the capitalist class. It is only this professionalism that allows it to have some autonomous power.

The Ehrenreichs' assessment is particularly interesting because it attempts to include in its theory of the PMC the concept of professionalization which, from a Marxist perspective, is a watered-down bourgeois class theory (Joppke 1985). In this however, the authors come to a rather puzzling conclusion. Initially they define the characteristics of the professions in the usual way as including "(a) the existence of a specialized body of knowledge, accessible only by lengthy training; (b) the existence of ethical standards which include a commitment to public service; and (c) a measure of autonomy from outside interference in the practice of the profession" (Ehrenreich and Ehrenreich 1977a, 58). From this they deduce a many-layered character of general professionalism as being elitist, anticapitalist, and anticollectivist in outlook. While professional activity is earmarked by a strict adherence to well-grounded scientific standards that in turn are obtained by specialized training and are based on norms of a professional ethic including an orientation to the common welfare, these professional activities also imply, in organizational and corporate terms, the search for sole power over education, the control over professional recruitment and criticism, as well as sanctions in cases of violation of professional behavior. Any outside social control is sought to be more or less eliminated. Objectively, the PMC seems to be striving for the enforcement of purely scientifically based and professionalized work processes and with this is oriented against stiff bureaucracy and the old capitalist-based organizational hierarchies. Subjectively, however, the representatives of the PMC, according to the Ehrenreichs, are following other interests. Despite the amazing heterogeneity of the composition of the PMC the authors describe them as a coherent class with a common way of life. On the basis of their professionalism some political behavior based on a collective mentality can already be recognized. This, however, as the above quotation points out, is said to be aimed at the maintenance of the capitalist order and class relations and thus is antilabor in orientation.

Various arguments can be made against this interpretation. Quite apart from their too widely constructed composition of the PMC, the Ehrenreichs do not take into account that a whole number of professional groups included by them are not suitable for professionalization or in fact oppose it (e.g., middle management in the profit sector). Secondly, they completely overlook the different organizational contexts and types of activities of business managers, technocratic engineers, and bureaucratic administration experts over that of the person-related service professions in the nonprofit sector. The difference between professional activities in the profit and the nonprofit sectors are generally disregarded by the Ehrenreichs and this prevents them from grasping possible processes of change taking place in these areas. By not recognizing sufficiently the anticapitalist impulse, not even that of the professionals in the human service area, the authors are lagging far behind their neoconservative colleagues. A neoconservative author like Irving Kristol on the other hand fails to appreciate the growing power of the New Class in the private profit sector and reduces the influence of the New Class almost completely to the public sphere. The Ehrenreich's analysis ends actually with a mere warning to the New Left and to a working class imputed with highly stylized political capacities, against the egotistic superiority of the PMC (Ehrenreich and Ehrenreich 1977b).[6]

However, the Ehrenreichs might not be dead wrong in their broad assignment of professional groups to the PMC. Bell has taken up two similar lines of development in characterizing postindustrial society as a new society dominated by professional services. In the transition to this new society, it was not only necessary to dispense with old holistic social concepts, but also to understand society as made up of three relatively autonomous spheres consisting of social structure, political order, and culture. With this he also wanted to take care of the changed character of social conflicts, which, after the loss of the Protestant ethic as an integrating power, now take place on the ground of an increasing autonomous culture in modernity. It is only when one promotes the knowledge of the New Class as a "knowledge class" with the requirements of cultural modernity that one understands its anticapitalist impulse. This impulse reaches back to the protest movements of the sixties with their hedonistic demands, where the wish to adopt a life-style completely independent of the logic of capital was the prime motive. The class struggle of former days has now become a cultural conflict in which the passion for the immediate experience and direct fulfillment of desires links up with a perceived necessity for a global impeachment of world-wide injustice. This type of knowledge of a counterculture is currently a part not only of contemporary new social movements but is also—though with significant restrictions—implied in the knowledge of the New Class per se.[7] Bell thus quite correctly states:

> It is true that, within an emerging postindustrial framework, a new professional and technical stratum has expanded in recent decades, largely in the knowledge field (education, health, research, engineering, and administration), and that the greatest growth in employment has been in the public sector. It is also true, though more

ambiguously so, that cultural and political attitudes highly critical of traditional capitalism (though more reform-minded than revolutionary) have spread among the educated classes and now seem to dominate the cultural periodicals. But the relation between these two developments is less clear. (Bell 1979, 169)

It becomes even more evident that this relationship is not clear, when he notes "if there is any meaning to the idea of a 'new class,' ... it cannot be located in social-structural terms; it must be found in cultural attitudes. It is a mentality, not a class" (Bell 1979, 186).

It follows that the emergence of the New Class cannot be fully defined in social-structural terms, but has to be approached more importantly in terms of cultural attitudes. An exact description of New Class membership using traditional class theoretical concepts is impossible. But even the assignment of professions to occupational groups is not only difficult but also of limited value. Instead it might be more worthwhile to examine more closely the intrinsic logic of professional behavior of the various professions in order to unravel the type of knowledge and behavior that is specific to them.[8] On the basis of this specificity, it might become possible to grasp the collective mentality of the New Class. In this way, the one-sided contrast of profit and nonprofit or public and private sector can be equally minimized as the New Class's presumed interest in growing government intervention in the economy. It is only against the background of the process of relative independence of economic interests and cultural attitudes, life-styles, and value systems that it becomes obvious why many authors have difficulties or are hesitating to certify the New Class with a clear political future. Indeed, this question seems to be open.

Steven Brint (1984) has tried to check different assessments of the New Class (Ehrenreichs' PMC, Ladd's New Class, Gouldner's New Class, and Kristol's New Class) against data from the General Social Survey on "cumulative trend explanations of the liberal, political attitudes of professionals." Brint comes to a partially different conclusion from the assessments he analyzed. His main point is that the other authors overestimate the measure of behavior that deviates from the norm and liberalism. Only young specialists in the social sciences and members of arts-related occupations would fit the image of an "oppositional intelligentsia." Otherwise, to him the New Class is only a "fictional entity," which he explains as the result of the "liberalizing effects of a much expanded higher-education system" (Brint 1984, 59). Brint's assessment of statistical material however seems to miss the phenomenon of the New Class, particularly since he does not take the type of knowledge nor the behavioral logic as an independent dimension seriously enough. The phenomenon of the New Class falls, as it were, through the holes in the net of his survey data. In a comment on Brint's analysis, Michele LaMont reported that she attempted to interpret the same data, to a certain extent more extensively, and found out that "Brint's data suggests that political liberalism among the new-class occupational categories varies *inversely* with the dependence of an individual's job on profit maximization and with the instrumentality of his knowledge for profit maximization" (LaMont 1987, 1503). But even her assumption that social and cultural specialists should be more liberal because their knowledge does not directly deal with profit maximization and that they are often met within public or semipublic institutions, does not seem to be particularly illuminating. Hans Peter Kriesi's remarks on the same issue are more significant when he points out that "it is not the instrumentality of knowledge to profit maximization that is decisive for the political liberalism/radicalism of certain parts of the new middle class, but the instrumentality of knowledge to the running of large-scale organizations in general" (Kriesi 1989, 1084). He quite validly sees a client-oriented difference in the behavioral logic of "technocrats in private enterprises *and* public bureaucracies who try to manage their organizations most efficiently" and also with respect to "specialists who try to defend their own and their client's relative autonomy against the interventions of the 'technostructure'" (Kriesi 1989, 1085). For him, therefore, the specialists in the private *and* public sectors constitute the New Class and it is they who contribute to the mobilization of new social movements. Yet even this characterization still misses important features of the New Class.

The decisive parameter for evaluating the New Class only becomes clear when we grasp the basic fact that the New Class's preferred cultural self-image substantiates itself in an attitude that in turn establishes a specific rationalist relationship to its clients. A simple assignment of New Class members to professional groups and fields of activity is misleading. The arguments of Kirkpatrick, Gouldner, and others, as we have seen above, point in the same direction. They all characterize the New Class's *habitus* in terms of "questions of legitimacy," "justification," "secular humanism," "the *Reflexionssyndrom*," "the system of reasoning by analogy," and "the specific ability to interpret and explain ideas to others." All these definitions share a view of the New Class as essentially characterized by a rationalist approach in its arguments and forms of criticism. Due to this approach, it is no coincidence that fields like education, health, social science, and research, are at the top of the list of New Class professions and that all of them are located in the public sector.

The key argument to be made is that the New Class—regardless of its professional location in the private or public sector—succeeds most easily in the seemingly unselfish enforcement of the rational discourse of permanent justification that is grounded in moral universalism. It is no surprise therefore that we find the professions that have direct contact with clients and services having to do with people in face to face relationships located at the center of the New Class.[9] Whether, as Gouldner suspected, the New Class will become a universal class, embracing the whole of society, consequently depends essentially upon whether this type of rationality will succeed in becoming predominant throughout all the professions and whether they succeed in peddling it to a wider public.

What is urgently needed then, is to examine more closely whether a social prevalence of this form of rationality is establishing itself. It is important to find out to what extent the "culture of critical discourse" as practiced in the different professions has taken hold in everyday usage. The ideology of the "culture of critical discourse" is the major "cultural capital" that the New Class draws upon to nourish their hopes and demands. In the attempt to enforce almost uncompromisingly their rationale of justification however, the counterculture type of knowledge recurs. The costs of this rationale are still hidden. There is for example the question of whether the New Class professionals' logic of action leads rather to a violation of the autonomy of their clients than to their claimed protection of it. In any case, depending on which self-image they have, the members of the New Class stand either on the side of an elitist claim to power or on the side of "emancipatory interests." It is at least an open question whether the New Class is striving, be it openly or secretly, for either more status and political influence or whether it indeed represents the interests of the common welfare. There are several signs however that the logic of the capitalist market economy is beginning to absorb the "culture of critical discourse" as well. While on the one hand, we do find a relative autonomy of cultural behavior and economic interests, on the other hand we have to realize that new forms of "joint ventures" between these two spheres are taking place, ventures that could signify a reintegration of social structure and cultural attitudes in an unexpected way. Whether New Class values will be absorbed tracelessly by capitalist business or will in fact change the face of the capitalist market economy in terms of a morally and politically enforced convergence must be left open.[10]

3

Modernizing Work: New Frontiers in Business Consulting

Hansfried Kellner and Frank W. Heuberger

Professional consulting offered on a market in the world of industry and organizations is by now an old trade. Though largely arisen only in this century, and in bulk certainly only in the most recent decades, it has become a much taken-for-granted element in our social environment. Not only are many people involved in it (more every year), but we hear and take notice of it everyday. Every newsstand reminds us vividly of its existence. Attention-catching covers of numerous journals point to an almost inconceivable variety of specialized worlds, among them the world of business. (In Germany, the number of journals devoted to the business world have more than quadrupled in the last ten years; at least ten deal exclusively with management consulting). A closer look at any of these journals makes us aware that consulting is by no means restricted to business affairs, but permeates each of the other worlds targeted by these journals as well. All sorts of "how-to" instructions, advice, and counselling are available. Almost no area of life seems to be left out; apparently nothing exists for which some "expert"[11] has not claimed competence. In this sense business consulting is a part of the "advice explosion" taking place everywhere. The massive spread of rational advice offered by what has been called the "service industry"[12] is a hallmark of our time.

The advice boom has made business consulting a major business in itself. Like McDonalds' or Benetton stores, management-consulting operations pop up all over the place, many come and many go, but on the whole business just gets better. New and promising avenues opened by some are readily occupied by many follow-ups. One set of rising consultants are the systemic practitioners, as we call them in our study. Their practice is peculiarly rationalistic in outlook and global in application. It is concerned not only with business proper, but also with nearly every facet of human affairs that could possibly touch on the business world. In fact, their major aim is to bring the human factor under control; interestingly enough not only for corporate interests, but also (putatively) in the interest of the individual employees. There is much talk in the business world these days about the need for a "corporate culture" and a "corporate identity."[13] Apparently the old forms of rationality no longer guarantee success, and business needs to place the human factor at the very center of its concerns. Systemic practitioners are the "engineers" of these new industrial ventures into corporate identity and culture.

The aim of this essay is to delineate the structural features of this new frontier. Our remarks are based on an extensive, book-length empirical research project on which we have been working for the last few years. This chapter presents major results of this study in compact form.[14]

Types of Business Consultants in the Market: Gurus, Exotics, and Technocrats

As is to be expected in a booming market, a number and variety of consultant entrepreneurs compete for a share of the demand. The picture of the entrepreneurship that emerges here is quite a bewildering one. Before we can attempt to make sense of it, we need to draw a distinction between two ideal types: "classical" and "modern" consulting.[15] In a nutshell both have to do with what may be called "the organization of organizations." In our understanding, classical consulting—important as ever—is more concerned with addressing the more technical problems of business, particularly those that crop up in the rationalization of the production and organization. Classical consultants give advice on such questions and problems as the implementation of new lines of production, expansion into new market areas, and mergers. When, on the other hand, a firm wants to overhaul its organizational structure, redesign its personnel system, or improve its outside relationship with the outside world and government, it tends to commission a different kind of consultant.

As soon as the consulting services are dealing with such issues as the "corporate image," the "firm philosophy," or the "corporate culture and corporate identity," they approach the borderline between classical and modern consulting. These services become truly modern, in our opinion, only when such issues are not primarily a matter of design and conception, but a matter of *internal de facto realization.* Modern consultants are contracted to bring about the *embodiment* of a firm's "image" or "philosophy" in the concrete behavior of its employees.

Modern consulting, therefore, has very much to do with the cultural, behavioral, and psychic aspects of people and events in the actual setting of an organization. From this "soft" side, it "organizes the organization" just as systematically as classical consulting does from its more technical side. Consequently, modern consulting includes activities that cannot be subsumed under the terms of "advice" and "counselling" in the classical sense. It also involves "coaching," and, particularly, "training." It aims to sharpen, modify, perhaps even to condition the clients' concrete behavior and self-understanding. For this reason one could equally well refer to modern consultants as trainers. We do so often throughout this text.

Next to good knowledge of the business world, expertise in modern consulting presupposes professional competence in the social sciences, especially psychology. Classical consulting, by contrast, derives its competence primarily from the fields of economics, business administration, engineering, and law.[16] At times, what we call modern and classical consulting do overlap. There is even a trend toward bringing both types of consulting under one roof to provide what can be called "global consulting." In this essay, however, we are exclusively concerned with modern consulting. We can now turn to the presentation of some of the major types of modern consulting, that are now vying for a share of this market, a market that seems to reward high standards and charlatanism equally. This presentation provides the background for subsequent discussion of the specific type of consultant we are primarily concerned with in our study, the *systemic practitioner*.

We want to begin with the more exotic and gurulike enterprisers. The specialty of the gurus and the exotics typically is the mystery of "body and soul," and their so-called services indeed prescribe mysterious treatments for both. Usually they advocate a body-centered therapy for more positive self-awareness, happiness, stress-avoidance, and so on. For example, we find, perhaps alluding to the success of Japanese industry and the alleged mentality responsible for it, peddlers of such Far Eastern "success methods" and "wisdom philosophies," as the so-called "Miyamoto Musashi method for managers." According to the Musashi method (based on the "paths of wisdom of Musashi the Samurai and philosopher" in the seventeenth century) behavior is mediated first by the body and only then comes under intellectual control; Only a body training that translates itself into a disciplined soul and mind, accordingly, can set one on the "true path toward success." This method uses ancient Japanese sword fight rituals (performed and taught, most of the time, in first-class hotels) and astonishingly large numbers of participants pay royal fees for this adventure. We are not able to judge the values of the philosophy of Miyamoto Musashi and the exercises he prescribes—at least in the Japanese context—but the way they are administered here in Germany inclines us to suspect charlatanism is not too far away. We extend the same evaluation to such "encounter" services as "fire walkers"[17] or religiously inspired "meditations," that promise success in life and business through unfolding the mysterious powers and potentials of human nature. Recognizing the frauds in this business, however, is not always easy. For example, few would expect to find the Scientologists behind the CCI method (coordination, communication, and innovation).[18]

Indeed, the *pseudo-scientific* model defines still another category of consultant firms. Two noteworthy examples are, the NLP method[19] (neuro-linguistic programming) and the TZI approach (topic centered interaction). Both claim to be able to restructure the neurophysiological "deep structures" or the "unconscious" by means of allegedly standardizable methods. "Mind-mapping," "reframing," and "rewriting the lifescript" promise clients' success in life and work. We needn't comment here on the dubiousness of such services.[20] Their visible success in the market, however, needs some explanation. First of all, they promise short-term results, and this by itself attracts some customers. Secondly, consultants of this sort are quite adept at staging their performances and equally adept at inducing trance like moods in their participants, at least for a short while. Even apart from the possibility of "spacing" out in a state of mildly pleasant narcosis these kinds of services offer welcome breaks in the daily routines of business people; particularly if the events take place in exclusive settings. In an interview, the personnel director of a large firm mentioned to us that even though he knows that the "gurus" bustling about in the market are mostly quacks, he nevertheless makes occasional use of them, "just to get some fire started" in the company.

A thin line divides these firms from those that ask to be taken at least somewhat seriously. These are the science-based forms of consulting, that typically use one or another "established" method derived from the social and psychological sciences: Gestalt-therapy, transaction analysis, and psychodrama in the psychological area; group dynamics, sociodrama, role games, and interaction analysis in the behavioral sphere.[21] Also very popular are the so-called "problem solving" methods and "creativity training."[22] We cannot elaborate here on the relative merits of any of these. It should be pointed out, however, that the theories behind them are often regarded as outmoded by contemporary social scientists. So their resurgence in the consultant field, we think, requires some explanation.

Because the consultants need to deliver results fast, methods derived from the sciences have to be abbreviated and transformed into a handy set of "quick-fix" instruments. All of these various therapies are quite amenable to such abbreviations and standardizations, yet retain the aura of scientific rigor. Where time is a scarce resource for both consultants and clients, the need for short-cuts presents itself almost unavoidably.

Because the science-based consultants usually operate with such quick-fix methods, a certain technocratic stance becomes an inherent feature of their trade. This is even the case when they loudly proclaim a "holistic approach," since the de facto use of their instruments turns their vaunted holism on its head. Against an overt technocracy, we would speak in this case of a form of *hidden technocracy*. The way technocratization proceeds under the banner of "wholeness" will concern us in a later part of this chapter.

Science-based consultants operate in the field in a variety of ways. Clients may contract their services for a single afternoon or for several years. In the more temporary assignments, consultants usually take the role of a mediator (e.g., in collective bargaining deadlocks) where their mediation between rivals uses such techniques as sociodrama and role playing, or the role of troubleshooter (e.g., in "communication crises") where they overcome the "barriers" by means of behavioral training. In longer-term assignments, we meet the consultants in the role of what we call the *systemic practitioner*. Their assignments involve the entire overhaul of segments of a firm (e.g., the sales department) or the firm as a whole. These assignments are particularly concerned with the institutionalization of a corporate culture and corporate identity.

The number of the last type of consultant has grown significantly over the last several years. This is not accidental. Modernization processes in industry strive for highly flexible yet still cohesive forms of production and organization. Thus the concept of *project management* has become central, as we will see later on. Project management, however, requires efficient teamwork and an amenable corporate culture. It is in this venture that the consultants we call *systemic practitioners* are brought in. Our study has predominantly been concerned with this type.

Reasons for the Boom in Modern Consulting: The Quest for Competitiveness and Social Adequacy

Before we present the reasons for the boom in modern consulting, we want to make a few remarks on its quantitative dimension. Since the consulting field is in constant flux, clear-cut data are rather difficult to obtain. Nevertheless, we can make a few estimates. Drawing from various sources, we have calculated, for the Federal Republic of Germany,[23] that (1) the total volume of business transactions for all the forms of consulting in 1988 exceeded DM 3 billion (world wide figure usually given is around DM 30 billion), that (2) the growth rate of the transaction volume of this business is well above any other, and much higher than that of the GNP; (3) from 1984 to 1988 the growth in turnover reached 12 percent per annum (in 1989 two of the major consulting firms we studied expected their growth rate to exceed 20 percent), that (4) manpower in this field in 1989 has been above 20,000 (that is, highly trained and educated personnel only); (5) about 8,000 of them are active in the area of "personnel development" (experts in the field we interviewed judge these figures to be on the conservative side). The picture would be incomplete without mentioning that all the above figures refer to *external* consultants, that is, free-lancing firms only. They do not include what is probably a large number of *internal* consultants who are employed by businesses to carry out the same functions that the external consultants do. Internal and external consultants are complementary counterparts since the former reinforce the work of the latter.

What are the major reasons for these rather dramatic quantitative developments? First of all, modern consultants have mostly been trained in the social sciences. These fields expanded dramatically in the last two decades, producing tremendous numbers of highly trained people, who found it difficult to obtain jobs in their field, at least in Germany. The pressure on them to carve out some sort of a career has led more than a few to try consulting. Our interviews with consultants and managers in firms suggested a number of other reasons for the consulting boom. On the macroeconomic level these are: (1) The dynamic changes, nationally and internationally that the contemporary market is undergoing; (2) because of these, firms are often in need of expert assistance to cope with emerging problems; (3) the increasing competition of the modern market, where success depends more than ever on innovative impulses; (4) when these cannot be readily generated within firms, they are brought in from without, particularly by creative consulting; (5) the need of modern firms to adapt continuously to dynamic market changes and technological innovations (not only in the high-tech sectors but in other areas of business as well) means that they are forced into frequent reorganizations and often rely on experts for the "organization of the organization."

One of the most important aspects of the modern market is the phenomenon of change in consumer habits, to which firms have had to react and change their production lines accordingly. Where older consumers could largely be satisfied with mass-produced items, the contemporary consumer wants better quality goods and pays increased attention to their aesthetic design and durability. What is more, he demands that these goods should also secure for him a desired "quality of life." The consumer has also recently become sensitive to the ecological compatibility of goods with the environment. The industry has learned to meet all of these consumer demands by various forms of "upscaling." At the same time, these dynamics have opened up quite profitable new markets. One could even maintain that the vitality of modern industry depends in part upon "upscaled" consumerism, and that business actually "commissions" the media to create and promote new consumer habits.

Modern industry is also forced to adapt to altered expectations in the wider social world. Here these changes are largely subjective. Most of our interviewees agreed that claims for the so-called "humanization of work" have to be taken seriously, not only because (at least in Germany) they have been promulgated by the labor movement, but also because they are seen as objective needs.[24] Firms have to seek intensified "participation" on the part of their employees. Firms have to overcome employee "alienation" that expresses itself in attitudes of indifference, "inner" resistance, withdrawal, and poor motivation. This list implies both value perspectives and, less readily apparent, strictly economic calculations. The value perspective, of course, emerges from the normative discourses that have come to the fore in the last decades. Inasmuch as these are highly esteemed, business must not only respond to them, but also incorporate them in such a way that they become compatible with business interests. This double relationship of business interests and value expectations is providing a major resource for the vitalization of business. Expectations carried into the situation by employees are being taken up by industry and turned into what is often referred to as "human resources" and "human capital." Business success no longer solely depends on capital and capital accumulation, but also on the optimal mobilization of the skills and motivations of the workers.

Since the task of motivating the workers is intrinsically related to their subjective expectations and values, these were referred to again and again in our interviews. The experts we interviewed more or less shared the opinion that the following modern expectations and values have to be taken into account by industry:

- the importance of an individual's quest for an "unfolded" personality;
- the justified demands for self-realization, autonomy, and authenticity;
- the prerogatives of the subjective life, emotional well-being, and intimacy against the demands of rationalized industry, with its controlling pressures, coldness, and abstractness;
- the rights of private over public life;
- the individual's search for "meaning" in a world that is held to be devoid of meaningful symbols, plausibility, and credibility;
- the individual's need for "spontaneity," "immediacy," and expression of hedonistic impulses;
- the importance of creativity and fantasy.

Our interviewees also made it quite clear that the functioning of industry could no longer rest solely upon traditional virtues, particularly those of the Protestant (and Prussian) variety. They shared the opinion that the old institutions, such as the church and (in Germany) the state increasingly fail to transmit values and therefore that new ways of institutionalizing values are necessary. They believe that by "humanizing" the world of work, (the task at which our consultants regard themselves as experts), they can reinstitutionalize subjective expectations into public life.

Certain parts of these transcripts read like pop social science paperbacks. This is not at all surprising, if we recall that modern consultants are coming predominantly from the social sciences. What is surprising, initially, is that the ideology of the "critical" social sciences is being carried out into and are applied in the very practical business world of capitalism. But of course, value-related and subjective issues are central to their jobs, and apparently they can make good use of this "critical" world view in their tasks. The flourishing of their business depends on their being able to sell a view of reality to their clients. At times, then, it is neither easy nor desirable for them to disentangle the objectively real from the ideologically valid. They rigorously opposed the suggestion that their world views legitimate their business interests and maintained with all seriousness that their descriptions of reality reflect the world as it objectively is. It is not for us to put their claims to the test. In as much as those conceptions are shared by others, particularly by their clients, they gain in objectivity. Whatever is held subjectively as true is certainly objective in its consequences. Consider for example the fact that the rhetoric of the consultants is also used by the vast number of their clients. It has become, so to speak, the vernacular of modern discourse. If consultants and clients cannot meet on wholly common grounds, then the consultants can at least assume their clients' preparedness to accept their presuppositions, or could sensitize them to similar forms of understanding on the basis of their shared vocabulary.

In talking both with consultants and organization people, we were astounded to find so much "emancipatory" and "inclusive" rhetoric in the world of business. We were used to finding this rhetoric only in the "critical" sections of society, where it was usually directed against business and the capitalist system as a whole. Obviously a change has taken place when the presuppositions of this kind of rhetoric become the starting place for advanced business interests. In this connection we made an interesting observation. In interviews with high-ranking union functionaries, we learned that the unions were very much caught by surprise to find their own rhetorical coinage being used by the other side. They feel a bit helpless in the present situation and are obviously caught in a kind of cognitive dissonance. On the one hand they must, of course, welcome such developments. On the other hand, they have to be frightened of losing their symbolic leadership as advocates of worker interests. Understandably, then, they claim that as soon as their positions are adopted by the other side, they are subverted and made to serve not the workers' but the corporations' interests.[25]

We can infer from all of this that modern consulting plays a double role. It keeps business and industry dynamic, vital, and perhaps even more competitive than before. But it does so by paying careful attention to the wider social world and the expectations emerging from it. It therefore strives for an adequate compromise between the world of work and the social life-world. Or, to put it differently, modern consultants are the agents and carriers who mediate between the world of industry and the world of the individual working in it. But as we will see, they are often enough on shaky ground.

Project Management and the Logic of Teamwork in Modern Industry

We noted earlier that business and industry need constantly to adapt to the pressures placed on them by both a changing social world and a changing market structure. Thus expert assistance is increasingly in demand. However, the required expertise is less and less to be found within modern firms trying to adapt to new situations. It has to be brought in from outside, and to no small extent from the market of the organized consulting. The enterprise of consulting in turn has been and is constantly growing and diversifying. Its continued viability, however, rests upon its ability to answer two needs simultaneously. On the one hand, consultants are called upon to promote, even to engineer, human capacities that are needed for increasing work efficiency and for running a successful business. These needs are intrafunctional, and encompass such "human resources" as engagement in work, cooperative habits, creative work styles, and a positive spirit of teamwork. On the other hand, they are also brought in to help firms meet the expectations and pressures posed by the larger social world. These needs are extrafunctional, and include value patterns, demands for the reintegration of subjective meaningfulness and a sense of wholeness into a hitherto fragmented and rationalized world of work, or the need for personal self-realization in the occupational life of individuals.

In the contemporary situation those two sets of needs have become dialectically related. Until recently the intrafunctional requirements of the firms and the extrafunctional value patterns were often seen as incompatible. Indeed, since the beginning of industrialization, it seemed that the need for meaningfulness and wholeness could be realized less and less in the rationalized world of work, and that the public and private sectors were growing ever more apart. Precisely because of this widening gap, the intrafunctional needs became increasingly difficult to fulfill. For quite some time this situation was bemoaned not only by intellectuals, unions, and liberal politicians, but by the business world as well. In some cases, depending upon the respective interests involved, political "participation" programs designed to reintegrate values into work, have been promulgated as often as educational training programs to promote more efficient work habits.

However, only when intrafunctional needs and extrafunctional demands are brought into structural correspondence can both the function and the meaning of work really be revitalized. It would be a mistake to assume that such a structural correspondence between external demands and internal needs could be accomplish in a merely strategic fashion, for example, on the basis of "symbol management" alone. Not even the most refined techniques available in this area—as they are masterfully applied in the areas of public relations, marketing, and advertising—can give, by themselves, a subjective plausibility to the interconnectedness of the two spheres. Attempts in this direction run the risk of being taken as either "ideology" or exploitative "indoctrinations." A viable plausibility structure arises only if the "superstructure" of the symbolic apprehensions of work can be linked realistically to objective moments in the "substructure" of industry. Precisely this, in our opinion, is taking place in the contemporary situation, and it is this that we have in mind when we speak of the emergence of a peculiar dialectical relationship between the intra- and extrafunctional requirements in industry. This dialectical relationship serves, according to our analysis, as the necessary background against which the consultants gain credibility among workers, who perceive them now as something more benign than symbol managers, ideologizers, and indoctrinators operating solely in the interest of top management.

The field for consultants of this type also opens up from a different direction. Contemporary firms are becoming increasingly less hierarchically and vertically ordered than in the past, choosing more often to organize themselves in a horizontal and divisional fashion. We cannot dwell here on the history of industrial organization forms and the development from functional to matrix organizations.[26] We want only to point out that in the present stage the most modern type of organization is what is referred to as *project management*.[27] It is with project management that the modern consulting business came into being. Project management organization divides firms into teams who need to be effective on the production side and at the same time to be efficient as organizational units in their own right. On the production side, teams handle all the necessary steps of product development from the beginning to the end: planning, engineering, designing, marketing, and sales. For this purpose, project teams have to be taken out of the regular divisional controls of the wider company and made at least partly autonomous. They operate like special task forces endowed with all the necessary jurisdictions, duties, and responsibilities. Nevertheless, they remain within the functional control of the firm. To reconcile the half-autonomy of the project teams and the company's need for control, it is necessary that an integrated system of interaction, that is, a network of relationships, come into being to accommodate both. Hence the position of the network specialist who organizes the teams and sets up a wider network within which teams remain under the control of the company. It should be quite clear that the key to successful project management is efficient teamwork. Or, to put it differently, the logic of project management is teamwork. Since firms rarely employee in-house teamwork specialists they have to be brought from without, and thus the market of systemic consultants opens up.

The use of the expert knowledge and the professional advice of consultants may become a survival issue for a company. Firms want consultants to do two things: to set up efficient project groups and to integrate these semiautonomous groups into the wider network of the firm. Only in this way can a company strike the right balance between project autonomy and management control. Later on we will show that the second task to a certain extent repeats the first. At the moment, however, we want to deal with the logic of teamwork as it occurs at the basic level of the teamwork in the firm. Naturally, the importance of teamwork as such is nothing new. Industry has made it a virtue for a long time.[28] What is new, however, is that today teamwork has become an object of "controlled" deliberation and even in some sense a manufactured product. Almost all external consultants in our study emphasized that until recently there was no systemic way to structure and produce teamwork. They alone, and for the first time, had at their disposal the necessary social-scientific competence and, equally important, the practical knowledge to set up teamwork structures. They maintain that they, by the virtue of their professional expertise, are uniquely able to grasp the inherent problems of teamwork in the field, and only they are able to find and apply the proper means of creating and maintaining it. Thanks to them, social interactions can now be diagnosed in relatively short time, and "disorders" and "obstruction" in the social network can be identified and cured through their intervention. At times they even claim to be able to "tailor" teamwork structure to the particular needs of any individual firm.

The technocratic stance in such claim is apparent. Yet, almost all consultants maintain that they are approaching their field not as experts who "impose" structures on people on organizations from "without" and "above," but merely as catalysts who "help" to bring about what is already potentially there in the field. It thus comes as no surprise that so many of them characterize their activity as "help toward self-help." Consultants typically enter their field with the professional habitus of a therapist, even though they very much insist on being seen only as trainers. In fact, they are careful to avoid giving their work any therapeutic connotations whatsoever, since this could easily create anxieties and fears on the part of their clients. As "catalyst" rather than therapist, a consultant typically maintains that he only helps others see their own "problems" and "communication barriers," that he helps "raise their consciousness," and makes them aware of their "latent motives and aspirations." This quasi-therapeutic self-understanding often expresses itself behaviorally. The modern consultant wears a doctor's comfortable clothing rather than a pin-striped suit, positions himself in the corner of the workshop (like the psychoanalyst behind the couch), rarely involves himself actively in the group situation, and offers himself only as a passive sounding board for ideas, all the while maintaining the attitude of being a "partner."

In fact, when characterizing themselves, the consultants use no term more often than "partner." By this they seem to want to indicate that, although they are highly qualified experts introducing functional steering measures into firms, their work in no way infringes on the autonomy of the firm or its members. Consultants insist that the decision to implement their suggestions remains completely with the management, and that they don't want to assume any managerial powers. By the same token, they refrain from assuming any responsibility for success and failure. They also insist that they are no psycho- or social-technicians, who "manipulate" the personality core of their clients. When we asked them whether their work doesn't inevitably involve a certain degree of manipulation, they regularly answered that their instruments were not capable of reaching down into the deep structure of individuals' psyches and that they would carry nothing into a situation that was not already there potentially and waiting to be expressed. All they do is assist others in achieving self-understanding and self-mastery. In addition, they understand the role of partner in a strictly practical sense, since they have to be partners in the objective tasks of the team they are working with. In fact, firms often set up planning teams in which external consultants cooperate with firm experts. A consultant commissioned by a firm for the construction and supervision of a "teamwork culture" in the social-psychological sense ought also to be able to be a competent partner in the actual work being done. His understanding should not be restricted to the how, that is, the speaking, thinking, and feeling of team members, but should also extend itself to the what, the content of their business. Accordingly the consultants we interviewed emphasized their practical knowledge of the businesses they work with in addition to their behavioral and psychological expertise.

Only on the basis of this dual competence can a consultant be accepted as a partner. To be fully accepted, he must also avoid any suspicion of being an "agent" of top management. If he were such an "agent" he would serve partisan interests only, and would address persons as professionals, not as *whole* persons. According to contemporary management and consultant philosophy, however, it is the whole person that has to be the focus of all the consultant's endeavors. The aim of this "new wholeness" is to foster intensified achievement-orientation, high motivation levels, and greater engagement and identification with the firm as a totality. The consultant accordingly has to operate in both the occupational and personal realms, and will only be successful insofar as he is able to bring them into a fruitful alliance. What makes this venture plausible is the contemporary expectation that such cultural and personal values as self-realization, participation, and autonomy should find expression in the world of work. As we have argued, it is precisely the contemporary desire to conjoin the occupational and personal realms that admits the consultants into both simultaneously. It is this conjunction of once-divergent worlds that gives the term "wholeness" plausibility for both the management and the individual employee, as well as for the consultants themselves. This sets up the tacit background against which the diverse actions and communications can take place; a background, however, which serves the interests of both the members of the firm and the consultants.

The alignment of business and personal interests can be best realized if the process is also mediated symbolically by means of a shared interpretive scheme. In addition to the ubiquitous "holism," consultants frequently refer to a common set of pragmatic maxims, often relating to corporate culture and corporate identity. One, we often came across, (mistakenly) attributed to Kant, is "I can do, because I want to do what I must do" (*"Ich kann, weil ich will, was ich muss"*). In this context, however, this maxim is not associated primarily with old Prussian ethics, but rather with the "new wholeness" in its professional, identificatory, and hedonistic components. The accent is on the term "want." It means that external demands are posited for the subjective self-understanding in such a way that a subject has to agree with already existing constraints and forces. The maxim therefore relates simultaneously to objective tasks, subjective self-realization, and strategies of conflict-avoidance implying that these are all of a piece. We have found that axioms of this kind are regularly used by consultants in both their brochures and in workshops.

If we look more closely at the instruments and tricks used here, we detect yet another dimension to the logic of teamwork. Since firms are very much interested in promoting the employee virtues of flexibility, engagement, responsibility, competitiveness, creativity, cooperative interaction styles, and identification with work and the corporation, the question arises how these qualities can be inculcated instrumentally and systematically. One critical phase in this process is the elimination of obstructions to interactive and communicative cooperation. In order to create efficient teamwork structures, consultants frequently set up series of workshops, group dynamics and conflict-avoidance seminars, collective weekend retreats, and the like spread out over an extended period of time. The underlying purpose of these get-togethers is to bring participants into a situation where they get to know each other intensively (to the outside observer these little "encounters" often had an almost childlike hand-holding quality to them), where psychological idiosyncrasies, latent aspirations, hidden fantasies and self-images as well as veiled forms of competitiveness are brought into the open "uncensored," so that they can later be better controlled.

In comparison to the usual therapeutic and encounter situations, however, these types of meetings obey time constraints. (Time almost by definition, can be supplied by the firms only in restricted amounts.) The picture becomes even more complicated when we realize that project management teams do not remain stable units over time, but, due to the various goals strived after, have a constantly shifting membership. This means that the individual and collective encounter processes should not become ends in themselves, solely subjective adventures, but should relate to the functional tasks and problems of the business. For this reason encounter meetings are often held in tandem with objective task-oriented workshops. So when consultants speak of "measurable success" in connection with these meetings, they mean a measurable improvement in the work of project the team, not simply the intensity of the "encounter" among its members.

While the tasks of project management teams are usually (at least initially) set up by top management, to a certain extent the teams define their goals for themselves. They are expected to be "creative" and "innovative," to set up independent objectives and to assume the responsibility for following them through. Consultants cash in on this expectation by developing their own techniques for "mobilizing" creative potential. Typical methods are "brainstorming," and "concept finding," "unearthing" unused but fruitful experiences, and any other techniques that all come under the rubric of "creativity training." In the application of such methods people are asked to "open themselves up" to new experiences and forms of thinking, just as they are asked to "open themselves up" to one another in the encounter groups. In this way task-oriented moments, creativity-oriented habits, and personal interactions are brought together. So that none of these projects become ends in themselves, they are linked together into a unitary structure with the help of what are usually referred to as "moderation techniques."[29] (In Germany the "Metaplan" and "Zopp" techniques are especially popular.) The moderation techniques guarantee that the opening up in various directions is stimulated in such a way that the practical tasks remain in the center. In this the tool of "visualization" is very important. Using flip charts, bulletin boards, and so on, "uncensored" and "creative" data and expressions are first linguistically condensed into labels, are sorted, resorted, discarded and retained, and then brought into final charted formulas that describe the task programs. Thus a process of "closing in" completes the process of "opening up."

This pattern of opening and closing was central to most of the group processes and workshops we observed. It makes it possible for team members to open up widely, and indeed they are urged to do so by the trainers. But because of the visualization techniques their "revelations" can later be retracted to quite an extent. This technique, with its ongoing sorting and condensing processes, allows all of the individual contributions and revelations, with all their anxieties, vanities, and idiosyncrasies to be subsumed into a collective product and thus to be made anonymous. As a result the individual has opened himself "freely and fruitfully." He has contributed to the achievement of the common goal, and can in turn identify himself with the collectivity.

In the vocabulary of modern team management the qualities of cooperation and competitiveness are stressed equally and not necessary seen as mutually contradictory. In fact, it is assumed that they are complementary. In teams, trained by consultants, no member is allowed to hide behind the achievements of others. He is constantly asked, even forced, to contribute as a responsible participant, yet at the same time he is not allowed to dominate group processes. A spirit of primus inter pares prevails. To cooperate means to compete with others for a common goal. Competitiveness, then, has to be stimulated and checked at the same time. The modern consultant therefore pays special attention to the balance between competition and cooperation.

A successful team demands not only that its members possess the requisite functional skills and know-how, but also that the personal "chemistry" among them be just so. Since stubbornness, impertinence, complacency, bossiness, intolerance, and poor verbal skills (and all of their opposites) play a significant role in group dynamics, trainers and coaches of teams pay attention to these qualities, trying to encourage certain personal traits, and discourage or even eliminate others. In this process, a general collective habitus is enforced, yet at the same time great emphasis paradoxically is given to individuality. Even when they are engaged in streamlining and standardizing, modern consultants claim to be contributing to the individuation process. This is no accident, since their acceptance in the field depends on their meeting the enormous contemporary demand for "self-actualization." Most do, of course, possess the formidable verbal skills to blunt the edge of this paradox.

Global Teamwork: "We—the Company"

Up until now we have dealt with the logic of teamwork as it is applied in singular teams. To complete the picture we also have to look at it from the perspective of *networks of teams* within the organization of the firm. To a certain extent the perspective now reverses itself. The application of the logic of teamwork to individual teams aims among other things at the production of intragroup cohesion. Strong group cohesion, however, carries the danger of isolation from, and even unproductive competition with, other teams and levels in the firm. As much as the firm favors the development of self-responsible and quasi-autonomous teams and welcomes productive competitiveness within and between teams, it needs to adopt countermeasures to reintegrate each team into the wider framework of the company. Top management therefore needs to secure *functional control* over teams; their participation in the broader life of the company needs to be promoted; and their position in the firm's information flow needs to be established. For these purposes, corporations have traditionally used measures like company circulars, periodical meetings, job rotation, and more recently "quality circles."[30] Today more systematic measures are used as businesses look to "corporate culture" and "corporate identification" to bring personnel into a flexible network of team relationships that allows for functional control, information flow, and employee participation at the same time. The double program of maximizing "human resources" and establishing vivid and effective corporate culture finds its expression in the attempt to set up and to achieve global teamwork: "We—the Company."

The challenge for the consultants is to create a network of teams that meets the needs of both individual members *and* the firm at the same time. What is needed is a *welding process* to integrate functional control, information flow, and participation. The logical place to begin the integration process is in selecting the members of each team. Teams have to be staffed by qualified *specialists*. Yet specialists can easily become narrow-minded and lose sight of the overarching structures within which their work takes place. Furthermore, they may not be sufficiently flexible in taking up new tasks or upcoming projects. For this reason, despite the pressure toward specialization, the demand for *generalists* is also great. Generalists become all the more important as modern firms have to adapt to survive in a dynamic market. No firm can afford to lag behind in terms of technical innovation, market transformation, or ongoing value changes in the wider social environment. To be competitive, they need not only to predict the future with some degree of accuracy, but, where possible, even to influence it. This process of the "management of future" (*Zukunftsbewältigung*) often determines a company's major reorganizations. In such reorganizations the proper balancing of specialists and generalists becomes critical, particularly in large firms. In addition to running team projects, companies also install special teams, either to research possible future firm activities or to introduce improvements into projects and teams that are not operating efficiently. Often, therefore, a particular company member (from the upper to the lower executive levels) will belong to several teams simultaneously, acting as specialist and generalist by turns. His multiple memberships make him a strategic information channel. Thus a network of teams with multiple memberships allows for a built-in institutionalization of information flow and control. The advantages of such an institutionalization are greater the better the "chemistry" of the various teams. External consultants are brought in to expedite the welding together of these two dimensions.

Top managers, including directors of personnel, repeatedly stressed in our interviews that the problems they are tackling these days are not only found in the areas of organization and technical production, but increasingly in the realm of the human "climate" in their firms. They need not only an efficient team network, but also optimally communicative structures within which this network operates. With respect to the latter they must deal with various kinds of deficiencies like communicative hindrances, manifest and latent stubbornness, and inconvenient aspirations toward authority and domination. One of the main tasks of the consultants is to cure such unwanted deficiencies. This is based, however, on the assumption that with the help of consultants a productive and promising communicative climate and corporate culture can be installed within which such deficiencies are eliminated in a lasting way. At the same time, such a structure would create an innovative atmosphere in the firm oriented toward providing a maximal use of "human capital" in the future, and also room for the "legitimate" demands for self-realization by its members.

Whereas basic teams are much more cohesively structured, networking teams are of a more diffuse nature. Memberships in them shift much more and are usually of shorter duration. For this reason the mutual confiding of team members is less dense and teams do not develop as many types of group identifications. In project management, collective cooperation must be brought about so that a "we" on the company level emerges. In order to arrive at such a level of corporate identity, a special technique is needed to master the kind of welding process presupposed here.

A Paradigmatic Case of Systemic Consulting

The following is a composite sketch based on a number of the actual cases we investigated. Our model is a theoretical construction that can nonetheless claim empirical accuracy. A company concludes that a global reorganization is in order. Departments can't agree with one another on the company's goal; teams are working poorly. The top management comes to ask itself whether measurable losses like falling profits, fewer clients, and more employee sick-days are connected with a less quantifiable malaise that seems to afflict the entire company. Are boredom, stress, aggression, inertia, and so on to blame for the firm's losing its competitive edge, or are these "soft" problems an outgrowth of the more measurable, more concrete ones? Whatever the answer, the company knows it needs to get outside help.

It should be pointed out here that not only ailing companies contract consultant firms. Simply suspecting that a competitor has been helped by a consulting group will often lead a company to turn to the same group. No firm can afford the risk of becoming a "sleeper" in the marketplace. The boom in the consulting business therefore owes something to the law of imitation, though other factors are involved as well. In fact, a successful firm is more likely to contract for outside help from consultants than an unsuccessful one. Apparently, to be dynamic means to be always on the lookout for new ways of increasing productivity.

A consulting group agrees to work for a firm only on the condition that its role be understood to be that of *neutral partner*. This is crucial if the consultants are to succeed. Even though they are contracted by the top management, they must avoid being cast in the role of "agents" for any faction of the client firm. They cannot ignore any group or partisan interests and must take each of them "seriously." Their initial activities consist in finding out what these interests are and where they collide (being careful to diagnose both their "manifest" and "latent" dimensions). For this purpose, they set up a series of conferences and workshops for each section and level of the firm. By means of interviews, observations, and "open" group discussions they arrive at what they call "is-profiles" and "ought-profiles." The process of deriving an "ought" from an "is" then serves as a streamlining filter in all subsequent training steps. During this initial stage, the consultants form teams among themselves and coordinate their activities with one another while they are working with various teams in the company. At least in theory, the conferences, workshops, and on-the-job observations yield data not only about the relationships and work patterns of employees within each group or level of the company, but also about the interrelationships and interdependencies of all parts of the firm from "top to bottom" (top management to the lower echelons) and from "bottom to top." It is just as important to grasp the "leadership styles" on top management as it is to identify behavioral patterns at the lower levels. Consultants make much of their "openness" at this point in their activities. If necessary, the top levels of a firm may even become the target of the improvements they suggest (a slogan, curiously taken from Mao Tse-tung, often used here is "the rotting fish first starts to smell at the head").

This first stage ends with an assessment of the "is-profiles" and the elaboration of the necessary training for arriving at the "ought-profiles" for each unit and for the firm as a whole. Consultant firms often claim that their programs are "tailor-made" to the needs of their clients. The term "tailor-made" suggests that the consultants' suggestions are individualized for the client, although to us it often appeared that the consultants were very good at applying the same general scheme to a wide range of clients. That scheme is usually aimed at creating the "corporate culture." This is the second stage of the consultants' involvement and once again a whole series of networking events in the firm is initiated: "basic seminars," "follow-up seminars," "coach-training programs," "short and long term behavioral training," "individual counselling," "family training," "on-the-job training," and so on. In all of these events, and always in the role of the "neutral partner," the consultant specialists operate as mediators, trainers, and coaches. In the area of individual and group "competences" they aim:

- to elicit "unused" or "suppressed" capacities and to inspire "dormant" powers;
- to strengthen intersubjective forms of understanding and sensibility;
- to make the participants conscious of how they appear to influence others.

In the area of "teamwork coordination," they try:

- to develop a spirit of teamwork;
- to practice successful styles of communication;
- to disclose latent group conflicts and adjust them;
- to teach cooperative and exemplary styles of leadership that move naturally between controlling and participatory forms of action;
- to develop flexible modes of thinking, to encourage employees to give up outworn habits of thinking, and to move into productive-visionary scenarios.

Finally in the area of the organization of the firm they aim:

- to improve knowledge of how information flows in the firm;
- to improve the knowledge of the tasks and needs of "alien" (that is, other) internal sectors;
- to promote understanding of the environment of the firm; to be able to estimate its market position and chances for development; to envision the wider social demands on the firm.

(The language used here is largely the consultants' own)

Since the major aim is not simply the behavioral training of teams as such, but rather the systematic welding together of teams into an efficient network ("We—the Company") all the workshops and seminars have to be organized in a special way. Whereas in the initial stage, groups and the segments were dealt with separately, now these groups and segments have to be "exposed" to each other. Members of different teams, subordinates and superiors, are put together and made to get to know one another, to learn common forms of thinking and acting, and to develop cooperative work habits. In this process the consultants employ a veritable barrage of "manipulations." The sense of manipulation is heightened when firm members themselves are asked to take on the role of trainers and coaches in the course of events, and to exert the same instrumental forms of action initially used by the consultant specialists, as the injunction "help toward self-help" demands. Thus do firm members internalize the instrumental logic of the consultants. They begin to thematize and organize things and themselves differently, and thus give way to forms of *self-technocratization* that are characteristic of the new modern age.

Depending on the duration of the consulting project (between one and three years), the average firm member participates in between ten and forty such events. No event has more than twelve or fifteen participants. If a firm, for example, contracts for a two-year consulting project aimed at its upper and middle management with a staff of, say, four hundred persons, and each member takes part in a minimum of fifteen events, then for the project as a whole a minimum of three hundred events have to be scheduled. As one might imagine, a project of such magnitude can become quite expensive. At the time of our study, each "man-day" worked by a consulting expert (communication trainer, psycho-specialist, sales trainer, etc.) cost the company DM 2,500 to DM 4,500 per day. Since consulting specialists themselves work in teams (sometimes three or four are involved in a single event), the total costs easily reach the million DM mark. We know of projects that cost as much as DM 3 or 4 million. Educational and training services that take place outside of the firm cost extra.

In tallying the number of events we have only counted those in which consulting experts are present to direct and observe. The number of events become even greater if we take into account the many events in which firm members—trained in the meantime as moderators, coaches, and trainers—themselves take on these actions. Especially in large firms, "centers for personnel education" are becoming increasingly common. In addition to advanced vocational, language, and computer training programs these centers organize programs to promote the corporate culture. Whether organized from within or without, the goal of these programs is to create and maintain an attitude of "We—the Company."

In all of these workshops and programs, time plays an enormous role. The consultant's time is money, but even more so is the time reserved by the firm for these events. The limited resource of time expresses itself also in the instrumental logic used. The consulting experts have to take the time factor carefully into account, since the success of a program depends on its ability to get relatively fast results. That necessity almost unavoidably leads to abbreviations and simplifications of the theories involved and consequently to a very *positivistic praxis.* The consultants of course have a rather different opinion. They place as high a value on the scientific foundation of their knowledge as they do on their holism. Positivism and holism, however, are traditionally considered to be mutually exclusive. The consultants resolve this seeming contradiction with a convoluted, vaguely emancipatory rhetoric. As one director of a company said, the workshops his consultants set up are "veritable orgies of humanity." Only under the cover of modern individualistic values does this reconciliation seem plausible.

What are the results of this kind of work? Ideally, the consultants will have succeeded in mobilizing human resources and made possible the achievement of a corporate culture. The firm will have benefited, and so also will the individual members. Firm interests and individual interests will have successfully been intertwined, and corporate identity will have emerged. The question remains, however, how long these results will last. As long as companies are capable of rewarding their members' intensive engagement with raises and promotions, we should not be pessimistic. Currently our German economy is very strong, and companies are affluent enough to remunerate their people handsomely for their ventures into corporate identity. What would happen in times of economic recession, however, remains to be seen. Here we have certain doubts.

It should have become clear that the success of systemic consulting rests upon the very intricate set of instruments that it sets in motion in its work. On the surface, it seems that their behavioral methods have solid scientific grounds and that this explains their results. But the real reason that these programs work, we think is because they so completely absorb the participants, who run from event to event being continually bombarded with impulses administered by the consultants. Different consulting companies use different behavioral methods (from transaction analysis to gestalt therapy). It made almost no difference which theories they were spouting; as long as they spun a tight controlling web of events, they all were successful. The scientific methods used are, by themselves, irrelevant. Any approach can become successful, particularly if it has a catchy name. The real instrumental logic lies somewhere else.

Supplementary and Reinforcing Services in Systemic Consulting

As we mentioned earlier, consulting firms will often provide follow-up or reinforcement services to a client company after the initial behavioral services are completed. Sometimes these refresher seminars are held on the site of the original consulting project. More often, however, they take place "off site," usually in expensive hotel conference centers. In fact, management training seminars quite apart from on-site consulting, have been around for quite some time. These older consulting establishments offer training in general management, business administration, organization planning, leadership styles, marketing, sales skills, rhetoric, and business ethics. Many of them are reputable establishments, though they have spawned some rather dubious successors. Classical management training (in leadership styles, marketing, etc.) is now combined with training in such things as sensitivity, creativity, conflict management, motivation, personal self-management, body language, positive thinking, and mental and physical fitness. According to a leading German magazine (*Management Wissen*) which runs a list of these seminars with information on time, place, and cost, about 700 of these training programs (usually lasting a couple of days each) are offered by more than 240 agencies each year. And the magazine does not even include the offerings of the more established large consulting firms, which usually schedule events continuously throughout the year.

Here we are concerned primarily with the events conducted to reinforce the results of on-site consulting. The advantage of off-site seminars and workshops is that they proceed without regard to the daily routines and pressures within the company. Because in this way they allow for exclusive concentration on the social and psychological dynamics of the group, they are particularly suited to "training" in sensitivity and creativity, mental and physical fitness, and the like. For consulting firms who offer both on-site and off-site services to the same companies simultaneously, the results of one can be applied to the other. In this sense, they too belong to the total program of systemic consulting.

Sometimes a number of techniques are packaged into the same event and offered as a "holistic treatment." A so-called "balancing seminar" described by G. Fischer in *Manager Magazin* provides a good illustration of the totalizing perspective involved here. Over a six-day period, in a fairly exclusive country club hotel, a group of eight to ten managers meet a team of six consulting experts and trainers in order to achieve a "balancing of body, soul, and mind." The team includes sports coaches and physical therapists for the body, psychologists and psychotherapists for the soul, and communication/behavioral trainers for the mind. Their sales pitch is "Each trainer is a specialist in his field. Together they are a flawlessly integrated team whose focus is the whole individual." The cost of this balancing seminar is DM 9,000 per person—about 4,500 dollars. As might be expected, the participants all came from the very top management levels, since no company could afford to send middle level managers to this sort of program.

The six-day program begins with the "test phase," in which the necessary requirements in the respective "departments" are assessed. In this stage the trainers prepare an "individual checklist" for each participant. The physical therapist and sports trainers conduct a complete "wellness assessment"; the psychologists and therapists find the "knots" in each psyche; the communication specialists try to lay hold of "dysfunctional patterns of verbal behavior and self-presentation." The results are entered on the individual checklists and used by the experts to determine the "intensity dose" to be administered to each participant in the subsequent training programs. Each of the six days is filled from morning to evening with exercises of various kinds. The day begins with gymnastics and sports. Later in the morning the participants hone their skills in communication and conflict-resolution. Then more physical exercises, this time emphasizing balancing, proper breathing, and body consciousness. After that, the psychologist and psychotherapist take up the mind-body relationship with exercises in autogenic training and meditation for the purpose of making "step by step contact with our body." In the evening, after further communication and meditation exercises, the participants and trainers talk about the day in group meetings as well as in one-on-one conversations, and work out the program for the next day. The aim of the program is to achieve a "holistic balancing" between the "departments" of body, soul, and mind, since only as a "whole person" can the executive meet the demands of his job without suffering physical or mental stress.

To whatever degree "packaged" events like this one transform their participants into happy, productive, and stress-free "whole persons"— we have our doubts on this score—it is certain that they have an impact. Insofar as participants commit themselves "body, mind, and soul" to such organized programs, their whole person is indeed called upon, since for the duration of the program they remain under complete and unrelenting observation and control. And this not only on part of the trainers, but also by the participants themselves who come to accept the implicit "encounter" logic. The structure here is very similar to the logic of teamwork we discussed earlier. Once again we find the process of opening-up and closing-in. And once again we see the whole barrage of workshop events forcing the individual into a collective web of perception and understanding. It seems to be this totalizing effect in particular that is responsible for whatever transformations in the participants do take place. Often enough, the participant himself becomes part of the instrumental directorship of the logic of teamwork without becoming aware of it. Since the maxims of wholeness are omnipresent this self-technocratization of the participants often goes unrecognized.

The Profile of an Optimal Consultant

What characteristics ought a modern consultant to have? Our interviewees listed a number of qualities they claim were essential. On the occupational side, a consultant should know the basics of business administration. He should also know the business of his clients, or be able to learn it quickly. In both cases, he should be aware of the latest trends so that he can speak convincingly of probable future developments. Obviously, he has to have a mastery of behavioral and therapeutic techniques; optimally he should have had a thorough training in one of the behavioral sciences. But precisely here, certain additional qualities are needed if he is to do more than apply these techniques mechanically. He needs to have intuitive abilities, a feel for persons and situations, a creative way of processing information, a restless imagination, and an abundance of ideas. In addition he must be able to interact flexibly and cleverly in different situations and, of course, to communicate well—most importantly, to persuade others, perhaps to charm, even seduce them into accepting a certain view of reality.

To do all of this, our interviewees said, the perfect consultant should not only be totally engaged in his work, but should derive joy and satisfaction from it as well. He should exude optimism, "positive thinking," and an air of reliability and credibility. That is, he should "live what he teaches." He should "like people," or at least take them seriously and respect them. As one of our interviewees shrewdly put it, he should "see people in the way they want to be seen and not in the way they really are." Because the consultant is working with peoples' self-images, a function of their innermost life, there is always the danger that the client will see a consultant as having overstepped the bounds of privacy. For this reason the consultant must always "assist" and never "manipulate," at least according to professional dogma. Where the line between these is drawn is another question.

Whether or not a consultant actually possesses all of these personal characteristics, he must in any case act as if he does. We have found that the professional consultant spends a great deal of time and effort on the presentation of a persona. The art of self-presentation is to make the ideal appear to be the real. And the longer the deception is practiced in the field the less necessary it becomes, hence the assumed person becomes the habitual one. In our observation, the longer the consultant had worked in the field the less he felt himself to be playing a role. In most cases, those who need to call up so much sensitivity, attention, sympathy, and engagement in their work need to rely on various forms of distancing and other compensations to let off emotional steam. For all the emphasis on "openness," certain emotional behaviors are off-limits on the job.

Conclusions

When we embarked on our study over four years ago, we were initially interested in identifying some of the "carriers" or "agents" of contemporary modernization processes. Since these, in an industrial age, are inevitably also *rationalization* processes, the agents who were of special importance to us were the very carriers of rationality. In the contemporary situation, often referred to (we believe erroneously) as "postindustrial," the "service professions" have become increasingly important. In this sector, business consultants, perhaps more than other professions, are agents of rationalization. They are working in the area, namely industry and economy, that has always been and still is visibly under the sway of rationalization of a *functional* kind. Yet, while the functional rationalization of industry continues, today something else is going on as well. Industry, as we have been arguing, has had to respond to external social demands that were hitherto more or less alien to it. And it has had to reconcile these social demands with the needs of the functional-rational logic governing the market as a whole. Modern consultants have become prime mediators and modernizers in this respect.

Our research often caught us by surprise. When we saw how effectively the modern consultants are at welding the needs of industrial firms and the subjective expectations of the firm members, we could not help but be skeptical. We wondered whether the consultants were not simply con men, however clever and refined. That impression remains with us, at least to a certain extent. The fact remains however that the persons who have worked with modern consultants often find themselves having benefited. The needs of firms and their members are indeed met in a double way: the members are taken "seriously" as persons, and given space for their individuality; the firm benefits from these more engaged employees who are ready to put their recently tapped "creative" potential to use in the service of the "corporate culture." Both sides are winners, it seems, when unapologetic capitalism and the demand for the "humanization" of the work world can be reconciled. This, however does not resolve our ambivalence. We are left with reservations.

For one, as we have shown, the "holism" so *en vogue* in the world of industry operates, often in a hidden way, on rather technocratic grounds. It forces people to regard themselves and reality in an instrumental fashion and, thus, can hardly bring about a "wholeness" deserving of the name. A manufactured unity cannot deny its synthetic nature. It is deliberately even clinically made up of elements that can be manipulated and rearranged like tiles in a mosaic. It is a wholeness lived in the grip of technical reasoning, both by the consultant technicians and the clients who have adopted their logic. Against all intentions, this new wholeness fosters *self-technocratization.*

Secondly, the conception of corporate culture and corporate identity in the sense of "We—the Company" is rather misleading. The term "we" suggests a sort of identity which usually exists only in primary groups. And the term "company" conveys the idea of family; indeed at times both terms are used interchangeably. Familial relationships, however, do in no way obtain here. Normally, the understanding of the family implies an unrenounceable membership, morally charged reciprocities, and deep emotional bonds. Even when the term "family" is used only metaphorically, those who push a philosophy of corporate identity nevertheless want to draw the common understanding. In this context, such an understanding is highly exploitative. A firm can hire and fire, renouncing an employee's membership at almost any time and for almost any reason. Its moral obligation to its members does not go beyond negotiated contractual conditions, and the emotional ties between employees usually last only as long as their employment does.

Finally the totalizing processes we have described level the distinctions between private and public life, personal existence and salaried occupation. People within firms that contract for systemic consulting are expected to invest themselves totally. Even their secrets are not their own; they are constantly asked to withhold nothing and to turn themselves inside out. For what they may gain in "self-realization" and the like, they pay a considerable price. The old distinction between the private and the public served as a shelter for the individual, where he could safely protect his personal autonomy at least to some extent. Deprived of this shelter, deprived of his autonomy, he may be on his way to becoming the perfect company man thanks to the absence of any individual life worth having.

In conclusion we may come back to our question of how the business consultants we studied are carriers or agents of the rationalization process in modernity. To us they are one of the prime mediators between the functional logic of rationalization and the social demands posed to industry in our contemporary situation. By reconciling these two, or seeming to, they promote a new kind of industrial logic. They are quite successful in anchoring subjective life-world demands in the internal structures of industrial companies, and are equally successful in exploiting the subjective capacities of individuals for the firm's interests. If the older type of industry ran on functional rationality (mechanization, bureaucratization, systematization) the contemporary industries now also make use of a different kind of rationality, namely that of the life-world. The life-world rationality, of course, refers to the matrix of expectations and assumptions that give meaning to an individual's life. In welding functional rationality to life-world rationality, systemic consultants transform both. The industrial world of functional rationality gains in flexibility, meaningfulness, warmness, and vitality if we see it as having once been rigid, cold, meaningless, and "alienating." The life-world, in our opinion, however, suffers in this process, not only in being exploited, but in being made to take on an implicitly technocratic nature when individuals under the sway of systemic consultants begin to relate to themselves and their private worlds in instrumental, mechanistic ways. In our opinion, the technocratization of the life-world amounts to a perversion of it. We do grant nevertheless that, seen from the other side, consulting specialists do contribute to the vitality of industrial life, and to some sort of humanization of the work world of capitalism.

4

Unexpected Convergences: New Class, Market, and Welfare State in the World of Art

Anton M. Bevers and Anton C. Zijderveld

The New Class in the Dutch Welfare State

In the 1970s Frank Parkin, Helmut Schelsky, Alvin Gouldner, and Pierre Bourdieu, among others, introduced the concept of New Class into sociological literature. Considerably earlier than this, however, various authors had drawn attention to this concept and the ideas lying behind it. What is common to the various definitions of and statements about the concept of the New Class is the idea that the contrast between "haves" and "have-nots" has lost its importance in modern societies, where income and property have become less scarce and more evenly distributed among people. At the same time, knowledge and skills, the power sources of the more highly educated, have become increasingly important, and this has created new types of inequality. The modernization process has led to such enormous changes in the Western middle class that it has become useful to draw a distinction between two classes. First we see the continuance of the bourgeoisie; the traditional propertied elite occupying important positions in trade and industry. This group is also significantly present in the more traditional occupations such as in the medical and legal worlds. These are the producers and the distributors of material goods and/or commercial services, who draw upon immediately applicable knowledge in practicing their profession. Second, we see the emergence of a new middle class, which Peter Berger has termed the "knowledge class," whose labor is directed at the production and distribution of cultural capital (Bourdieu's term), or symbolic knowledge. Highly educated, the members of the knowledge class work mainly within the noncommercial sectors, including the civil services, educational and health care institutions, and the media (Gouldner 1979; Wilterdink 1981). They are trained above all in the rational approach to the analysis and the regulation of societal processes and phenomena with special attention to the application of this knowledge in the advancement of what is well stated as the "quality of life." Schelsky fittingly refers to them in *Die Arbeit tun die Anderen* as *Sinnproduzenten* and *Sinnvermittler* makers and transmitters of "meaning" or "value." While the old middle class continues to remain strongly associated with the mentality and values of traditional capitalism, the life-style of the New Class is best described as hedonistic and consumption oriented, not only regarding goods and services, but also ideas, values, and social relations (Adriaansens and Zijderveld 1981). All of this is well illustrated by the goods and services proffered by this sector of the economy, a rich assortment of material and immaterial life-style articles catering to the desire for "well-being and happiness" (Achterhuis 1980).

From 1975 to 1985 the Netherlands experienced an increase in the number of jobs in secondary and higher education (from 45 percent to 58 percent in relation to the total employment opportunity). The increasing significance of knowledge and skills does not automatically lead to more power for those possessing them, since the strong growth of this New Class alone caused diploma inflation, blocked promotion opportunities, and created a glut of academics (Wilterdink 1980). The members of the New Class are permanently pressured by professionalization demands and thus are constantly pushed into internecine conflicts over the recognition of and appreciation for the cultural capital they possess. Since they derive their societal position mainly from the support they enjoy from the government and the strongly developed state apparatus, they occupy a unique position along the political spectrum of those possessing cultural capital. The assumption is usually made that the members of the New Class are politically and ideologically left of center, and plead for an expansion of government for reasons of self-interest, since those who benefit from the welfare state are also the clients of the knowledge specialists (Konrád and Szelényi 1982; Brint 1984). It is also true that the more highly educated wage workers are mainly dependent on government jobs and subsidies. They, therefore, form an important power factor in the battle to maintain and expand the welfare state. National research in 1982 showed that public sector employees tend to vote for liberal candidates and causes much more than their private sector counterparts. This was particularly true for higher income groups, which at the same time constituted the more highly educated. Of the best-paid civil servants, more than 30 percent supported left-of-center political groups, for example, the Labor Party, while no more than 15 percent of those with the highest incomes in the private sector did the same. It has also been shown that the more highly educated civil servants and students are strongly overrepresented among those sympathizing with and taking part in new social movements such as environmentalism, feminism, and the antinuclear and peace movements (see table 4.1).

Although the New Class prefers to vote for left-wing parties, they raise serious questions about the welfare state. They are highly skilled in critical argumentation and are particularly critical of their own role in the welfare state. The wave of publications by sociologists, political scientists, economists, and public administration specialists bears witness to the concern the New Class has about the ideas and ideals of the same circle of basically left-wing specialists employed in civil service. For many, their faith in social engineering and the blueprints of social technocracy had proven to be an illusion. Some Social Democrats have admitted that government had little room within which to maneuver when attempting to "guide society." Thus, thanks to empirical criticism, radical education reformers have been pushed out of the debate, social/cultural work and health care have suffered from harsh spending cuts, the number of social scientists has seriously been reduced and special subsidies for art experiments have all but ceased. The left-wing political hobbyhorses of idealists and world reformers were tested by critical research and were debunked more than once. The most recent examples of this have been in the fields of affirmative action policies and foreign development aid. The reaction from members of the New Class itself has had a sobering and purifying effect. Nothing bears better witness to that effect than the moderate position now taken by the largest political party in the Netherlands: the Social Democratic Labor Party, which learned its lesson in disillusionment during its period of left-wing political radicalism.

TABLE 4.1
Percentages of Adherents (Aged 18 and Older) of Some Social Movements in the Netherlands in 1986

| | | A Sympathetic to | | | | | B Participated in | | | | |
	(N)	I	II	III	IV	V	I	II	III	IV	V
All	(1.355)	65	40	49	16	2	42	32	36	14	4
Men	(655)	67	39	44	16	3	45	32	36	9	5
Women	(695)	64	42	53	17	2	38	31	36	18	4
Youth	(665)	70	46	56	19	4	58	45	52	19	7
Elderly	(685)	60	34	42	14	1	26	19	21	9	1
Lower educated	(550)	59	40	48	14	2	22	20	21	7	2
Higher educated	(790)	70	40	49	18	2	55	39	46	19	6
Rural population	(650)	60	35	46	14	1	40	29	33	13	2
City population	(705)	70	45	52	19	4	43	34	39	15	6
Civil service employees	(185)	71	45	50	23	1	59	44	45	20	5
Private sector employees	(355)	68	40	49	12	2	52	39	46	12	6

The transition is also noticeable in the decreasing interest in the new social movements. As Hanspeter Kriesi has shown, the protest potential among the Dutch population declined in the second half of the 1980s (Kriesi 1989). Participation in all social movements during this period has fallen; the more moderate environmental movement and women's movement have maintained themselves by becoming more pragmatic and business oriented (Van Noort 1988). Today, according to the Social and Cultural Planning Office, Dutch opinion

TABLE 4.1 continued
Percentages of Adherents (Aged 18 and Older) of Some Social Movements in the Netherlands in 1986

| | | A | | | | | B | | | | |
| | | Sympathetic to | | | | | Participated in | | | | |
	(N)	I	II	III	IV	V	I	II	III	IV	V
Self-employed people	(85)	*51*	25	*38*	16	3	34	27	32	9	1
Unemployed and physically disabled	(80)	69	*59*	59	25	5	47	41	42	13	5
Senior citizens/early retirees	(250)	65	38	46	15	*0*	*15*	*10*	*13*	6	*1*
Pupils and students	(50)	77	44	60	24	*12*	76	49	63	28	16
Others, namely housewives	(335)	*60*	40	50	16	2	*36*	30	34	*18*	4

Percentages italicized are significant at p < 0.05.

A. Generally is very sympathetic to the movement's goal.
B. Participated in or is likely to participate in the movement's activities.

I   Environmental Movement
II Antinuclear Energy Movement
III Peace Movement
IV Women's Movement
V   Squatters' Movement

Source: NKO 1986/SCR 1988, 403 *Sociaal en Cultureel Planbureau, Sociaal en Cultureel Rapport.*

generally reflects a "prudent" progressive attitude. Critical reflection within the the ranks of the public sector and criticism of the public sector from industrial, trade, and commercial circles have jointly led to a change in climate over the past few years, contributed to a positive reevaluation of markets and private initiatives, and even encouraged a more reserved stance by government. In countries such as Holland with a high degree of governmental intervention in so many segments of life, the discussion of the possibilities and limitations of the welfare state—authors have used such terms as "crisis" and "stagnation"—has strongly stimulated interest in the potential cooperation between government and market. In comparison with the last two decades, the representatives of the typical New Class professions now exhibit a much less anticapitalist attitude. In their present positions, many of the anticapitalists of former days work to restore and strengthen market relations in sectors that recently were fully the concern of the government. The arts sector is a prime example.

A broad front of administrators, industry representatives, scientists, publicists, and the public continuously testifies to the ever-growing interest in anything that concerns the arts and culture. After the era of "welfare thinking" and debating the welfare state, "cultural thinking" now seems to be taking its turn at offering élan to societal discourse. In many sectors at once we see how "welfare" problems are now placed within a cultural context. Social and economic inequality and income differences more often are being defined as cultural problems and replaced by the term cultural inequality, meaning the differences among the levels of education and development. The internationalization of culture offers politicians, particularly the "Eurocrats" among them, more than enough rhetoric for debate on the question of cultural identity. Corporations refer constantly to their corporate culture and cities to their urban culture (Zijderveld 1983, 1988). And philosophers have announced that the aestheticizing of our existence should be seen as the postmodern phase of Western civilization. Even within the walls of the university, social scientists demonstrate more and more interest in the domain of culture in the more narrow sense, the world of art, while at the same time, the arts are less recalcitrant in considering social approaches to art studies (Van Berkel 1986). Recently a growing number of universities in Holland have begun offering special areas of concentration in which sociological, economic, and policy issues on art and culture are included in cultural studies.

Why this increased interest in art? Is it compensation for the continued encroachment of rational and technocratic ways of thinking and doing? Or, given the rationalization process, did this thinking and doing also spread to the arts firstly by, declaring this sector a problem in order, secondly, to attempt to get a grip on it by using policy and organization? The answer to the first question may be found in the expansion of the new middle class. The increased importance of the culture sector is twofold. The Dutch government has had an art policy since 1945, resulting in a strong growth of some of the typical New Class professions during the expansion phase of the welfare state. The art world thus became an increasingly important object of concern to policymakers, managers, education workers, and art publicists. Secondly, moreover, the art world provides the bearers of the cultural capital with the desired supply of leisure-time products and entertainment possibilities. The forms and dynamics of cultural transmission belonging to middle-class groups in modern welfare states could explain the growing interest in art among the members of this New Class. These developments contribute to the convergence of the value-orientations of representatives of the art world, of government circles, and of the market and corporate spheres. Being members of the same class, they share an increasingly similar value system, with rationality at its core.

The Welfare State and The World of Art

There are indications in Dutch society that, following a period of divergence in the 1960s and 1970s, the political and ideological dividing lines between the old and new middle class and between factions within the New Class have begun to blur. This is especially so between the more highly educated social and cultural specialists in government service on the one hand and technical specialists and managers in the market sector on the other. It was particularly so in the subsidized segment of the art world where the previous contrasts were made manifest in words, images, gestures, and sound. The art world was the forum as well as the model for the protest generation and their disgust with anything related to capitalism. It is, therefore, logical to turn to the art world in order to see whether our characterization of the shift in relations and the convergence of value-orientations prompted by the entrance of the New Class into both the public and private sectors is justified.

This report is based on research conducted on the professional positions and professional conceptions of Dutch functionaries working in the world of art: civil servants concerned with art policy on the one hand, and, on the other, experts employed by art institutions in the field of the visual arts. It was within the art sector, one of the extensive "care" areas, that close ties were created between the government and its citizens. This research, therefore, must not neglect historical developments that have led to the extensive interpenetration of the government and the world of art so characteristic of their present relationship.

Since the Netherlands never experienced a true royal court culture, the government and its citizens were never separated by too great a cultural distance. This lack of distance helped the government and citizens to cooperate easily in an early stage of the development, organization, and consolidation of what is now termed the welfare state. This is demonstrated very clearly, for example, in the history of the Netherlands' many national, regional, and local cultural institutions. The initiative for founding and building these institutions usually came from enthusiastic and self-interested art lovers from the class of well-to-do citizens, the old middle class of trade, banking, industry, and the professions. But the private initiative so essential at the turn of the century soon proved incapable of or unwilling to maintain the existing cultural facilities, such as museums, symphony orchestras, monuments, and theaters. From the very beginning, therefore, a small group of well-to-do citizens, scientists, artists, art lovers, and art collectors worked on persuading the government to give full financial support to the arts. These members of the bourgeoisie usually and quite successfully presented their case to the public administration, who, if not congenial spirits, at least were members of the same social rank or status group. Philanthropists, Maecenases, or patrons of the arts were never significantly present in Holland. Incidentally, under certain conditions art collections were handed over to the state, or, in exchange for public acclaim, funds were donated to cultural institutions but the elite of prosperous families and rich entrepreneurs left their care to the state (Kemeps 1989).

We see then that the government first reluctantly, then actively, lent support to the arts and, already in the early decades of this century, expanded its tasks and to take on the role of defender and patron of culture. It is safe to say that from the last quarter of the nineteenth century until the middle of the twentieth, the Dutch concern for culture was almost totally a state matter. This state care, however, was limited to a very particular type of culture, that of the upper ranks of the established citizens, old nobility, and nouveaux riches. Fully convinced that their own values were representative of the common values, the "better" citizens launched a "civilization offensive" in order to spread their own culture among the lower classes with the purpose of fighting cultural poverty. By portraying their group interest as a general cause and by calling upon their own sense of obligation to cultivate an appreciation for beauty among the populace, the "better" citizens offered the government the necessary arguments for taking cultural concerns upon itself—in other words to fully finance art and culture. During the period preceding the welfare state and in addition to numerous popular concerts and educational exhibitions, many other citizen initiatives were organized with the express purpose of leading those deprived of art and culture, namely the labor class, to a higher level of civilization. The hierarchically biased word choice is intentional: all these activities in this period were seen as contributions to the "vertical spreading of culture." Additional arguments for this dissemination of "high" culture were found in the attitude of the upper class toward products of mass culture, which were in large demand among the populace. Because the bearers of the culture considered themselves defenders of culture, they understood themselves to be charged with the task of stemming the rising tide of taste deception caused by the expanding culture industry.

What effect did these culture-spreading idealists have? The information available allows for only one conclusion: the activities of these culture bearers, taste-educators, and art providers, from both denominational and socialist backgrounds, drew little response from among the populace. Attendance in museums and concert halls remained limited to the art providers' own circles. Initiatives on behalf of "art to the people" were not valued very highly. Although everybody was invited, not everybody felt themselves involved and included, and most definitely not the labor classes. Within the culture bearers' own circles, however, interest grew rapidly. Those first decades of this century can quite justifiably be seen as the blossoming period of cultural dissemination. The qualification should be made, however, that this success was limited mainly to the class of "better" citizens, who were actually feathering their own nests.

From the very beginning, the culture spreaders—the well-to-do propertied citizens, the church pastors, and the teachers—were the heralds of the rising class of professional functionaries. In the postwar period, these professionals found employment in increasing numbers with the government or government-subsidized institutions. These institutions were now under the flag of official policy designed to provide for the sustenance, development, and dispersion of art. After 1945, we see a period of expanding culture policy. The cooperation of government, the art world, and private initiative resulted here in a solid network of dependency relations thanks to the recognition, subsidizing, and regulation of professional activities. Official and professional circles thus become more and more intertwined. The result of all these efforts did not go unnoticed. Relative to its population Holland enjoys a larger density of cultural facilities than any other country: over a dozen subsidized symphony orchestras, more than 600 museums, an estimated 10,000 artists, 500 galleries, and a national network of theaters.

As a result of "governmentalizing," new professions have been created in and mainly around the arts. Apart from the familiar professions such as art dealer, art historian, conservator, impresario, and administrator, typical in the traditional world of the old middle class, the government-created and sponsored secondary institutions have stimulated the rise of new specialists: art educators, art civil servants, researchers, and advisors, of whom a great number are academically trained as musicologists, dramatists, political scientists, literary specialists, or sociologists. Bankers, entrepreneurs, and other notables of the well-to-do citizenry who were interested in and had a certain knowledge of art gradually lost their positions in the various administrations, advisory organs, and commissions, making room for a rising class of experts. Relying on their professional knowledge they took over and expanded the tasks of their predecessors while also demanding a monopoly in matters of artistic competence and judgment.

The diminished role and influence of the old middle class following World War I is not the sole contributor to the rise and expansion of new, generally government supported professions in this sector. At the same time, the new generation of artists and the more highly educated in the rising middle group began to question prevailing practices and concepts.

The artists' protest at the end of the 1960s drove the established artist off the stage and the bourgeois public out of the audience. The rebellious artists and their sympathizers wanted to create socially relevant art that would capture the attention of the populace, exposing the prevailing conception of art as a pleasant pastime for the elite that only contributed to the confirmation of the capitalist system. This art for the public at large aimed at enlightening these deprived groups, making them aware of their socially, economically, and culturally disadvantaged position. Insofar as they obtained any hearing at all and came to penetrate to some degree the policymaking and executive organs of the government and the art world, they were able to redefine existing functions and tasks so as to translate art into a practical policy of social well-being. With the total cooperation of the new (1965) Ministry of Culture, Recreation and Social Welfare (note that Culture is listed first)—the "experimental garden" of society—a new offensive was launched to promote the well-being of everyone particularly the weak and disadvantaged. The theater turned to educational drama, renewal projects and experiments were conducted in the concert halls; museums were given an educational task; artists went into the streets and neighborhoods to add a political tint to urban renewal and other neighborhood activities. This culture policy, ideally, would become the main instrument for the redistribution of knowledge, power, and income.

When the balance was drawn up for these stirring years, it was concluded that even though few of the ideological goals were realized, the protest actions did result in an expansion of the number of jobs with the government and art institutions. Thus the protest generation initiated the march through the institutions. Some have argued (Drion 1986; Mooij 1987) that since the French Revolution, Western bourgeois culture has always managed to absorb within itself the consequences of rebellion against itself, and that this generation and absorption of rebellion runs through the history of bourgeois culture like a continuous thread. In actuality, the insurgents have merely propagandized the same values as the bourgeois: individualism and rationalism.

The Recent Convergence of State, Market, and Art

In all modern, democratic, prosperous states the interest in art has grown steadily over the past decades. Already in 1964, Teffler wrote about the "culture explosion" and a "culture hunger" when drawing attention to the significant increase in the number of cultural facilities in America after 1945. Since 1955 the number of museums in the Netherlands has increased by an impressive 87 percent to a total of six hundred. Even more strikingly, the number of theatrical companies increased fivefold in the same period. In contrast to the 1960s and 1970s when art and politics found one another on the same side of the cultural-political battle against consumer society, the past ten years have been dominated by a depoliticizing process. Some observers considered this development a transition to a new era characterized by the aestheticization of the life-world. But apart from such interpretations, statistics indicate a growing market for art and culture products. The increased interest in this sector is clearly demonstrated in employment figures. In almost all countries, as shown in table 4.2, employment in service professions, such as government services for the social and cultural sector, increased tremendously in the period from 1965 to 1986.

Within this same period the percentage of the professional population working in industry generally dropped significantly. The numerically strong, well-educated, and prosperous middle class provide the art world its public. This reservoir has grown thanks to an increase of more than 100 percent, since 1969, in the number of people with advanced professional or university education. The number of the highly educated increased to 26 percent of the population. They constitute two-thirds of the public for the performing arts (Knulst 1989). This middle class forms the social layer that not only demands, but also creates culture products. A good illustration of this is the popularity of professional art education among the members of the middle groups.

Thus, the number of institutions offering education in the arts of painting and sculpture grew from eight, (with two thousand students) in the
1950s, to sixteen (with eleven thousand students) in the 1980s
(Haanstra 1987). Today one out of five students chooses painting,
sculpture and/or music as a final examination subject in secondary
schools that offer these fields (Hoogbergen 1989). This growing interest in the arts is not limited to the Netherlands. In America there were
80 percent more artists in the 1970s than in the previous decade—from
0.75 percent to 1.04 percent of the professional population (Ziegler
1986; Collins 1979; DiMaggio 1988).

For those, who are neither interested in nor capable of working as
artists, but who want, nonetheless, to work in the arts, there are those
professions in and around the art business, particularly those with the
government. In the relationship between the government and art world

Table 4.2
**Percentage of the professional population working in the public service sector
(government/market:social, cultural service).**

		1965		1975		1986	
1.	Sweden	19.8	(32.4)	30.7	(28.0)	36.9	(22.9)
2.	Denmark	19.4	(28.2)	30.5	(22.7)	34.8	(20.3)
3.	Holland	-	-	28.6	(25.0)	34.2	(19.2)
4.	Norway	17.6	(26.3)	24.5	(24.1)	33.1	(17.2)
5.	Belgium	20.7	(35.3)	24.5	(29.3)	32.2	(21.9)
6.	U.S.A.	26.8*	(27.0)	30.1	(22.7)	30.9	(19.1)
7.	England	21.5	(35.0)	25.6	(31.0)	29.9	(22.5)
8.	France	18.6	(27.5)	23.0	(27.8)	29.8	(22.6)
9.	Canada	32.2*	(33.2)	27.0	(20.2)	29.2	(17.3)
10.	Finland	18.8*	(31.9)	21.3	(27.5)	28.1	(22.7)
11.	Germany	15.7	(38.2)	21.1	(35.6)	25.9	(32.2)
12.	Australia	20.9	(30.5)	24.7	(23.4)	25.5	(16.4)
13.	Austria	16.7*	(29.1)	18.8	(30.2)	22.6	(28.2)
14.	Spain	17.1*	(25.8)*	14.5	(26.7)	22.1	(22.8)
15.	Portugal	17.0	(21.9)	14.7	(25.0)	22.0	(25.0)
16.	Japan	17.2*	(24.3)	20.1	(25.8)	20.7	(24.7)

In parentheses is the percentage working in the industry.

Source: OECD (*Economic Outlook*, 1987)
* Data from a year other than 1965

these new professional groups hold key positions. How close these ties are can be seen, for example, in the frequency with which experts switch employment from one sector to the other. The more highly educated within the humanities and social sciences have the required expertise in the fields of art policy, art management, production and distribution, arbitration and public relations. One can predict a further growth of the promotion sector, because the professionalizing of the art business means that more and more specialists selectively appeal to specific publics.

Consumer research repeatedly reports that the growing interest in art is basically a horizontal expansion. The consumers belong to the growing middle class where cultural interests and involvement are clear aspects of the life-style. This public is an important factor in the network of relations between the government and the world of art. Art officials and art experts benefit from favorable consumer research findings since they can legitimize their policies and argue for continued maintenance and expansion of cultural facilities.

Those who observe the recent changes in the relation between government and the art world will see that the substantive discussions have had increasingly to make room for complicated matters of policy and administration. The edifice of cultural care with its high degree of bureaucratization has thus taken its toll. This situation has also led to further reflection on the possibilities and limitations of governmental care for culture, though exactly how the power is divided between the experts in the state apparatus and those within the art institutions and which shifts are taking place, are matters on which empirical research still needs to be done (Freidson 1986). What research has shown (*Sociaal en Cultureel Rapport* 1988) is that discussions between the worlds of art and government have become more demanding and more businesslike, which means that they are being dominated by specialists in financial, economic, and administrative areas. These specialists insist on more independence and emphasize that government-subsidized institutions and individual artists have their own responsibility. The extent of financial support shows how dependent the Dutch art world has become on the government. In 1984, for example, the performing arts (theater, music, and dance) were 90 percent government subsidized; income from tickets and other sales, sponsors, royalties, and gifts covered the remaining 10 percent. In the same year, museums enjoyed 85 percent government sponsorship, and raised the balance of 15 percent through their own activities.

In the past few years, the Dutch art world has committed a great deal of time and energy to finding ways of increasing their financial support. Some institutions have raised admission prices, some have opened gift shops, others have established special support funds for donations, and still others have pursued corporate giving. Whereas previously many of these fund raising activities might have been pursued informally by an individual director of a museum, or business manager of a symphony, now they are a fixed part of the activities and policies of cultural organizations, almost all of which now employ specialists in these areas. The arrival of art managers and administrators has also helped to professionalize the activities of promotion, fund raising, merchandizing, marketing, and sponsorship recruitment. Additionally, the educational services of the 1960s have now become departments of public relations and communications. Above all, following the lead and long practice of the United States and England, art sponsorship in the Netherlands is now being seriously cultivated. Estimates indicate that since 1980, when art sponsorship began to generate serious interest, approximately 25 million Dutch guilders per year have come from these activities, amounting to 10 percent of the total financing beyond government subsidies.

This does not mean that, in the short term, the historically developed governmental subsidy policies will markedly change. The vast majority of political parties in the Netherlands agree that it is the state's responsibility to care for the maintenance, development, and accessibility of art and culture. At the same time reevaluation of the role and tasks of the government has already led in several areas to a weakening of the financial, organizational, and ideological ties between it and the government. For example, the government is less involved in cultural politics. In careful but clear wording the policymakers are adjusting the goal of art-to-the-public better to fit the facts. We can still read in the official communiques, for example, that art must "reach as broad a public as possible" but that art "for broad layers of the populace" remains a "utopian wish." It is seen as far better to serve "those circles where an already existing interest in art exists" (*Ministrie van Welzijn Volksgezondheid en Cultuur*, WVC 1985).[31] Thus the idea of the broad dissemination of art has gradually been exchanged for a more commercial policy based on quantitative consumer figures. The government no longer cares *who* is seated in the theater, but *how* many: the percentage of theater occupancy counts more than the social constituencies represented.

In organizational terms, the government is reacting in favor of increased privatization. In order to allow more room for the market sector, the government's role and tasks are diminishing or have already been discontinued. Subsidized facilities and organizations are given more and more administrative freedom and greater responsibility for their own operations. They are also strongly encouraged to adopt a businesslike and market-oriented approach, such as by raising funds in the private sector and from their own publics. These developments have extended beyond the world of art and culture. Schools, for example, have also adopted a more businesslike approach. Marketing and public relations efforts of schools have led to a competition for students and pupils, and more and more emphasis is placed on the management qualities of school leadership (SCP 1988).

A change in the mentality of art specialists and civil servants is evident across the entire spectrum. Functionaries working in government service, the art world, or industry exhibit more and more similarities. This is due partly to their confrontation with identical problems in administration, organization, and financial management and partly to a similar professional attitude and corresponding professional conduct. Does this mean that the tension between art and commerce is disappearing and that the art world will be catering to client's demands? Not at all. To the contrary, the more the art world, the government, and the market interlock, adopting increasingly similar goals and means, the more each party involved will want to determine its own position in relation to the others. Artists and the art world have been successful at this to the extent that they contribute to acceptance of the autonomy of art (which today goes without saying) and succeed in monopolizing art criticism. These two elements, the autonomous character of art and its critical evaluation, are the heart of the professional orientation in the art world. Government and public opinion recognize totally the art world's autonomy. This recognition even determines the relationship between the concerned parties, as the following case study demonstrates.

An Empirical Case: The Art Museum

Of the 600 museums in Holland, 200 are directly managed by the government (national, provincial, and municipal) and 300 are controlled by near fully government-funded foundations. The remaining 100 museums are controlled by corporate and private interests. The Dutch government's total budget for museums in 1987 came to 270 million guilders; an estimated 15 percent of that amount was raised by the museums themselves through ticket sales (8 percent) and other income sources such as gifts, donations, sale of catalogues, and reproductions, or contributions from friends and supporters. The latter source offers a yearly income of 8 million guilders. According to available figures, 80 percent of the Dutch museums depend on government subsidies for 80 percent of their budgets and most of their employees enjoy the status of civil servant. This strong dependence on the government holds true for more than fifteen modern and contemporary art museums, whose directors are representatives of the New Class in the art world.

The art museum is only a limited part of the total infrastructure for the arts, even though it has expanded over the past decade thanks to heavy government investments. An art-development policy refined and developed over the years makes it possible for 4,000 artists per year to receive subsidies from acquisition, assignments, or scholarships. Three hundred experts in government commissions are called upon to serve as judges and advisors on these potential grants-in-aid. This policy also provides for the founding of art-lending centers in 100 out of an estimated total of 600 communities with a total of 100,000 subscribers and members. It has also led to a considerable increase in public interest in contemporary art showings and exhibitions.

Although the Dutch art world may have already become state-run, in the early 1980s the relationship between the arts and government began to change as both expressed more and more interest in private initiative, the market, and industry. The private sector in turn has become increasing aware that a good cultural climate is an important condition for successful entrepreneurship. But the closer relationship between government, the art world, and the market cannot be explained by motives of self-interest alone. The government's budget deficit forces spending restrictions, industry wishes to profit from art, and the art world enjoys income from whatever source. Moreover thanks to society's increasing complexity, the organizational and institutional framework of government, the art world, and the market are becoming more interwoven. Growing mutual dependency leads to the diminution of differences and shared emphasis on problems of policy, management, and administration, as well as the norms of rationality and efficiency.

Confronting similar problems, and tending to use the same rational way of thinking and acting to solve them, the government, the art world, and industry grow more and more alike. The civil servant as pen pusher, the artist as bohemian, the capitalist as profiteer; little remains of these stereotypes. They have been replaced by a singular type of professional: the highly educated expert employed by government, art institute, or corporation. Understanding and evaluation across these sectors now takes place from the vantage point of the same professional position. The market sector, in particular, is now the model for the government and the art world.

The following analysis of the attitude and behavior of the directors of art museums attempts to show some of this convergence among the three sectors and the role of the New Class of professionals in each. We pay special attention to the position of the museum directors as it relates to artists, the public, the government, and the market. This position combines the financial dependence on government and the professional autonomy so characteristic of the New Class. In addition to drawing upon government documents and publications by and on art specialists, we also make extensive use of information obtained from fifteen open interviews with directors of small and medium-sized museums of modern and contemporary art.

Attitude and Behavior of Art Experts, towards Artists, and the Public

The profession of museum director formally belongs to the group of strong autonomous professions who are recognized for specific competence based on scientific knowledge. In social interaction, however, they derive their status from their *particular* expertise. A museum director plays the role of mediator between artist and public.

He maintains contacts with the artists, often visits local and international exhibitions, organizes exhibitions, and selects and purchases art. In all of these activities he relies on his personal artistic judgment and the wielding of his power and authority. The career and reputation of most artists does not necessarily reflect public opinion, but rather that of art experts who meet in various commissions and advisory bodies to make decisions on subsidies, purchases, assignments, exhibitions, and honors. Museum directors hold a key position in this circle of art specialists. Their almost exclusive authority to pass judgment in matters of art gives them something of the aura of the works of art themselves. They take their task very seriously. In establishing a collection these art directors see themselves as "showing the way" and offering culture a standard for judgment. They defend art's autonomous position, cooperate in its development, and are thus writing art history. They legitimize the art museum's existence primarily by referring to the autonomy of art and to the museum's forefront position in this regard. They unconditionally side with art and the artists. Success is not measured by the number of visitors, but by the museum's role as a judging and standard-setting institution. The museum and its staff will have made their name and fame by discovering talent, or at least by claiming to have noticed talent in its early stages. This is mainly true within the circle of experts, who usually form each other's important audience. As Manfredi points out, "the most important audience to the professional in any field are other professionals, speaking not to the world at large, but primarily to other professionals" (Manfredi 1982).

The development of modern art which has clearly been characterized by "taste insecurity" has driven experts and laymen apart. This is not the place to elaborate on the origin of this gap, which in fact is not only the cause but also the consequence of the autonomizing of art. Professionalization and the growing distance from the public are manifest in art history and art criticism. The experts who legitimize statements about art create a limited universe— open to only a small public. Artists themselves are also, to some degree, responsible for this development, although Barnett Newman once said that "aesthetics is for the artist as ornithology is for the birds." The interested among the public want to be informed and ask for explanations. They want support from art specialists, who possesses the cultural capital that will distinguish them from the half-initiated and the completely uninformed.

In the contemporary arts of painting and sculpture in particular, but also in music and certain forms of theatei and literature, the strongly professional attitude of the artists and art experts creates an unbridgeable gap between the initiated and the outsiders. These circles of expertise, which in an artistic and sociological sense are almost hermetically closed around the art by artists for artists, themselves create what de Swaan calls "Artificial Art" (de Swaan 1987).

Doesn't all this contradict the growing interest in modern and contemporary art among the middle-class public? Perhaps, but with regard to the public and the public service tasks the museum directors have taken on an ambivalent attitude. It is important to draw attention to this because it shows a changing mentality within the New Class of art experts. First of all museum directors assume that this interest in modern art could not possibly be authentic since most visitors lack the required expertise. One conservator stated: "As far as visiting large exhibitions is concerned, I think that it is manipulated. Big articles in the newspapers, of course, are helpful, since people always want to see something special. It is a highly stimulated form of forced consumerism. It sounds elitist, but these people naively gape in admiration and see nothing, they ask themselves no questions. It has become a form of mass tourism, a way to spend leisure time, nothing more." This notion of people walking into art museums for, in fact, the wrong reasons came up repeatedly in the interviews. Nearly all of the museum directors mentioned that the majority of the visiting people had insufficient knowledge of the arts, so as to set their own expertise and taste off against the aesthetic ignorance, insecurity, and incompetence of the lay public.

At the same time, few saw good taste as so exclusive that it could not be cultivated by those who sincerely desired to be trained. They tended to emphasize the exclusivity of the aesthetic disposition when it came to judging and selecting art, but also needed to believe in the transferability of this magic touch when they were serving the public. When asked who constitutes the public and who among this group actually visits museums, they drew a clear distinction between types of publics. This was particularly the case among the representatives of the museums with mixed collections (archaeology, ancient and modern art). For the museumgoers not interested in modern art the museums have nonetheless arranged their collection in such a way that even they have a forced confrontation with modern art as they walk through the museum to the collection of their choice: "The people are forced to walk their way through it. They sometimes react with, 'Why do I have to walk by all this trash first?' Well, because I tell you to, that's why!" Those museums offering only modern and contemporary art primarily appeal to the already interested and initiated visitors.

Choosing a public already favorably predisposed to contemporary art usually means attracting lower numbers of visitors. Most of our interviewees said that it is not difficult to follow a completely different policy in order to attract more people, but that, for their part, they had decided not to do so: "You then would get those heavily educational exhibitions." The quality of visitors was important to most, since everyone is pleased with a large turnout for the exhibitions organized by one's own staff and the extensive press coverage it might receive. Crowds also benefit the museum's relationship with its subsidizers. At the same time many were suspicious of high attendance rates. As one museum director said, "It is not true that an exhibition is good because forty thousand visitors came to see it, it often may have been a bad one. The very good ones which are historically important exhibitions, have always drawn very few visitors."

The ambivalence is clear. The public's interest should not be so slight that it hampers the legitimizing of the art museum. Too large a public, however, hurts the exclusive character of art. A public consisting of initiated people, that is, of artists themselves and of interested people from the circles around art, such as students, professors, art experts, collectors, and art lovers, has proven to be large enough to ensure the museum its continuation and to maintain its exclusive character. Just as lawyers, doctors, and psychologists are aware that their professions do not lose status when lay people imitate the basic principles and concepts—we may call this the juridicalization, medicalization, and psychologization of everyday life (de Swaan 1988)—art specialists try to keep sufficient professional distance from the aesthetization of everyday life.

Occasionally exhibits with tourist appeal are mounted to boost revenues and attendance figures. The museum, however, should not become dependent on such shows else it risks becoming too like

American museums with their infamous "blockbusters."

Unlike some sectors where the members of the New Class can with relative ease win government support for their own interests by appealing to the welfare and the needs of their clients, specialists and interested parties in the art world are having a much harder time. Over 60 percent of the population is against the expansion of subsidies for art, while another 20 percent has no opinion. As recently as 1970, 41 percent favored expanding art subsidies; 36 percent opposed. It seems that the majority of the population now feels that the art world must manage on its own. Expenditures have strongly increased since 1970. The number of voters in favor of halting increased public funding has risen particularly among the middle-class groups, who are increasingly enamored of a marketing approach. The lower classes in fact have always been opposed to subsidizing something from which they are excluded (SCR 1988).

Museum directors acknowledge the growing tendency to organize exhibitions that draw large crowds: "If a few museums are doing that, you cannot remain behind. You then also will have to try and draw more of the public in order not to be lost sight of by the subsidizers. When a few colleagues make an effort to improve management, public relations, and fund raising, others will have to follow shortly, not wanting to stay behind." Apart from this sociological law of imitation, the movement to cut back governmental expenditures in general was instrumental in this shift in the art world. These circumstances forced museum directors to employ a more public-oriented policy. The above quotation, however, demonstrates how this attitude toward the public and public service projects differs considerably from the attitude held only a few years ago. Whereas in the 1960s and 1970s art was expected to be socially relevant to broad layers of the population, we now see a strong desire to draw large crowds in order to acquire more financial support for the museum. Whereas previously, art subsidies were justified on the grounds of appealing to enhancement of welfare, particularly that of neglected groups, the public is being recruited today not for the sake of education or other cultural-political ideas, but for reasons of healthy management.

This "*l'art pour l'art et l'artiste*" attitude, combined with a business-minded mentality in regard to public service, represents a complete about-face from the attitudes of a decade ago in the heyday of the welfare state. In those days the New Class in the art world strongly believed in a technocratic-developmental policy of *Machbarkeit* ("Makeability") according to which man and society could be improved through art. Now they concentrate on an informed, interested public and appeal to the autonomy of art. Government subsidies still offer the best guarantee, but there is an increasing willingness to consider a market orientation and various forms of collaboration with private initiative and industry. Nevertheless, the political orientation and ideas have remained largely unchanged in the art world: left wing, liberal, and progressive. But this self-image of progressiveness does not really fit any longer with the obsolete image of the political left. Cultural progressiveness today no longer coincides with the technocratic-developmental ideas of the welfare state. It relates better to a notion of the autonomy of art, which is more easily achieved by creating ties with the private sector.

The Attitude and Behavior of Art Experts Toward Government and Market

To a great extent artists and mediators owe their autonomy and reputation to the ignorance of a large part of the public. The relationship between the art world and the government is determined also by the exclusive character of the professional knowledge in the artistic fields. According to the museum directors, this often leads to tiresome contacts with politicians and civil government: "You are dealing with a kind of inability regarding modern art, thus you have to try twice as hard to be taken seriously. You discover time and time again that you have to really lobby, much more than representatives of other professional sectors. Everyone understands that you need a baker but you have to keep explaining that modern art is also important!" They ask for more understanding, but pointing out the incomprehension of others is also an expression of distinction. Moreover, as far as the lobbying struggle is concerned, it hasn't been that difficult over the past few years. The popularity of modern painting and sculpture and, in fact the popularity of the visual arts culture as a whole has increased strongly at least for part of the population, in spite of its difficult accessibility. The art world knows how to use this situation to its advantage when searching for financial support from the government and private sources. But, apart from this special case, we can conclude that the following more or less double bind characterizes the relationship in the Netherlands between the art world and government: when matters concerning the content of art arise, artists and art mediators, appealing to their professional autonomy, usually form a closed front against the state and its civil servants, who consider it their task to promote art and supply the necessary financial means, but who cannot and will not express their opinion on the content and quality of art. Everywhere in democratic welfare states the government refrains from involving itself in matters of taste and style, preferring instead to watch and wait, and to delegate the evaluation task to experts. This has led over the past years to an extensive system of intermediate facilities between the government and the art world in which art specialists of the New Class play a leading role, and constant reflection on art and artistic criteria controls the debate.

We can now ask how the relationship between government and the art world can be maintained if, on the one hand, the art experts have been able to monopolize artistic judgment, defending and strengthening the autonomous position of art in relation to other life spheres and when, on the other hand, politicians and officials—not willing to be judges of art—distance themselves more and more from a politics of culture in which art is used as a basis for a policy aimed at societal reform and the promotion of welfare. To a considerable degree the ties between the government and the art world, of course, will continue to exist based on historical practice, but the recent changes in mentality and behavior usher in a new phase in which both concentrate on the shared value of rationalizing organization, administration, and policy. Art specialists and art officials give high priority to the economics and management of culture. The idealistic technocratic-developmental philosophers of days gone by have had to step aside for today's realistic "makeability" technocrats. In many cases these are the same official people who continue to interfere and steer, but now do so with a businesslike, no-nonsense attitude and a conviction that the possibilities of social engineering are limited. It is, therefore, not surprising that this New Class of experts employed by the state and state-subsidized art institutions quite easily link up with representatives of the New Class in the market sector. Their rationality and functional approach are considered the most important qualifications for success. The New Class of art specialist is no longer averse to the old virtues of capitalism once so libeled by these very same people, this entry of government and art world into the market or, better, their recognition of the values that prevail in the private sector, in turn, has led to the restoration and strengthening of the ties between industry and the art world. The following recent examples from the plastic arts offer proof.

From the beginning of the 1980s, the collective sector has been more interested in market processes. Members of the New Class in the art world and in politics, as well as governmental bureaucrats, have become less wary of competition, commerce, and cost-control. Their vocabulary now includes the concepts of flexibility, client-orientation, and efficiency, which assist them in redirecting art policy. They demonstrate more caution in their undertakings. In exchange, there are financial constraints on artists. The government has forcefully questioned whether the traditional subsidy flow has not disturbed the balance between supply and demand and led to a cultural overproduction. During the past few years, budgets have shifted in favor of art distribution and the sale of art productions, not all at once or to a remarkable extent, but in increments over time. Thus, in 1986, the government abolished the almost twenty-year-old Beeldende Kunst Regeling (analogous to the American Works Progress Administration) and replaced it with a series of market-expanding measures intended to stimulate the independent entrepreneurship of this group of artists. The BKR offered a guaranteed income to artists who were incapable of providing for themselves, which enabled them to continue practicing their profession independently. In return, they were obliged periodically to donate one or more works of art for display in government buildings. The impossibility of financial and organizational control of this arrangement, and the increased dependence of over 3000 artists on government subsidies, led the government to change policies by the beginning of 1980s. With part of an available budget of 130 million guilders, it has now attempted to stimulate the market for the arts of painting and sculpture. Lower authorities receive about 100 million guilders annually to purchase art, commission works, finance art lending centers, and to make possible promotional activities such as exhibitions. A number of regulations also encourage the public to buy, rent, or borrow works of art.

Museums for modern art are directly involved in these policy changes. Directors are expected to be more market-oriented. Those professionally socialized in the world of government subsidies now have to try to find other sources of income. The fact that it takes a considerable amount of time to convince corporations and private citizens to continue to be interested and supportive is experienced as an added burden. It is to be expected, however, that these new kinds of tasks—fund raising, searching for sponsors—will eventually constitute the museum director's new job description. Sponsoring art is a fairly recent phenomenon in the Netherlands. Today, corporate sponsorship of museums and the performing arts is estimated to be about 25 million guilders. Governmental spending in comparison stands at over 600 million guilders per year. The art world's attitude toward sponsorship is willing, yet cautious.

While museum directors are zealously searching for sponsors, they also warn against adopting the American model, in which museums depend totally on trustees and where sponsorship is no longer a matter of good will, but based solely on calculated profitability. None of the Dutch art mediators see the American model as a true alternative. They feel that governmental guarantees should continue to back Dutch museums, and want private support for culture in addition to and not instead of government subsidies. They welcome developments like the flourishing "friends of the museum" associations and the marked increase in the number of volunteers. In 1980, only 3 percent of the people working in museums were volunteers. In 1984 volunteers represented 46 percent of the total personnel (CBS 1988). Budget cuts, of course, played a role but this does not diminish the positive meaning of volunteer work.

Initiatives for more forms of cooperation with the private sector have come from the side of industry as owners and managers of private enterprises are discovering art as a valuable product for improvement of the corporate image. Particularly, enterprises and organizations representing extensive capital, such as banks, pension funds, and insurance companies, form an important group of clients and principals for the art world. Competition leads to imitation once such a trend is underway. The growing demand for art creates a need for new professions in the field of art mediation and distribution. Ten years ago "art agencies" and "art consultancies" were quite unknown in the Netherlands. Now, they offer cultural programs during company dinners or offer product presentations. They create sponsorship programs and design new company offices. They advise on the purchase of "corporate art collection" and they provide companies with works of art to adorn everything from the president's suite to the employees' cafeteria.

Just as the Dutch corporate world now wishes to link its corporate image with culture, cities are playing the culture card to improve their image as well. The topic of "urbanity and culture" now receives more interest from city administrators than ever before, and offers a good example of cooperation between the collective and the private sectors. Instead of the old-fashioned terms "city beauty" and "city beautification," the modern slogans of "urbanity" and "city marketing" have become increasingly popular. Competition among cities at the national and international levels draws attention everywhere. Million-guilder and even billion-guilder plans roll off the desks of politicians, officials, architects, and project developers. The budget estimates of these plans can run so high simply because city administrations want to follow a policy model of a "public-private partnership."

There also is an increasing awareness that cultural facilities and undertakings are not just or mainly an expense, but that they are economically productive as well. In 1987, Amsterdam calculated that the city's culture generated over one billion guilders worth of economic activity. This economic multiplier-effect is difficult to quantify and can easily be exaggerated, but no one dares deny that cultural facilities have a favorable effect on urban life. The city forms the natural environment for political, economic, and cultural elites who take up residence and maintain contact with one another there. These elites, members of the New Class of highly educated professionals, are the main consumers of culture. Museums, concert halls, theaters, parks, and city squares form the infrastructure of the knowledge economy (de Swaan, Olsen, et al. 1987).

Increasingly, culture has become a weapon in economic competition. Within a short period of time, almost all Dutch provincial areas have presented plans for the cultural enrichment of their inner cities. The national planning service recently warned that cultural development need to be made a priority in order for the Netherlands to remain competitive; the Ranstad (the urban region stretching from

Amsterdam, through the Hague, to Rotterdam), therefore, as one large megalopolis, should compete with cities such as Düsseldorf, Frankfurt, Brussels, and even London.

Be it for left- or right-wing administration policies, the contrasts between the collective and private sectors are becoming less noticeable thanks to these forms of cooperation. In the future, the emphasis will be placed more often on joint activities of the government and the market.

Conclusion

According to Daniel Bell, the New Class is not a "class" in the social-structural sense. One can speak more convincingly of a new mentality, rather than of a New Class. We would add to that the supposed mentality of the new professional groups—left,progressive, anticapitalistic, change-oriented, and with a strong belief in the "makeability" of society by means of governmental interference—has, since the beginning of the 1980s, become increasingly less distinguishable as such. The value orientations of the old and the new middle classes, and of the representatives of the New Class, converge and cut across the old contrasts of left versus right and collective versus private sectors.

In *The Cultural Contradictions of Capitalism*, Bell emphasizes, the contrasts and tensions among the spheres of economics, politics, and culture. But as differences become fewer the three spheres start to look more and more alike, particularly within the domain of organization and the means-goals way of thinking, technological progress and growing rationalization increasingly determine the image of social reality. This is, by and large, the domain of the New Class of professionals wishing to utilize their knowledge capital in a goal-related way. They are aware that they are limited by controllable elements from the cultural, political, and social environment. Thus the *"Machbarkeit"* philosophy is no longer openly propagated, but a belief in limited "makeability" is still found in day-to-day thinking and practice.

The convergence of attitude and behavior among the New Class employees of government, the art world, and industry is stimulated by a type of standardized professionalism that they all share by virtue of their training and position. The convergence is also enforced by the special circumstances of the autonomy of art. The more one accepts that only the art specialists are competent to judge in matters of artistic content, the more one will emphasize functional rationality in matters of policy, management, and administration. A new appreciation for the market and consensus on the retreat of government in favor of a more active private sector can also be seen as signs of convergence. Convergence, however, does not mean that actual changes are taking place in the welfare state. More room for the market does not imply a diminished government. The government's recovery policy in the 1980s has proven that. In relations among government, art world, and market, one should speak of a periodic adjustment of policy and of small course-corrections by the New Class of "hidden technocrats." In this context one justifiably speaks of selective shrinking and growing of government budgets.

Sponsorships, fund raising, volunteer work, and a more market-oriented way of thinking and acting by art and distributors shift the dependency relationship between the government and the art world. We do not expect the balance to tip to the other side in the near future. The government's share in the cultural concern remains significant. But this support affects a larger social arena thanks to the converging value-orientation of government, market, and art world. These changes remain mainly psychological and political. Institutions are being stimulated to expand existing budgets through private initiatives. This is politically important for the legitimization of art subsidies. At the same time, it also further ensures the continued existence of art institutions which can call for assistance from private sources whenever governmental interference threatens.

5

Symbolic Knowledge and Market Forces at the Frontiers of Postmodernism: Qualitative Market Researchers

Bernice Martin

Proposition 14. Contemporary Western societies are characterized by a protracted conflict between two classes, the old middle class (occupied in the production and distribution of material goods and services) and a new middle class (occupied in the production and distribution of symbolic knowledge).

Proposition 15. *The new knowledge class in Western societies is a major antagonist of capitalism.*

—Peter Berger, *The Capitalist Revolution*

"Daddy ... what do you do?"

What did he do?

"Do? What do you mean sweetheart?"

"Well, MacKenzie's daddy makes books and he has eighty people working for him."

...

"Darling," said Judy, "Daddy doesn't [make books or] build roads or hospitals, and he does not help build them but he does handle bonds *for the people who raise the money."*

"Bonds?"

"Yes. Just imagine that a bond is a slice of cake and you didn't bake the cake, but every time you hand somebody a slice of the cake a tiny bit comes off like a little crumb and you can keep that."

...

Judy launched into a description of his Giscard scheme. Then she said to his father, "Pierce and Pierce doesn't issue them for the French government and doesn't buy them from the French government but from whoever's already bought them from the French government. So Pierce and Pierce's transactions have nothing to do with anything France hopes to build or develop or ... achieve. It's all been done long before Pierce and Pierce entered the picture. So they're just sort of ... slices of cake. Golden cake. And Pierce and Pierce collects millions of marvelous"—she shrugged—"golden crumbs."

...

"Perhaps I ought to try decorating. Excuse me, interior designing—It must be fun getting pouffe curtains and polished chintz for—who were those people?—those Italians you did the apartment for?—the di Duccis?"

...

"Even if it's for people who are shallow and vain, it's something real, something describable, something contributing to simple human satisfaction, no matter how meretricious and temporary, something you can at least explain to your children. I mean, at Pierce and Pierce, what on earth do you tell each other you do every day?"

—Tom Wolfe, *The Bonfire of the Vanities*

Pringle's was definitely a business dealing in real commodities and running it was not in the least like doing literary theory, but it did strike Robyn sometimes that Vic Wilcox stood to his subordinates in the relation of teacher to pupils—he would have been surprised to be told it but he used the Socratic method: he prompted the other directors and middle management and even the foremen to identify the problem themselves and to reach by their own reasoning the solution he had already determined upon. It was so deftly done she had sometimes to temper her admiration by reminding herself that it was all directed by the profit motive.... Furthermore, he showed no reciprocal respect for her own professional skills.

A typical instance was the furious argument they had about the Silk Cut advertisement.... Every few miles, it seemed, they passed the same huge poster on roadside hoardings, a photographic depiction of a rippling expanse of purple silk, as if the material had been slashed with a razor. There were no words on the advertisement, except the Government Health Warning about smoking. This ubiquitous image, flashing past at regular intervals, both irritated and intrigued Robyn, and she began to do her semiotic stuff on the deep structure hidden beneath its bland surface.

It was in the first instance a kind of riddle. That is to say, in order to decode it, you had to know there was a brand of cigarettes called Silk Cut. The poster was the iconic representation of a missing name, like a rebus. But the icon was also a metaphor. The shimmering silk, with its voluptuous curves and sensuous texture, obviously symbolized the female body, and the elliptical slit, foregrounded by a lighter color showing through, was still more obviously a vagina. The advert thus appealed to both the sensual and sadistic impulses, the desire to mutilate as well as penetrate the female body.

Vic Wilcox spluttered with outraged derision as she expounded this interpretation. He smoked a different brand, himself, but it was as if he felt his whole philosophy of life was threatened by Robyn's analysis of the advert. "You must have a twisted mind to see all that in a perfectly harmless bit of cloth," he said.

—David Lodge, *Nice Work*

It is curious that while most contemporary sociologists are inclined to regard the New Class debate as passe, the war between the "old" and "new" middle class provides the central narrative pivot of the most popular novels of manners in the 1980s. Indeed, a contest between the "knowledge class" and the "business class" has been so central to the politics of the Reagan/Thatcher decade that it could hardly fail to find its popular chroniclers. The two novels from which I quote above, one American and one English, were instant best sellers: *Nice Work* (Lodge 1988) has been adapted for television and *The Bonfire of the Vanities* (Wolfe 1987) was filmed. Both novels draw their main protagonists from the ranks of specialists in the new symbolic knowledge. David Lodge's story might have been devised to illustrate Peter Berger's propositions 14 and 15 (Berger 1986). Tom Wolfe's central character is by no means the archetypal knowledge class antagonist of capitalism but a ridiculously well-rewarded junk-bond broker, yuppie chic at the heart of finance capital. *The Bonfire of the Vanities* demonstrates how new forms of specialization in symbolic knowledge are by no means monopolized by the knowledge and communication industries or by the welfare professionals who together have usually been regarded as the core cadre of the knowledge class.

The high satirical style in which these novels are written—full of the sly irony that intellectuals often employ to mock their own kind as well as class antagonists—offers the sociologist certain valuable pointers, not least because it revels in the very ambiguities that pose the trickiest problems of classification to the social scientist. Consider the apparently more straightforward of the two novels, *Nice Work*. At first sight it directly illustrates the New Class propositions. The University of Rummidge involves its dons in a joint scheme with the local captains of industry whereby the managing director of a small engineering firm, Vic Wilcox, and a feminist literary theorist from the university's department of English, Robyn Penrose, "shadow" each other, that is, sit in on each other's work one day a week. David Lodge draws the two in even-handed comic caricature. Vic is a philistine, embedded in the traditional mores, a first generation entrant into the business class who never acquired "high culture" en route. Robyn is the daughter of an academic, able to take high culture for granted and thus to deconstruct it without mercy or inhibition, a feminist and trendy lefty, a pure postmodern in her project of continuous self-monitoring. What begins in war and mutual contempt ends in rapprochement and mutual respect thanks to the old narrative device of the sexual encounter. Lodge uses the plot to blur one distinction after another. He starts from the dichotomies that are the stuff of the New Class debate—useful versus useless labor, material versus symbolic knowledge, hard-headed market principles versus anticapitalist assumptions, the unselfconscious habitation of a taken-for-granted "life world" versus narcissistic "self-actualization," cultural philistinism versus cultural elitism—and makes them change sides (and exchange "signs" since much of the joke depends on some understanding of semiotic analysis). His portrait reminds one that "new" versus "old" middle class need not be the same as "knowledge" versus "business" class. Vic is "new" in being a first generation captain of industry, and in that he resembles many of Mrs. Thatcher's most loyal supporters. It is Robyn, the specialist in purely symbolic knowledge who is "old" middle class in the sense of being a second generation member of the professional class. David Lodge is not merely being perverse, since all the evidence suggests that management in manufacturing industry is a major and continuing source of social mobility in Britain, one that has not significantly depended on education and, therefore, on acculturation into "old," that is, elite, middle-class style and taste. So Vic is properly representative of a large stratum of a literally "new" middle class that is also "old" business class in the sense of being based in manufacturing rather than in services or finance. Vic, the culturally proletarian , more resembles the self-made iron masters of the early industrial revolution than their descendents who have been thoroughly gentrified in the characteristic British fashion by all the high culture (symbolic knowledge, cultural capital) that money has been able to buy over several generations. Robyn also accurately reflects a stratum in British society. It is that of the offspring of the established professional classes *and* of the already successful business class that takes the gentry options in education and provides the core of the intelligentsia at the top of the professions that deal in the most purely symbolic forms of knowledge. David Lodge's personification of the war within the middle class thus begins by putting a question mark over the parallel between the new/old and the symbolic/material dichotomy. With good empirical cause he makes the two binary oppositions work in reverse.

Lodge muddies most of the other distinctions too. In the passage quoted above, for example, Vic's managerial skill is depicted as relying on exactly the same processes as Robyn's teaching of literary theory. Then her feminist semiotics are demonstrated as the undergirding "knowledge" behind the advertising strategy of a leading brand of cigarettes. The apparently lucid distinction between the knowledge base of "the production and distribution of material services" and that of the "production and distribution of purely symbolic knowledge" is thrown into question.

Tom Wolfe takes the paradox a step further. In the extract quoted above, we observe a small passage of arms in the marital warfare between Sherman McCoy, the bond broker, and his wife Judy, the interior decorator. Judy, another professor's daughter, baits Sherman about the status gulf between serious knowledge like that of her historian father, and the parasitic manipulation with which he makes mere money, "golden crumbs." Yet Judy, the "intellectual aristocrat," plays cruelly with the distinction between useful, material production (which even embraces the "pouffe curtains" and "polished chintz" which she assembles for the superaffluent) and Sherman's labor, which adds nothing to material production. Tom Wolfe leaves us in no doubt about the centrality of symbolic knowledge and cultural display in Sherman's work. The invisible but indispensable factor on which money markets depend is confidence. Bond brokers have to inscribe this professional "confidence trick" on their persons. Where the old business class, like Sherman's father, exuded dependability through their sober suits, their restrained manners, their control and moderation, Sherman and his yuppie confreres demonstrate their success through a personal style that is extrovert and exhibitionist. Sherman has to pump adrenalin, optimism, and persuasiveness into every professional interaction with colleagues, customers, and underlings alike.

This performance, which gives off the crucial symbolic message, is as vital as the moment-to-moment knowledge of the movements of bond prices that information technology delivers to his fingertips. The strutting, the conspicuous consumption, and the snazzy dressing are all essential parts of his stock in trade: they are the dramatic props, the material scenery in the plausibility structure that sustains his self-identity as a Master of the Universe, and it is his own belief in that identity that is his most valuable asset. Once his *self*-confidence slips he starts to make losses, not profits, because any failure to sell *himself* every moment of the day leads to loss of confidence in his professional predictions and assurances—and in order to sell his own *self* he must also *buy* it. All of this makes Sherman eligible for membership of the New Class of specialists in symbolic knowledge. Yet it all takes place on Wall Street. Sherman's father, an "old-style" affiliate of capitalism (a corporate lawyer), has doubts about the solidity of his son's business world, in particular about the pivotal role of spectacular debt (leverage) instead of financial solvency at both private and corporate levels. Within this old "bourgeois" family there is a shadow of what New Class theory postulates as the war within the middle class.

These two narratives throw into sharp relief three particular ambiguities: one, the precise nature of symbolic as distinct from other kinds of knowledge, that is, a distinction *intrinsic* to the knowledge itself; two, the distinction between knowledge that is oriented directly or indirectly toward material life and knowledge that isn't, that is, a distinction *extrinsic* to the knowledge base and concerned primarily with its application; and three, the distinction between occupations employing symbolic knowledge that are "affiliates" of the business class and those that are not. These ambiguities are intensified by the growth of service sector activities that may operate as part of the state provision or may offer themselves in the private market, but that in either case characteristically involve a mixture of material goods and nonmaterial services. It is all very well for the dealer in fiction (a prime specialist in symbolic knowledge, of course) to play with such problems and ambiguities, but the sociologist must at least try to lend them coherence. We need, therefore, to turn briefly to the debate on the New Class.

A sociological literature on the emergence of a New Class or knowledge class in Western capitalist societies grew up in the 1970s, largely in America but with some European input (e.g., Parkin 1968; Touraine 1971; Bourdieu 1977, 1984). Certain broad empirical tendencies in Western economics and their corollaries in the social structure formed the starting observation. The growth of the service sector, both public and private, at the expense of manufacturing and primary production led to a decline in blue-collar jobs, both in absolute numbers and as a percentage of all employment, while white-collar occupation expanded proportionately. In particular, the number of claims to expertise based on the creation, distribution, and application of symbolic knowledge expanded dramatically. The second feature was a tendency for specialists in symbolic knowledge to be highly visible in leftist and radical political and social movements. Indeed, in an important sense the theory of the New Class was a response to the countercultural movements of the late sixties and early seventies, in which Peter Berger's proposition 15, "the new knowledge class in Western societies is a major antagonist of capitalism," was more than plausibly illustrated. New Class theorists mostly came from right-of-center (Bell 1974, Schumpeter 1942, Kristol 1978, for instance), but those on the left (Gouldner 1979, Bourdieu 1984) also took for granted the *fact* of the leftist tendency of the knowledge class. The explanations advanced were very diverse. Some, like Gouldner, saw the media of symbolic communication as intrinsically liable to foster critical stances: the concept of "the culture of critical discourse" was his key explanatory variable. Bell offered a cognate argument that rested on a theory of how in "postindustrial" society, the "axial principles" of the cultural sphere diverge from those of the social structure and make self-expression the privileged goal of cultural enterprises. The cultural sphere attains this degree of specialization and relative autonomy through a developmental process familiar in functionalist argument. It also depends on a high level of material affluence that can protect the cultural sphere from the direct impact of the market forces. It is important, perhaps, to note that Bell did not assume that all the new knowledge specialists would take an adversarial stance. Indeed, his primary argument suggests that in postindustrial society the *majority* of the jobs will be based on services rather than material production, and that theoretical knowledge will perform the role taken by material capital in the previous stage of industrial society. This theoretical knowledge embraces everything from nuclear fission to principles of bureaucratic organization.

Thus, for Bell, the knowledge class comprises more than the culture specialists. Indeed most contributors to the debate tend to differentiate the culture specialist from the "technocrats" who manage the economy and its technical needs. Bell even suggests that vertical divisions in the new white-collar labor force will become more important than the old horizontal class division: the extent of a knowledge specialist's oppositional sentiment will be affected by whether he works for the state or for private enterprise, in the cultural or in the economic sphere, in manufacturing or in services. This Bell calls "situs" rather than "class."

This is not the place to pursue a minute critique of New Class theory; that is, in any case, the subject of another chapter in this volume (Heuberger 1991). I simply want to show that the ambiguities exposed in the novels of David Lodge and Tom Wolfe were problems from the start of the sociological debate. Even the attempt to write a simple description of empirical developments involves constant slippage into conceptual and category problems. More people are employed in the service sector; but this "service sector" covers those who serve in the obvious colloquial sense—hairdressers, flight attendants—as well as those bureaucratically organized mediators between the state and the citizen—civil servants, state welfare professionals—and between capital and labor—managers, technocrats, white-collar clerks. In all these occupations knowledge is the primary requirement—symbolic, theoretical, technical, and cultural in various combinations. Among these folk certain groups are notoriously inclined to be critical of capitalism and to join and lead radical social movements—social workers, teachers, mass-media communicators, academics, writers, artists, popular musicians. Technocrats, administrators, and managers are far more likely to be supporters of capitalism even though they also depend on symbolic knowledge, and even when they are functionaries of the welfare state. Attempts to explain the different propensity for adversarial stances among the various sectors of the knowledge professions as systematic manifestations of objective interests have a certain plausibility (Kriesi 1989). They do not, however, eliminate ambiguity; moreover, they acknowledge that these objective interests are far from unitary across the whole putative "class." There is a persuasiveness in Peter Berger's contention that a large proportion of radically inclined culture specialists are employees of the welfare state and so have a built-in interest in the distributive machinery of government as against the production system (Berger 1986). Yet many of the administrative and technocratic personnel, who tend to be found on the more conservative end of the political spectrum are also welfare state employees. A similar problem applies to Berger's argument that the knowledge class needs to emphasize educational certification rather than raw economic achievement in order to claim privilege and status for itself: again, this should have as much force for the managerial and technocratic employees of the state as for the culture radicals. It is also difficult to identify the professions that in Berger's term are "affiliates" of the business class and those that are not. He suggests that the old professions, accountants and dentists, for example, are in some special way allies of the business class since they have historically served it and thus have an indirect relation to material production. But why not therapists, who today sell their services to members of the business class? Moreover, there is no good reason why the old professions that deal in the more purely symbolic forms of knowledge—academics, lawyers, the clergy—should be immune to the leftward pull that characterizes the newer knowledge-based professions. Indeed, there is good reason to believe that leaders among the cultural radicals, in Britain at least, come disproportionately from families in the "old" professional groups even if the "other ranks" are more obviously from the petite bourgeoisie.

Furthermore, throughout the 1980s some twists appeared in the story, unanticipated by the theorists of the seventies. One hot political controversy in Britain, for example, centered on the not-altogether-implausible accusation leveled by the New Right at elite schools and universities, and at institutions of high culture generally (traditionally seen by Marxists as docile lackeys of capitalism), that they have systematically eroded "industrial values" and the "entrepreneurial spirit" by insidiously gentrifying both the privileged children of the business class and the educationally mobile children of the humble and obscure. (One important academic study underlying this political argument is Wiener 1981.) On this argument, patrician contempt for mere money-making is as damaging to the spirit of capitalism as is the chic radicalism of the privileged. We have witnessed a decade of struggle between the Thatcher government, which has been intent on bringing market principles to bear on every sphere of public life, and an uneasy and intermittent alliance of both old and new knowledge specialists intent on resisting that pressure. Much of this resistance is, as on Berger's argument we would expect, defense of the welfare state, and is premised on the view that market principles are largely inappropriate in that sphere—yet it is seldom an outright opposition to capitalism but a narrower disagreement about how to distribute the wealth that capitalism generates. Some of this resistance is also the reaction of professions, old and new, to direct onslaughts on their autonomy, particularly when the government seems almost to regard certain established practices (in law, medicine, and academia, for instance) as conspiracies in restraint of trade. At this level, the battle lines seem somewhat less ambiguous than they were in the early seventies, since the professional experts in symbolic knowledge, old as well as new, have taken up similar defensive stances in a contest with the political spokesmen of the business class, though this resistance has been markedly sectional and fragmented.

At another level the picture is much more confused, in that the radical knowledge specialists have invaded the business class. Much of what the culture industry offers—from therapies to rock concerts— is provided on the open market and is a rip-roaring commercial success. Bohemianism, radicalism, symbolic raspberries blown in the face of capitalism frequently make a great deal of money, not only in the service sector but in the production of material commodities. Katharine Hamnett became a millionaire by selling teeshirts printed with radical slogans. Anita Roddick's fortune comes from providing ecologically friendly cosmetics. Richard Branson made his millions by selling rock music, and was able able to do his bit in the campaign against AIDS by subsidizing the sale of condoms.

Three obvious processes are at work here. First, many services based directly on the creation and distribution of symbolic knowledge are themselves bought and sold in a straightforwardly capitalist market. This applies as much to correspondence courses in international marketing as to astrological advice services. Symbolic knowledge creates businesses and entrepreneurs. Second, few services are entirely unconnected with the provision of material commodities— even therapies can sell books, unguents, and macrobiotic foods as bye-blows of their symbolic operation. Third, the antagonists of capitalism among the knowledge specialists constitute a market for products and services tailored to fit their values and self-images. Thus, it becomes possible to identify a significant sector of radical-friendly business enterprises selling the services and commodities to this particular public and to find enclaves of laid-back, leftist, anarchist, countercultural accountants, business executives, marketing managers, and the rest working within this self-selecting band. Therefore it is not only individual entrepreneurs like Hamnett and Roddick who cross over from the radical knowledge class to the business class, but all the other experts whom they go on to recruit. They may also experiment, as Roddick has, with forms of profit sharing and worker participation that shift the inner workings of a capitalist enterprise in a leftist direction. In this process it may well be that certain knowledge bases undergo radical revision: a "management science" for nonhierarchical firms will look very different from one based on principles of hierarchy and unidirectional information flow. On the other hand there may be bodies of professional knowledge and practice, like accountancy perhaps, which remain essentially the same even if the personal style and cultural values of their practitioners take on a bohemian look.

Tom Wolfe's Sherman McCoy may be a good example. He is no political leftist, but in many ways he looks more like the knowledge class than the old business class of his father's generation. Sherman and his ilk are immoderately and calculatingly hedonistic; they pay the barest lip service to the older principles of respectability, control, and moderation; their aesthetic is more postmodern than Biedermeier; and their vocabulary, if not their accent, can rival that of the street wise guttersnipe (Wolfe 1990). But how far is Sherman operating with a qualitatively different set of *skills* and *professional values* from those used by respectable older bankers? How far is he simply employing an unchanging technical knowledge base in an electronically assisted marketplace and within a cultural style that proclaims success and confidence by a new set of signals? I suggested above that his thespian attributes and displays of conspicuous consumption were an essential part of his professional skill in handling symbolic communication. Are these *intrinsic* changes or mere performance details? Even on a minimal definition that renders them *just* changes of packaging, a nagging query remains. Exactly why and how should such a "style" have taken root in the heart of finance capital particularly when so many analyses of capitalism have attributed the success and stability of the system to the very "bourgeois" values it undermines—

moderation, discipline, the stable family, saving rather than debt? *Is*
there a canker at the heart of capital and if so, where did it come from
and why does capitalism tolerate it?

It would be tempting but unsatisfactory to close the issue here by
asserting that these paradoxical developments are simply instances of
capitalism's power to co-opt even its opponents. I believe that
something more profound and interesting is happening, because the
co-option is a *two-way* process. I am more intrigued by the question of
why so many milieux close to the heart of contemporary capitalism
should look like cultural offshoots of the 1960s avant-garde than by
why the children and grandchildren of 1960s radicalism should have
adapted to capitalism and adopted its market strategies. The latter is
banal; the former is a genuine intellectual puzzle. The problem lies in
the precise ways in which these two antagonists *need* and *use* each
other while nevertheless being at war in a sense so culturally obvious
that it spawns best-selling satirical fiction.

The key, in my view, lies in recognizing the transformation that
capitalism itself is undergoing in its latest stage of development. The
New Class theorists of the 1970s tended to use Bell's term
"postindustrialism"; the sociologists of the 1980s were more likely to
call it "consumer culture" or even "postmodernity." But at bottom they
were all attempting to conceptualize the latest mutation of a supremely
adaptable system, one premised on a permanent drive for innovation in
the productive system and therefore on endemic change in the cultural
system within which it exists. It is, after all, capitalism rather than
communism that has turned out to be the permanent revolution—just,
indeed, as Marx and Engels claimed in that ambivalent paean of praise
to the heroic bourgeoisie, *The Communist Manifesto* (Berman 1982).
The term "consumer culture" alludes to two of the primary elements in
capitalism's most recent transformation, that is, the economic
prominence of consumption in the service economies of the West and
the cultural construction which energizes and legitimates the drive to
consume.

The paradoxical role of the New Class as the missionaries of the
consumer imperative is a third element. The fourth is the mutation of
the relatively clear class structure of the manufacturing stage of
capitalist industrialism into a more fragmented and volatile patchwork
of subgroupings identified by self-chosen consumer "life-styles."

The sheer capacity of capitalism to generate wealth is in itself an endemic incitement to consumption, but the primacy of capital accumulation in early capitalism coexisted with the familiar cultural injunctions to self-discipline. That, after all, was the burden of Max Weber's analysis of the *absurdity* of the spirit of early capitalism which turned the *making* but not the *enjoyment* of money into a moral imperative. As mature capitalism begins to percolate its unprecedented wealth down to the average private citizen in the form of expendable income, ever-increasing standards of material comfort, and a consequent escalation of legitimate "needs," so the brakes on consumption begin to weaken. Most analysts of consumer culture suggest that it is a stage reached in America by the 1920s and in Europe by the 1950s in which the urban landscape comes to be inscribed by the iconography of consumption. Its temples are department stores and shopping malls; its bibles the mail-order catalogues and advertising sections of the newspapers, magazines, and later, television; and its priests are the advertisers, marketers, and designers, the creators and distributors of the imagery of the consumer good life. (See, e.g., *Theory, Culture, and Society* 1, no. 3 [1983], especially Featherstone, Leiss, and Chaney.)

I have suggested elsewhere (Martin 1981) that in Britain a ritualized "culture of control," historically rooted in conditions of scarcity for the blue-collar and the routine white-collar population as well as in the bourgeois tradition of disciplined capital accumulation, was still in place at the end of the 1950s when it was, in purely economic terms, becoming anachronistic. In this context the countercultural carnival of the late 1960s acted inadvertently and ironically as midwife to full-blown consumer culture. Although a major theme of these radical movements was ideological opposition to capitalism (including its bourgeois insistence on self-discipline, work, and moderation) it was also a dramatization of the protean possibilities of desire, which in practice fueled the flames of consumerism. The counterculture served to popularize, initially through shock and outrage, the apprehension that the narrow, ritual limits within which desires had been contained in the interwar period of the Depression, were out of date by the affluent 1960s. People could afford to want many things that had never been regarded as available, affordable, or acceptable outside an elite and/or bohemian margin.

This applied to both consumer commodities and experiences. Thanks largely to the impact of youth culture and the popular media of communication, much that had been shocking and unthinkable in 1968 had become taken for granted by mainstream society by the late 1970s. This process greatly assisted the expansion of markets for all kinds of goods and services, from fashion to foreign holidays, sex aids to exercise bicycles.

We thus arrive at the central paradox of the role of the New Class. As is shown in the Hunter and Fessenden chapter of this book (Hunter and Fessenden 1991), they led and still lead the burgeoning single-issue movements that oppose unbridled market forces. Yet they also distributed and still distribute a cultural message that personal hedonism is a legitimate, perhaps even *the* legitimate goal of life. It may even be that something like this globalization of desire is a cultural prerequisite of economic growth in that stage of advanced capitalism that Walt Rostow once called "the era of high mass consumption"—an era at which the population of the Eastern Europe is demonstrably eager to arrive today. In a recent interview, Umberto Eco neatly summarized the element of excess and escalating "need" that this entails. He recalled the ice-creams of his youth:

> They came in two sizes: one scoop for 10 lire, two for 20. Sometimes our parents allowed us two scoops and when they did, I always asked them to make two separate cones, not one big one. Each time they said no. It was immoral. And so it was. Today everything is about excess, about having the right to more; not just a cassette player but a cassette player with auto reverse. In those pre-war days two cones were excess, and excess was immoral. (Eco 1989)

Making desire and excess legitimate—and thus paving the way for Sherman McCoy—was perhaps the real revolution of the 1960s. As Tom Wolfe recently remarked, it released "an affluence that has reached down to the level of mechanics and tradesmen which would have made the Sun King blink." (Wolfe 1990)

Consumer capitalism may "need" a hedonistic consumption ethic, but capitalism has historically also needed a work ethic, and society of any kind needs a modicum of stability, continuity, and culturally sanctioned altruism if it is not to spin out of control. The political conundrum for advanced capitalist societies is how the balance between these two forces should be drawn.

The market as such is amoral; given its head *any* desire will find its way to the cash nexus. Who, if not the market, is to decide *which* desires are legitimate, and how are the forbidden desires to be stamped out? The current Western governments of the New Right have set themselves the problem of how to reprogram the young inheritors of the hedonistic consumption ethic so as to suppress certain desires (for drugs, for instance) and to reestablish the old bourgeois value of restraint without killing the goose that lays consumer culture's golden eggs. One compromise message seems to be "work hard, play hard, and you have the right to enjoy the fruits of your labor." Normative asceticism is definitely out of fashion. But the governments of the New Right are caught between the desire to resurrect bourgeois values (through education reform and control of the mass media, for instance), and the inherently libertarian principles of the free market. The result is a chronic contradiction and a *political* focus on the institutions of culture which are, of course, the heartland of the New Class professions.

The institutions of cultural communications are *economically* strategic in another sense. Under the impact of general affluence, markets fragment: instead of standardized mass products, minutely subdifferentiated products within one general category (tourism, clothing, food, whatever) are targeted at specific audiences. This differentiation depends as much on the cultural packaging as on material differences in the products. Commodities and services thus acquire complex layers of meaning through the symbols and imagery in which they are clothed. It is for this reason that some theorists characterize the current stage of capitalism as "postmodern" and see its basis as the exchange of images or simulations—"simulacra," in Baudrillard's term (Poster, ed. 1988). This process puts the New Class specialists in symbolic communication right at the hub of the postmodern *economic* system because they are the professional creators and distributors of these all-important images.

Mike Featherstone (Featherstone 1987a), one of the most convincing exponents of consumer culture/postmodern theory, was probably the first to argue that the New Class is the essential carrier of consumer culture, beginning with its advance-guard among the advertisers, designers, and market researchers whose professional lives are precisely devoted to the creation and manipulation of the symbolic meanings of items of consumption and of the act of consumption itself. Because the New Class stands structurally between the owners of capital and the proletariat, between the state and the citizens, between the older professions and the routine white-collar workers, it is faced with the need to establish its own distinctive status. Consumption is the arena in which it engages in this struggle for status, just as Weber anticipated. Its expertise in symbolic communication enables its members to assemble a bricolage of goods and symbols into customized packages that are in some sense unique: the constituent elements come from the commercial marketplace but the uniqueness resides in the ensemble and acts as a symbolic assertion that the New Class is *self-created*. This process is the main dynamic by which the older class-based patterns of consumption are disrupted. A democratization of consumption occurs in that "the less powerful are able to emulate, within the limitations of mass fashion, the consumption practices and styles of the powerful." (Featherstone 1987c) Yet the style wars of competitive consumption are also concerned with establishing ever more minutely differentiated status distinctions. Destabilization therefore becomes endemic: the meanings of items constantly shift as affluence and the activities of the advertising and marketing professions make available to the many what had been exclusive to the few, and in so doing, change its status signification. The old business and professional classes may disdain the competitive consumption game, but they are forced to respond when the markers of bourgeois or gentlemanly culture are expropriated alongside the transmuted products of working class, "ethnic and mass culture in the jumble sale of life-style construction." One indubitable member of the old gentlemanly class (higher ecclesiastical branch) recently remarked to me that in order to avoid being mistaken for a yuppie today it has become necessary to live among considerable decay, sagging 1920s sofas and the kinds of ugly heirlooms that no self-respecting bond broker or television producer would be caught dead *buying*. The Judy McCoys of this world are, of course, acquiring the rest for their interior design businesses.

In constructing his argument, Featherstone draws on Norbert Elias' theory of the "civilizing process," on Simmel's richly suggestive essays on fashion, and on Pierre Bourdieu's anatomization of taste as the articulation of power and status competition (Featherstone 1987b). He shows how the "consumption practices" of postmodern culture need to be understood as involving far more than the mere consumption of commodities and services. They rest on patterns of taste, modes of feeling, styles of understanding—including self-understanding—and presentation of identity. The New Class not only set examples in their own lives, but through their professional activities provide the teaching, training, and therapy by which the rest of the world learns to adopt these new modes of thinking, feeling, and being.

One effect of this may be something approaching a feminization of economic culture. Donald Bell (Bell 1985) and Peter Stearns (Stearns 1979), for example, have both suggested that one corollary of the shift from manufacture to services is a switch from "masculine" to "feminine" skills as knowledge and *feeling* become the main components in postindustrial service occupations. Arlie Hochschild takes the argument a step further in her analysis of the "emotional labor" in labor intensive service sector jobs—"the work of trying to feel the appropriate feeling for the job." (Hochschild 1983) She estimates that roughly a third of the American work force is currently subject to substantial demands for emotional labor, and that of all women roughly half have such jobs. Hochschild's analysis perhaps overstresses the costs to the worker—particularly to lower level participants, the heavily supervised men and women on the "human assembly line" (Hochschild 1989)—of demands for the deployment of the private self and for conformity to the "feeling rules" of emotional labor. Nevertheless, the increased incidence of this kind of work, (in particular when it is *self*-monitored at the professional level, as in the case of therapists or social workers), is surely a component in the power of the New Class as missionaries of new structures of feeling and being-in-the-world delineated by Featherstone. The power of the New Class lies not only in the fact of its members' expertise in communication and their location in the higher reaches of emotional labor, but in their role as *gatekeepers*. Teachers, for example, are the gatekeepers of marketable certification; social workers are the gatekeepers of redistributed material resources. The provision of such resources normally entails a process of acculturating recipients into the structures of feeling and understanding pioneered in the New Class and privileged by it. This constitutes an additional reason why the institutions of culture have become a site of political contest as the representative of the business class in current governments of the New Right seek to halt or reverse this acculturation.

Clearly not every sector of the New Class occupies an identical strategic position in these matters, although the stratum as a whole is characterized by its *mediating* role in the social and economic system. Scott Lash and John Urry see this mediation as a key element in the general tendency toward "disaggregation" in what they call the "disorganized capitalism" of the West today (Lash and Urry 1987). Like Featherstone they interpret the growth of the New Class which they call the "service class," as a crucial causal dynamic in the transformation of capitalism. The service class *performs selective, disaggregated functions of capital and/or of the state.* Its class position is therefore shot through with contradictions and its objective interests combine, in enormously varied subpackages, some capitalistic and some proletarian elements that are more often than not wrapped in a rhetoric of professionalism. Lash and Urry, for example, cite evidence of the decline of class voting patterns in the last two decades and show how this reflects the emergence of significant sectors of the middle strata whose objective class characteristics contain contradictory indices. They use the term "class fraction" to indicate the disaggregated clusters of objective interests that lie beneath the fragmentation and status competition within the "service class." They also show that the historical emergence of the service class varies greatly from one country to another. The advance guard in the United States were the scientific managers of Taylorism, while in Britain, where the service class was more a product of state than of private sector sponsorship, management did not seriously professionalize until the 1960s. By that time the other professions had long been assimilated into a gentry rather than a bourgeois model—"status" rather than "occupational" professionalism. Hence the status dilemma of the Vic Wilcoxes of British industry.

If Lash and Urry are correct it would follow that there is no simple resolution of the ambiguities in the criteria by which the New Class has variously been identified. It is perfectly possible to map for each "class fraction" the precise combination of features, both historically specific and structural, that give rise to the particular levels and manifestations of shared interests with capital and/or of antagonism toward those interests. But it is not feasible except in the most general and abstract way to characterize the position of the New Class as a consistent and unitary one. The mapping of specific constellations of interest among the constituent fractions does not, of course, preclude the attempt to model certain general processes or tendencies within the class as a whole while recognizing that these tendencies will not be found evenly across the board. This is precisely what Featherstone and Hochschild have both done. Kellner and Heuberger have undertaken a similar exercise (Kellner and Heuberger 1987-91). Their argument appears in another chapter, but it is necessary to comment briefly on the approach here since it forms the final piece of the jigsaw puzzle.

Kellner and Heuberger elucidate the rationale of the postmodern consciousness, of which the New Class is the major carrier. They root their argument in Max Weber's typology of rational action, and in an extension of his hypothesis that the progressive application of the principle of functional rationality results in the increasing dominance of experts and expertise. This dominance spills over from economic life into culture and everyday life. What distinguishes the postmodern from the classical applications of the principle of functional rationality is that the new forms "seek to penetrate ever more deeply into the private life-worlds of individuals." This is "life-world engineering." It involves actions in which the "rationalistic problem-solving attitude even embraces those spheres that are usually regarded as the province of the nonrational, as the worlds of immediacy and spontaneity in everyday social and mental life (therapeutic work, for example, is a case in point)" (Kellner and Heuberger 1988). These new forms tend to violate the traditional distinctions between the public and the private spheres, and between the world of work and the world of everyday life. (They also tend to require what Hochschild calls "emotional labor," and to result in the new structures of feeling postulated by Featherstone.) Experts of this kind are "hidden technocrats." Certain modern professionals such as those in the media, the health and therapy professions, social work, and consumers and ecological movements are the most obvious cases of this new style of functional rationality—their knowledge base tends to lie either wholly or partly in the social sciences, sometimes in combination with more traditionally "technical" knowledge. Although the professions most centrally concerned in "life-world engineering" are those welfare professions that first attracted the attention of the New Class theorists, all professions can be divided into "traditional" and "new" types of expertise. Thus, for example, in the Kellner/Heuberger model "traditional social workers have an instrumental understanding of their work as curative, geared to reintegrating the client into the traditionally accepted structures of psychological and social normality, while the new type has an equally instrumental understanding of the work but as emancipatory, geared to challenging inherited definitions and structures of normality and enabling the client to become self-defined." In the case of advertisers and their adjuncts like market researchers, the "traditional" approach is to collect and transmit data in a documentary fashion whereas the new approach is to construct scenarios, create data, and transmit new images and models of life (Kellner and Heuberger 1987a and b). Kellner and Heuberger see the "life-world engineers" as adversaries not of capitalism as such but of those elements of functional rationality which result in Weber's "iron cage" of modernity. Life-world engineers see themselves as a humanizing force, as nonconformists, devoted to "beating the system." They provide the tools by which the members of the New Class can become, in Featherstone's term, unique and self-created. They set up more personalized modes of work and seek out the interstices between public and private spheres in which to operate.

In short, Kellner and Heuberger propose a distinction between two types of functional rationality: "formal rationality," that is the classic Weberian bureaucratic type, and "material rationality," which designates the application of problem-solving analysis to the material "life-world." Not only are the two forms of rationality in chronic tension with each other, but the second is inherently problematic. The life-world as understood in phenomenological sociology indicates the taken-for-granted classifications, understandings, and habitual practices which make up everyday life. The notion of intervening in this by rational analysis and manipulative intervention is problematic since it seeks to make visible to the rational understanding processes that root human beings in structures whose stability and normality depends on their invisibility and taken for grantedness. The importance of the social sciences is immediately clear, not least the popularization over the last two decades of interactionist, phenomenological, and semiotic theories about everyday life. These revelatory but potentially ironizing tools of understanding and self-understanding give the postmodern expert *both* what Kellner and Heuberger call "a sense of privileged access to reality," and at the same time, a conviction that "reality" is not a unified, objective entity but a creation of "discourse," "communication practices," and so forth: a destabilized life-world (or "habitus" in Bourdieu's term) is the result. Attempts to "design existence" involve constant reflexivity and the perpetual reexamination of the life-world and its components in what Kellner and Heuberger term an "incessant pressure of justification." A type of rational analysis is employed in the vain hope of recapturing a wholeness in the life-world, which has been disrupted and distorted by the historic processes of formal rationality. For this reason the *constructed* life-worlds (or "life-styles") remain precarious because always provisional and never truly taken for granted. Absurd and self-defeating as this is, it is an extension of the historic process of occidental rationalization whose "contradictions have to be put up with" (Kellner and Heuberger 1988).

Qualitative Market Researchers: The Prime Case of a Postmodern Profession[32]

Qualitative market researchers have many virtues as the fraction of a fraction of the New Class on which the British study focuses. They are knowledge-class migrants to the business class. This new profession constitutes a provocatively awkward case for the original New Class theories since its core cadre seems to consist of cultural bohemians who nevertheless perform certain functions of capital and have even proved to be ready converts to entrepreneurship. They are also, of course, a key case of Mike Featherstone's argument about the New Class as professional carriers of the imperatives of consumer culture. Their economic functions give them a high level of shared objective interests with capital, but in terms of their social origins, cultural formation, and primary knowledge base they look more like the natural antagonists of capital. They mostly come from Bourdieu's petite bourgeoisie and owe their entry into the knowledge class more to state-sponsored education than to any significant inheritance of either economic or cultural capital. They are mostly graduates from the humanistic end of the social sciences or of the liberal arts, and the social sciences are certainly their primary professional knowledge base. From the 1970s onward, as openings for academic careers virtually disappeared under Thatcherite higher education policies, many high-achieving social scientists entered market research as a substitute for the "real" research jobs they had originally hoped for. They took their adversarial sensibilities, their effortless familiarity with the symbolic workings of popular culture, their cultural kinship with consumers in their own class of origin, and their armory of fashionable theory—Schütz, Garfinkel, Foucault, Gramsci, Derrida, Kristeva, Lacan, Raymond Williams, and the rest—into the heart of consumer capitalism. They used all of this to make money and, quite often, to become capitalist entrepreneurs themselves.

The object of the present study was to identify clear cases of the postmodern type of expert, the life-world engineer. There was no intention to measure the extent or distribution of this type, only to clarify its component elements, to examine the tension between "formal" and "material" rationality, and to see how the contradictory indices of class interest work out in practice. Some thirty interviews were conducted among practitioners regarded by others in the business as successful, innovative, and creative. It quickly became clear that almost anyone in this business, from established company heads to new recruits, was likely to display a good many features of the postmodern type—the differences were of degree and consistency. The analysis below is a composite model drawn from the most vivid expositions offered by a notably loquacious group of people whose profession and pleasure it is to reflect the self and its endlessly fascinating states of being and doing.

The Structure of the Industry

The emergence of qualitative market research parallels the transformation of the advertising industry in Britain. Advertising which had been dominated by large American conglomerates, was revolutionalized from within during the early 1970s by a number of aggressive new agencies, notably Saatchi and Saatchi, who changed all the old practices. Most of the innovations began in small consultancies, grew into agencies, and, through takeovers and amalgamations, became multimillion pound businesses, some remaining independent like the Saatchis, but differentiating their operations, others becoming absorbed as sectors of existing companies in publishing and other related fields, like J. Walter Thompson (Kleinman 1987; Wright 1972).

Market research companies grew in tandem. Most market research, even today, is quantitative. As markets have expanded and fragmented the research process has required ever more sophisticated typologies of particular groups of consumers. One consequence of this has been investment in expensive information technology by quantitative companies, and a tendency for such companies to become larger and more capital-intensive. The other consequence has been the emergence of qualitative market research as the separate exercise of analyzing data about the meanings and uses of product and of brand images from which more sensitive typologies can be derived. Independent qualitative companies and consultancies began to appear in the early 1970s, though the fastest expansion occurred later in the decade. Qualitative sections also emerged within many large quantitative companies and in some large commodity companies.

Estimates suggest that there may be anywhere from 200 to 500 independent qualitative companies in London alone. Few are very large enterprises—in qualitative market research "large" means, say, twenty researchers, including executive directors, plus as many as secretarial and administrative support staff, and only two companies are as large as this. The norm seems to be five to eight researchers; the largest category of companies are really partnerships of two director/researchers with perhaps one other researcher and three support staff. In short, it is a cottage industry.

The typical genesis of a company seems to follow a pattern of this sort. Two colleagues who have worked as researchers in an existing large or middle-sized company for, say, eighteen months, become restless as they realize that they are bringing in a high proportion of the business but are not getting a proportionate share in the profits. The profit margin on most individual jobs is between 50 percent and 70 percent. They decide to set up a partnership/consultancy on borrowed capital. They probably need between 25,000 and 50,000 pounds sterling in credit to cover office rent, office furniture, word processors, a company publicity brochure and stationery with designer logo, and to create an immediate float for salaries until the business begins to flow. As one young company head put it, "given that your average bank branch manager has an average 50,000 pounds credit responsibility, he can actually give it to you. You don't have to go to Head office. I mean it's dead easy, and the bank encourages you." The partnership may need to take out life insurance or second mortgages but the procedure is simple. The process of fission is so normal, however, that many companies seek to inhibit their researchers by requiring them to sign contracts in which they promise not to take clients with them if they set up on their own. The main danger to a new company comes in the first year: if they cannot keep a steady flow of jobs coming in they will be unable to meet their salary bill, which is by far the largest outgoing cost. The proliferation of successful companies suggests that the risks are not unduly serious. It seems to be fairly normal for design companies and advertising agencies (potential clients, of course) to invest in these promising small partnerships on the basis of personal friendship, trust, and successful prior business relations.

The highly personalized structure is one of the most important features of the qualitative research business. It is pure Daniel Bell: the "capital" of this new "knowledge" profession does, indeed, reside in the know-how rather than the hardware, and, more crucially, in *individual* practitioners' interpretive "feel" for the business and in their personal, face-to-face relationships with their clients. Typically clients bring business to an *individual researcher*, not to a company as such, they expect that researchers do all or a substantial part of the research and, above all, present the findings to the client at the "debrief." Reputations, therefore, are individual reputations first and company reputations second.

Most individual jobs for clients bring in between 5,000 and 10,000 pounds and each one takes only a few weeks. Fast work and a continuous stream of jobs are thus the essence of success. The difficulty of having companies grow much beyond partnership size is a common preoccupation in the industry. The problem is twofold: the tendency for experienced researchers to set up on their own, and the difficulty the executive directors have in withdrawing from the research function because it is their proven success in research as *individuals* which brings in the work. Only one London company—the largest—seemed to have solved both problems, though it has a reputation for higher-than-average staff turnover. Its founder's policy was to expand laterally by recruiting extensively at the senior level. Its image with other researchers in the field is that it does not want "creativity" in its researchers, and that it gives a "predictable," "bread-and-butter" service by standardizing the formula that researchers are constrained to use. It may be one example of a qualitative company in which "formal rationality" has prevailed over "material rationality" or the more typical postmodern, laid-back style of this industry.

The industry's own founding myth is that it was created by "old hippies" in the 1970s. Its current members are typically young. Some senior researchers and company heads are in their fifties, but I should guess the median age of the profession as being the early thirties. It is also a fairly glamorous profession, although interviewees tend to regard it as far less glamorous than advertising, planning, and marketing. Yet the company brochures and offices give a different picture. The brochures almost invariably carry studio photographs of all the members of the company—typically posed and poised but also indefinably informal, hinting at spontaneity. Aspects of their professional qualifications, experience, and private personas are often strung together in accompanying captions or mini-curriculum vitae, thus: "John Smith, psychologist, film buff, father. Research executive. New product development: primarily food, beverages, and pharmaceuticals." No strict separation obtains between the private and the professional aspects of self.

The profession is probably 70 percent female, as is quantitative research. It is attractive to ambitious female graduates who want to break out of the ill-paid feminine ghettos of the welfare professions. I encountered many broadly "feminist" sentiments among interviewees, but they were mostly concerned with the importance of women as consumers and with the dilemma of young women researchers in planning the optimum mix of work with child bearing and child rearing (with or without marriage). Many of the women believed that not enough women became executive directors or could afford to take the risk of setting up their own companies. Nevertheless, many companies are headed by women.

Most of the interviews took place in company offices, so I was able to observe a range of styles and spatial layouts. The typical sartorial style of qualitative research is informal elegance: they do not want to be confused with city types in old school ties and dark suits. They are also quite open about the importance of dressing "up" or "down" depending on whether they are meeting clients or interviewing groups, whose social composition determines the self-image the researchers present. Dress is, in all events, one of the recognized props of the job. Office decor ranged from the immaculate restored Georgian to the aggressive minimalist. A few offices might even have been mistaken for any academic department office, overflowing with paper and decorated with topical newspaper cuttings, cartoons, and posters. A great deal depends on whether clients normally visit the office: more commonly, the researcher goes to the client. Office decor, therefore, is mostly important for the presentation of self *in-house*. "Not bothering" was one style; another involved the display of recherché Australian prints; several offices made a great feature of displaying products which had been researched or memorabilia of contracts with large corporations. The display of the insignia of corporate clients and products on which the company has worked is a common feature of the company brochure and advertising too. All the offices I visited were either completely or partially open plan. Even the senior executives do not typically have their own private offices. This reflects a style of work that favors openness, flow (of ideas and of persons), egalitarian relationships (instant first-name terms), "bouncing ideas off each other," gregariousness. There was a general acceptance that this fluid and apparently chaotic arrangement "really works best." One young company founder explained his rationale for designing the company's new offices in a semi-open plan:

> Jim [his partner] and I will each have a desk in one of the two main offices and we will have two or three researchers in there with us. It keeps us all on our toes and, anyway, in this business you have got to talk to everybody else all the time. The doors are never closed, you know, and hardly anybody actually sits on a chair at the desk much of the time. We prowl and perch and drink endless cups of tea and coffee while we pick each other's brains. And that is how we [the partners] keep an eye on how the juniors [researchers] are doing.... Everybody is working on half a dozen different jobs at the same time.

He went on to argue that this constant interaction also served to bind the members of the company together. He was very anxious to head off potential secession (like his own) and was considering all kinds of ideas from profit sharing to bonus schemes to make it possible for the company to grow rather than split. One company had taken a Thames river boat for an evening—the Yuppie version of the "works outing" of course—to see whether drunken license might help diffuse the tension that the partners recognized as a function of the real differences of power and reward underlying the egalitarian surface.

Time structures are fluid and apparently chaotic too. Almost no one observes strict office hours although the more junior the researcher the more likely it is that attendance nine to five will be required. The real discipline is geared to delivering the findings to the client on time; *how* that is done is of less account. Researchers have to travel around the country a great deal in order to conduct the interviews (usually of groups rather than individuals) that provide their main data. Most researchers expect to work late (up to midnight) at least two nights a week and estimated actual weekly hours of work at well above the national average—eighty hours or more was normal—though it was clear that few of them had ever sat down and counted the hours before I asked. Early starts at the office are not important, though being prepared to give up your "free" time is a sine qua non of being good at the job. Many researchers also expect to find the privacy and quietness necessary for shaping the first draft of the report at home rather than in the office. Researchers in smaller firms frequently criticized the larger bureaucratized company for its inflexible office discipline and its damping of the flow and bustle. One researcher, who had never worked for the company said, "It must be awful. Great rows of desks like a factory with T.G. (the founder) keeping her beady eye on you. 'Heads down, now write, one, two, three....'"

These time and space structures reflect a fundamental, dynamic tension between individualistic ideals, on the one hand, and on the other a recognition that the creativity and imaginativeness that everyone in this business prizes so highly do not come unequivocally from "inside" the individual, solitary consciousness but through constant mutual stimulation and exchange. Qualitative market researchers are doing precisely what Kellner and Heuberger have defined as the postmodern project: they are reflecting professionally and persistently on the life-world of consumers *and* of themselves. Their work practices are geared to creating and maintaining a life-world that members of any one company team, as microcosm, and all members of the profession, as macrocosm, can share. The frenetic interaction is not just about "stimulation" and "bouncing ideas" but about establishing and constantly repairing the plausibility structures that underpin the confidence these practitioners must have in their own interpretive procedures. Other features of the organization of the industry strengthen the forces of postmodern resistance to "formal rationality." In the first place, there is no formal certification, no professionally prescribed training, no powerful professional organization, and no established tradition other than what the postmoderns have themselves created in the last fifteen or so years. Virtually all the recruits are graduates and many have higher degrees or failed to complete them when grants ran out and the pressures and pleasures of full-time market research intervened. The ideal of graduate entry to the profession seems to command wide assent, but I spoke to no one who believed that it should be a formal entry requirement.

Quasi-professional associations do exist. The Market Research Society is a voluntary association to which most market researchers belong. It publishes a monthly newsletter, runs conferences, administers prize competitions for research papers, offers frequent short courses, usually two or three days, and mounts isolated lectures. The MRS has also developed a Code of Conduct, mostly concerned to protect the anonymity and the interests of the subjects of research activity. The MRS has no legal or professional sanctions of any substance, however, and is thus more a talking shop than a professional guardian of ethics or quality. Independent of the MRS, an Association of Qualitative Research Practitioners runs conferences and short courses, but has an equivocal reputation among some of the more recent recruits to the field as a cabal of half a dozen "big names in the field throwing their weight about and electing themselves to be the industry's teachers." Although many researchers believe they know what kind of training they would like to see in the field, very few want to see formal certification. Even those (many) who were certain that their own methods were the best available also acknowledged that pretty well everyone else who was any good thought *theirs* were the best too, and concluded that variety and permanent openness to change were superior to standardization.

The Nature of the Work

Qualitative market research companies are essentially consultancies. The work comes to them from advertising and design agencies or the marketing or development sections of producers of goods and services. Increasingly they are also being used by government departments, local authorities, welfare agencies, and charities. Most of the researchers I interviewed had worked on what they tend to refer to as "the social side" (to distinguish it from "the commercial side") in projects that involved aspects of prison administration, the hierarchy of needs as seen by elderly recipients of welfare, health and housing services, and public attitudes to sex and violence on television. The great bulk of their work, however, remains in the commercial field. The qualitative researcher is typically brought in when a producer wants to know why a brand is losing market share, or how to retain the market share on an established and successful product, whether to differentiate a product to serve several submarkets rather than one mass market, how to update a brand image, whether and how to market a new product or sell an established product to a new category of consumer, and so on. The client is not asking for numbers—how many will buy X?—but an analysis of processes and meanings: if I want to sell my low-alcohol beer, my new small car, or my pension scheme to young artisan-class consumers, what images do I need to deploy in advertising and marketing it?

Every job is a separate contract and every report is strictly confidential—none of it, including the social policy analyses, is in the public domain unless the client who bought the research chooses to publish all or part of it. Although a client company may commission several pieces of work from the same research company, this cannot be assumed. Moreover, clients relate to individual researchers, not to companies as a rule. Vice-versa, the "client" is similarly not I.C.I. or Courtaulds as such, but Jim Bloggs in I.C.I.'s marketing division or Mary Smith in Courtaulds' advertising section. Even the continuous relationships with clients have a natural term, since Jim Bloggs and Mary Smith are typically mobile either within the company or between companies. Yet this mobility itself also serves to extend the professionalized networks between client and researcher so that they criss-cross a wide swath of the commercial field. There is also some movement between quantitative and qualitative research and between research and the advertising, planning, and marketing fields. All this means a considerable overlap of professional life-world between researchers and potential clients: they often go to the same parties, eat many lunches together, and drink in the same pubs and wine bars.

Most qualitative research companies see themselves as all-purpose performers, as capable with frozen peas as with laptop computers. One company chairman explained to me the advantages the qualitative companies have over the research section of producing companies. "The qual. guys at Colgate, lets say, know everything there is to be known about *toothpaste*, but they know fuck all about the consumer. We know about about *consumers* and it does not matter a shit that I have never researched toothpaste—I bet I can do a better job of it than they can." (The scatological language was a frequent feature of communication in this project—part of the nonconforming self-image and of the quasi-bohemian style: Tom Wolfe reports his own amazement at finding the same phenomenon in Wall Street [Wolfe 1990].) Despite this generalist claim, most individual researchers present themselves as particularly good with certain kinds of work: the researcher quoted above saw himself as best with work on male-defined commodities because he had a "feel" for masculine imagery; many of the women researchers had specialized in women's and children's commodities.

In their publicity, the qualitative research companies also often like to stress their special competencies. Consider this example:

O Wad Some Pow'r The Giftie Gie Us
To See Ourselves As Others See Us!

If only, if only! The impassioned words of Robbie Burns rang obsessively in the researcher's brain. And then, in a flash, it came to him. No, to be brutally honest, that was not how our Salient Multi Attribute Research Technique came into being. The reality involved months of complex development work. But the end result was certainly dramatic. XY International can now officially offer you the pow'r to see yourselves and the service you offer, as others see you. It's called SMART for short. And it's the only research technique specifically designed to assess customer service rather than products. Encouraging your staff to give customers a smile might do more than restructuring your entire distribution system. It's now almost impossible to maintain a competitive edge based on price or product in many businesses: improved service is the only way of standing out from the crowd. (MRS Newsletter, May 1989)

This is a rich piece of prose. The style is chatty. It begins with the image of a flash of genius (nonrational vision), disarms us with its honesty in admitting that hard work, not inspiration, is the real backbone of the company's offering (formal, technical rationality), blinds us with technique, with an image of infallible precision in that unique research tool, rounds off the Robbie Burns metaphor ("We're literate and imaginative") and goes on to show how *precise* fine tuning of customer service is the most crying need of any producer worth his salt (and his market) today. It is a very shrewd mixture of promise and threat—and a perfect piece of corroborative evidence for the Hochschild hypothesis about the spread of "emotional labor" in consumer culture.

Interviewees typically maintained *both* that everybody in the field uses pretty well similar methods *and* that their own were better, subtly special, more sensitivity deployed. The latter claim takes two forms, often at the same time: the first is patenting, as it were, a specific technical tool like SMART in the advertisement quoted above; the other is the claim that it is the *quality* of the interpretation rather than the fieldwork technique that matters. One advertisement for a qualitative company takes the form of a full-page drawing of an iceberg with the sliver of surface ice labelled "the fieldwork" and the vast submerged hulk of ice "the interpretation." Companies take pains to assure clients that they are flexible and pragmatic and will make the client's specific needs their primary concern: it is very counterproductive to be too "academic," to sound profound but give no practical advice.

Many companies do a certain amount of telephone work, especially business-to-business interviews. Several companies have recently begun to branch out into management and personnel consultancy, advising on issues like employee morale, company image, or "corporate culture"—the subtler features of the "life-world of work." Such consultations involve direct observation and individual depth interviews. Most of the work, however, takes the form of group interviews with targeted customers. The groups will be anything from eight to, say, twenty people, depending on the subject. They will be chosen, in consultation with the client, to represent a specific type of consumer. The groups are normally recruited across different parts of the country by a field recruiter who may work for several companies.

The group interviews will take place in the recruiter's home or sometimes on hired premises. The groups may be divided between two or three researchers. The researcher acts as a "moderator" in the group discussions, which are always tape-recorded, and may take up to four hours each. As well as talk, all sorts of stimulation techniques are involved: some groups run like encounter or therapeutic groups; some use batteries of psychological tests, processes of word and image association ("write an obituary for this brand," "pretend this product is a blind date—how would you describe him?"), role-play and improvised drama; others use "creative" techniques with plasticine, bricks, clay, drawing, and painting; still others play games, including board games which groups may be asked to create as well as to play. The objective of these various techniques is to get at what consumers "really feel" below the level of conscious rationality. They aim to elicit feelings, symbols, and meanings, that is the elements of the nonrational which make up the *unconsidered* structure of consciousness—the material of the taken-for-granted life-world or what one interviewee called "Pandora's box."

Individual researchers may often type up these tapes themselves as a part of the process of developing interpretations. Others use office typists to transcribe the tapes. Several researchers of considerable experience admitted that they seldom even read through the full typescript because they will already have sifted the significant from the insignificant in the course of the group interview itself. (This is the subject of recent debate in the MRS newsletter where "formalist" versus "postmodern" opinions on the ethics of research methodology clash without possibility of reconciliation.) The data collected in these interviews is then discussed in the endless to-and-fro of the office, both within the team responsible for the project and with other members of the company, before being finally written into a report. The climax of the research process comes with the "debrief," when the senior researcher on the project, sometimes with the active, often with the passive assistance of junior colleagues, presents the report to the client, usually at the client's office. This is a big performance where all the skills of self-presentation on which the researchers pride themselves come into play. One young female company head said:

I love the debrief. It's the real dressing up time, you know, the works! Hairdo, makeup, smart dark suit, even high heels, real Maggie Thatcher, would you believe? Oh, and briefcase—leather of course. When I do groups I might carry my stuff in an old Sainsbury's bag but you have got to look the part for the debrief. Then I give it to them. Cool competence, they like that, and a surprise or two, and a bit of sex appeal. [Parody of crossing her leg.] It's a cabaret act, a one-women show, but you have *got* to believe yourself or it won't work. It doesn't matter how good the research—I mean the real work—*how* good, if you can't put it across—you will never make it in this business.

A female researcher, a PhD with a considerable academic research experience described the typical debriefing: " Oh yes, it's a gig. Everything's a gig. A presentation is a gig. A group's a gig. I wouldn't mind if it was a case of out performing each other in terms of quality but it's just a one man band wagon." She went on to argue that these thespian performance values were often a cover for unoriginal research. Her own performance took a simpler approach, "telling the story to the client as if he were your mother." She added: "the best people don't need to stuff a debrief full of projectives that make the client think they are terribly, terribly witty and a great psychologist."

Yet even she agreed with the common view that it was the debrief performance that secured repeat contracts. She believed that this was because clients were the last people capable of judging the objective value of research findings. They therefore had only the "board room cabaret" to convince them. The problem, she argued, was that those who commissioned the research did not usually have the responsibility for acting on it—that would often be another branch of the company or another firm. Sometimes even the client would not know if, or how, the research was used. Many researchers said that it was rare for clients to report back to them on the use to which their research is put, but few agreed that the client could not tell useful research from mystification. One researcher argued that clients were in a good position to know because they often have more than one research company working for them and can compare the service they get. He added:

I suppose I am sufficiently arrogant to say that I'm good.... It's like a doctor/patient relationship, part of the deal is about your confidence. If you have no confidence no one is going to believe what you say, because it's regarded as soft data and therefore has an element of subjectivity in it. So your ability to convince the person relates obviously to *the amount of confidence you put in and the amount of soul, if you like, of your soul and personality that they see embedded in it. You know there is a lot of personality involved.* There is a performance element to it. I mean if you ask me "What is the best thing about doing qualitative research?" a lot of people will say "going out with the team and doing the field work." I would not agree with that at all. I—it's doing the debrief. I think that is the best. You are on the stage and people are paying you for standing up and telling them what's right in this world. What a big ego trip! [My italics.]

There is a very important element of rewarding the self for a job well done in these performances: it's a ritual assertion of self-esteem. These performances, which everyone sees as pleasurable climaxes, are an indispensable aspect of the plausibility structure of the whole enterprise, and one that draws clients as well as researchers into a liturgy of life-world manifestation—analysis and shared subjectivity all in one. It is all very reminiscent of Sherman McCoy.

The Knowledge Base and Skills

Everyone I interviewed believed that somewhere in the center of the knowledge base were the social sciences. Some firms specialize in psychology—everything from Jung to behaviorism—some in sociology. Most are eclectic, one might almost say magpie, in their approach. Several interviewees told me that there were companies committed to one rigid theoretical frame (usually "deep Freudian stuff"), but no one I met was anything but cheerfully catholic. As one researcher put it:

It's basic social sciences but it's broad church and you can take models from anywhere as long as it seems to make sense and is useful to you. I mean, we don't analyze things and say "there is an interactionist account of what we have been talking about." That isn't the point, the point is to actually provide the guy with something he can use.

It is worth looking in some detail at this eclectic sociologist's view of research method.

It's not just social sciences.... Essentially what you are after is someone with a good brain. I mean frankly it doesn't matter much what they have studied at university but they must have a good brain.... We do have two postgraduate doctorates in this company and it is interesting to see how they have to change. They have to adapt a lot to go from the sort of very nice longitudinal studies that they're doing. It's got to be delivered on time and it's very focused and more—shall we say—quick and dirty research that we do.

I then asked if he felt that this made his research less reliable and he responded, "No, I don't. No, I don't, certainly not." "So quick and dirty can still get it right." I asked. "Oh God yes! Oh God yes! I mean, it just needs a bit more nerve I suppose is what you are talking about." He believed that "a technique is just a technique" and explained his view of the knowledge base of research in terms of his own "personal style."

My personal style is about gaining knowledge, right? So I use the people in front of me [in the groups] as a way of increasing my knowledge, so it's a lot of interaction between me and them and around the group and then back to me again, whereas other people will implant an idea, or plant a subject and then just let them talk and sit back and not do much, just listen. I don't like doing that. I like to be in it grabbing and it's very much a sort of "I want to know, I want to know, I want to know" system that I operate under because it's just what I feel comfortable under.... One of the first things I say to [new recruits] is, "look, it doesn't matter how you get out the result as long as you get them out and they seem to have some form of validity in terms of their usefulness, they take you further and the main thing is just to feel comfortable because then the people will respond to you." If you are feeling anxious or feeling "Oh God! I don't want to do it this way" then don't do it that way because they will cotton on very quickly to your feeling of discomfort and the group won't be worth anything.... Fun is important too. I mean—God—you're asking people to give up an hour and a half of their time just to talk about something remarkably trivial really that they don't really want to talk about, although they do find it fun and interesting as they get into it.... You know they come along and talk about frozen peas. I mean, you know, who gives a toss frankly. No one. *And yet you have got to make it so that they do and they actually start to look at facets of their life that they never look at really* and you've got to take them into that process. And you know they do find it fun. So humor, jokes, laughter, sex appeal, play...."[My italics]

I asked how he knew when he had got to the nub of the thing. He answered:

I think it's a number of things. I suppose a part of my training will always say to me, "you've got to go in with some form of hypothesis," and, you know, that hypothesis is a rolling one. I go in with ideas in my head and then it changes as you go along. It's just experience. Tough. A lot of it's confirmatory. And each project is cumulative. Your knowledge over the years is cumulative and so is each project. I mean this is a point about the Americans. They will insist on you having a sort of topic guide following from A to Z in exactly the same format so they say, well, every group's going to be the same. Well, I mean that's just daft, it's stupid.

The features of this account that I would underline are first, the personalization of the answers—"I do it this way" as an answer to a question about the knowledge and skill required in the job in general. That was typical. It was also typical to find an attitude to the work that was analogous to "driving by the seat of my pants." Most of the market researchers had a standard theoretical and methodological knowledge of the social sciences but were impatient with the meticulousness, abstraction, and precision they associated with with "academic" research—"formal rationality." What this interviewee graphically described as the "quick and dirty" approach was favored by the most senior and commercially successful of my interviewees as *superior* to self-indulgent, expensive, overtheoretical academic research. The quoted passage's references to "validity" and "usefulness" justify this approach. Validity is not used in a strictly scientific sense. What it seems to mean is "convincing to me and to the other qualitative researchers whom I respect in that it makes sense of the client's problem." Validity is tested by "bouncing the idea around" in the office and "performing" it for the client. In short it is the shared professional life-world of the qualitative researcher that tests "validity." Also typical in this account was the dislike of formally rational, standardizing procedures of which the Americans are reputed to be so fond. (This same interviewee also spun a long satirical trope on the American fondness for equipment, the use of one-way mirrors, and video-taping groups. It was laughable in his view because the routinization and mechanization of the procedures squeezed out the analysis: "they love hardware and activity but they've no balls when it comes to analysis.")

Others were even more vehement in their rejections of standard "scientific method," or rather, the *vocabulary* of scientism. One particularly innovative woman researcher, who had a psychology background, rejected a large number of other "taken-for-granteds" of the profession and went out of her way to deny *any* scientific basis to the work. "Sure we use all the standard psychological tests but its bull shit really. You just go out and let your imagination fizz in the groups." Of the process of interpretation she said: "That's what I love. It's just like having a three hour gossip session with your mate in a cafe. You know, 'Did you hear what that one with the awful dyed hair said? Do you think it really means ...?' It's great. It's not science, but it's a lot of laughs." I asked if she thought her findings had any validity and she was emphatic that they did. "They may not be the *only* way of seeing things but, yes, *of course* it's real and valid. After a while in this business you just *know*."

Even the most emphatically "academic" of the interviewees were in the end reduced to similar assertions. One woman researcher discussed the methodological importance of the process of recruiting and selecting groups, and the skill required in moderating groups so that the researcher could "build up participation in the group to such an extent that we could reach some stage of honesty." I asked how she knew when she had got down to that "honest" layer. She talked for a while about techniques and hypothesis-generation then finally said with a laugh, "But it's a click that happens, something goes [snap of the fingers]. You simply *know*. All your antennae tell you you're getting the real stuff."

What goes on in the group is obviously the heart of the whole enterprise because that is where the data is generated. Let me take another individual case. This is a company founder with a sociology background. He began by arguing that the key to his current work was "wrestling with the epistemological issue":

> This is a whole industry in which people say what you do is you go out and talk to people and you come back with data and that's the answer. They exploit, they misrepresent Popper. "This is a scientific enterprise" kind of thing, "this is objective knowledge" kind of thing, and it's all bollocks.... there was this conference about reliability in research. The biggest nonsense I have ever heard. They *never* ask about the epistemological status of the data.

He argued that what was needed in groups was:

> To create the kind of environment in which hopefully you can empathize with the situation of the punter. You get inside their flesh, their mind. It's actually quite promiscuous in a way, because it's all one night stands. You go in there and get deeply into people's lives, a bit of their lives, the part you know that is about deodorant or lager [an] intimate stranger kind of thing and if you can do it well then people will own up quite a lot to you. I mean, I have discovered amazing things that women do with ice cream in foreplay.... People sort of open up to you.... There are all the things you pick up in terms of body language. You don't have a specific scheme for interpreting it. You feel it almost because you've done it so much.

He was quite open, as were many researchers, about enjoying the power the moderator had in the groups. He talked about it as dangerous, as "laying *yourself* on the line too if you are asking the punter to let go his civilized controls." It was essentially seduction and the element of play was vital.

What you're really interested in doing is creating little explosions in there, little disruptions so things fly off here and there, various bits of culture and feeling.... I think what you are trying to do is kind of coming at things from around the side and say—"let 's not be serious about this, let's not be totally rational, let's not try and be absolutely objective and let's not speak the accepted wisdom of this marketplace." ... Over time you learn various subtle ways of getting people to do things they might not otherwise do. I could get someone to shit in a bag if I wanted to. I believe that. I could do that. And there are probably few other people in the business who could do that.

He believed that the process also "liberated the punters" who "go through this kind of cathartic thing and say 'We can now do and say anything. Wheeee!'"

He had little time for systematic analysis of the data, regarded working through transcripts as "something you give to juniors to kind of train them." For him the process of interpretation was "serendipity really." "You have all the stuff. You are swimming around in it, you just immerse yourself in it and suddenly things will just jump. You make that leap into some new territory and say—'Hey! the world is not like *that*, it's like *this*: it's an entirely new configuration,' and then you just work your way back."

He explained that he now subjected his own life to constant reflection, which was seamlessly extended from his own research work:

What you are interested in is what people do with their lives. I go out—you sort of go out and look at what people, you, your friends, buy. You look at the logic of their lives, the illogic of their lives and how things fit into that, not necessarily with a critical sort of eye, just as part of understanding. Going out and interviewing people in Hemel Hempstead on Wednesday night is a sort of surrogate social life. There's an overlap. And then when I go out with my mates to the pub and shift a few beers, I'm acutely conscious of the fact, thinking about it now, that there are different brands on the bar that they are drinking and there's a particular pattern of drinking going on—grown up, mid-thirties yobbos you know. These things infest one another. I don't see it as problematic.

Many of the skills in qualitative research, he noted, are those an actor uses.

I borrow a lot from the academic sort of background. But it starts before that and it isn't rooted in that, the academic thing is rooted in something else which is about being compulsively nosy and compulsively analytic—all that stuff back then when I used to act.

One of the clearest and the most complete cases of postmodern consciousness, this interviewee made little or no differentiation between public and private world, was "compulsively analytic" about his own and everyone else's "life-world." He valued his own bohemian nonconformity and saw himself as a maverick within the business, had no compunction about the dangerous "emotional labor" at the heart of his work, and was staunchly against routinization and bureaucratization in the work and in training.

Another respondent referred to the object of the work as "asking consumers to change their lives, just a bit, even if it's only about frozen peas." The same idea was frequently presented. A paper by three colleagues in one qualitative company, *New Product Development and Paradigms* (Chandler, Henry, and Owen 1988), makes the implications fully explicit. The argument is that products and services exist within established "paradigms" for consumers: they have been built up over a long time.

> Consumer culture is not an abstraction, it is a social reality in which people live. Being a consumer involves a long process of socialization in which people learn to feel and behave in particular ways, in which they acquire a common set of assumptions about what the world is and what it means. These commonly held assumptions make life manageable, they make it possible for us to interact with other consumers because we agree on a more or less common definition of the meaning of cars, drinking, washing powder, frozen foods, clothes, and so on.

> What we have here is a portrait of consumer culture as essentially "paradigmatic"; comprised of a vast web of interlocking meaning structures defining the significance, qualities, and role of different products and brands.

The paper goes on to argue that these paradigms are a constraint on new product development and that research should be geared to helping producers overcome these restraints. It gives examples of how new products have a typical "life history" and what can be done to assist "brave marketers" to introduce new products. What is needed is "to develop new elements within the framework of existing rules [within the paradigm]" and "to develop and advance new ideas by breaking out of the existing framework of rules [that is, creating new paradigms]." The latter will involve a "restructuring of the marketplace." "The trick of truly innovative NPD work is ... to identify the directions in which the world can be successfully restructured." Research aiming at this should therefore "identify and map the contours of the existing paradigm(s). Recognize that ... new products will first be taken up by radicals and individualists, then form 'cult' followings, then achieve subcultural status, then perhaps find a mainstream position." All of this requires "the adoption of more creative research approaches which can turn the consumer world upside down and inside out, then restructure it and reorder it in new constellations. This demands research approaches which, on occasion, actually disrupt, disorient and confuse the consumer, a style of research which is more provocative than therapeutic."

The postmodern project could hardly be more openly avowed. A woman researcher who was quoted earlier denying the "scientific" status of the work was almost equally explicit, but in a very different style. "I don't know where I read it. Perhaps a psychology textbook, I can't remember, but it's what I believe. Somebody said, 'The real problem of life is how to fill in all that time between birth and death.' That's it! Well, that's what commodities do. They fill in that time. I'm all in favor of commodities and I want to get consumers to have fun with them.... There is nothing wrong with useless commodities. They are good for a laugh, a game. I just want people to have more fun and that's what this business is all about. Showing consumers where the fun can be." Her style with the groups was gentler but it was equally geared to "liberating" them.

A few researchers expressed strong disapproval of the disruptive techniques of the kinds recommended in the NPD paper. One woman researcher said some of them were "no better than rape really." The problem involved both a moral dimension—the public should not have to suffer that kind of assault on its personal privacy—and a technical dimension—they don't work anyway because they inhibit the public. The subject was part of a wider disagreement or confusion about how "the public" should be regarded. There is a long running controversy in the business over whether the good researcher needs "empathy" with the consumer. I met violent agreement and equally violent disagreement on that point. One researcher said "I don't need to *empathize*. They might be the most awful yobs. They're *objects* to me—my rats in the lab for a couple of hours." Yet he also went on to say that beyond a certain age it was hard to continue with research because "you lost touch with the consumer who's typically C1/C2 aged 20 to 39." He was rejecting the *emotional* identification indicated by the word "empathy" while accepting that sharing some aspects of life-cycle (and life-world) was a foundation for the work. What researchers seem to agree on is the need for Weberian *verstehen*, but they disagree on the nature and depth of the "emotional work" that is desirable in the interaction with the public and colleagues, and on the legitimacy of aggressive or disruptive techniques in the group interviews. Some openly despise "the punter" but still describe the kick they get out of the interaction in the groups—the adrenalin, entertainment, and power still carry them through. Nevertheless, it is clear that the area of the work that provokes most controversy—and is a problem for the MRS Code of Conduct—is that which most openly seeks to "turn the consumer's world upside down."[33] (MRS Code of Conduct 1990)

One area of agreement among the researchers was the satisfaction they get out of the job. Few would do the job if it were not enjoyable. Many described themselves as "on a permanent high." "If it weren't a permanent party I wouldn't do it." That it pays well is part of the enjoyment, but would not be enough if the intrinsic pleasure did not exist. The ability to feel this pleasure was inextricable from having the "personality" and skills that made them good at it. There is a palpable sense of professionalism in that everyone believes he or she can tell a good researcher from a bad. Creativity, imaginativeness, saying something new are good, but so is giving the client practical advice. To the question "How do you know your work is good?" there were two standard answers. One: "I just know." The other: "because the client comes back for more," or in another variant, "we make profits." The touchstones are inner integrity and the operation of the market, in that order.

Many interviewees however had problems with the idea of "a profession" since it suggested routinization. "We are not a profession, we are an industry. Professions end up having their own entry examinations and all that sort of rubbish."

This same researcher disliked the idea of formal training of any kind. To the idea of M.B.A.'s in qualitative market research he retorted, "Ah, come on! I mean if you needed that you ain't very good." Yet he also had very clear ideas of what constituted "amateur" work or "unprofessional behavior," such as simply confirming the preconceived ideas of a client even if he represents a company that has investments in your own firm. All interviewees were acutely aware that they needed to reckon with the internal politics of client's companies and that their findings were often counters in such power games. This was the subject that provoked most ethical unease and prevarication among these otherwise shameless postmoderns.

I met no one who wanted the training process taken over by a professional body. A few of the more recent entrants said they would have welcomed more formal courses but not as "professional certification." All the more experienced researchers told horror stories about how they were "dropped in the deep end" with little training and less supervision but uniformly concluded that that was the best way to learn. The dominant ideal was an apprenticeship model in which experienced researchers work alongside new recruits and induct them into the ethos of the job. Specific *techniques* can be learned from formal courses but the heart of the work can only come from inside, teased out by the virtuoso seniors in the field. It is a "craft," a sort of secret society where "feel" comes from good example, benevolently intentioned shock tactics and strategic neglect of the new recruits. It's a mystique. In short, it is a process of steeping the entrants in the life-world of a profession which favors individualism and despises routinization, bureaucracy, and certification. Hence the ambition of so many company founders to find a way of fostering the talents of the "the shit hot new graduate" within the unique "tradition" of the firm without either suppressing his or her creativity or encouraging the newcomer to go it alone at the first opportunity. It is a very precarious balancing act, but it is obvious that many firms have created a "tradition of iconoclasm" into which they induct recruits. I have little doubt that the disorientation that most new recruits experience has the same function as that which is induced in the early stage of joining a religious cult—it makes the resulting identification with the life-world of the profession all the more intense, particularly since it also leaves each individual with the strong sense of *having defined it for him or herself* in a taxing initiation ordeal. It is akin to Featherstone's idea of the New Class as "self-created," and a world away from the views of professional ethics and research methodology that the proponents of "formal rationality" reiterate regularly in the M.R.S. Newsletter in a vain hope of imposing on qualitative work the positivistic tradition of the quantitative field. (Goodyear 1989; MRS Newsletter, March 1989, 34)

Life-Styles and Life-Worlds

The group of clear postmoderns in qualitative research has many elements of personal style and self-presentation in common. They share a generally hedonistic approach to life, an assumption that anyone who belongs with them will have a tolerant view of the vagaries of sexual preference and personal relationships. They are informal in dress, uninhibited in speech, and liable to assume instant intimacy; they have an easy familiarity with the minute movements of popular culture and are typically involved in those modern art forms (from avant-garde rock music to modern dance and photography) that Bourdieu noted as belonging to the milieu of the New Class "petite bourgeoisie." They see other professions as their natural peers but advertisers as immediate status rivals. It is impossible to tell from the stylistic signals what the *political* preferences of any individual will be or the nature of his or her social networks. Among the interviewees sexual partners included doctors, a bond broker, bankers, school teachers, and social workers, as well as others in the research, advertising, and marketing world. Friendship patterns were often rooted in relationships made at university and therefore tended to range through the whole professional spectrum, both "new" and "old," from shipping brokers to media producers, bankers and accountants to charity administrators.

The postmodern stylistic package seems able to accommodate with ease every political position from the anarchistic left to the libertarian right and to tolerate considerable contradictions. Friendship and association easily cross the political divide as long as there is a postmodern life-world in common. Some of the most exuberantly procapitalist researchers had accepted without demur the common assumption among the qualitative research tribe that it is unethical to work for "the tobacco lobby." Those on the political right nevertheless prided themselves on their unstuffy, libertarian views and on their willingness to admit that they liked money and the things it can buy, from property to private education. They often make fun of those in the business who are uncomfortable about making money: one researcher called them "the social workers"; he himself preferred to be "one of the robber barons."

Several interviewees explicitly described the profession as having a "social work dimension" and, indeed, some researchers were clearly ill at ease with some aspects of consumer materialism and apologetic about serving capitalism. They preferred to do work for the state or local authorities, for charities, for radical pressure groups, or for left-of-center political parties. While they saw their emancipatory potential as attached to welfare issues and anti-Thatcherite politics, they justified their purely commercial work on the grounds that, as one woman put it, "it educates the producer about what consumers really want and that can't be all bad." Although among my interviewees these were not the group most obviously dedicated to purely commercial "paradigm shifts," they were enthusiastic about interventions designed to alter political images or to promote ecologically sound or socially beneficial products like alcohol-free beer.

The most complete postmodern case among the respondents described himself as an "anarchist ex-socialist" and put himself firmly on the bohemian end of the spectrum, claiming that the majority in the business were like him. He loved the work because it was competitive, a hand-to-hand contest with "the bastards in the old school ties" to be more creative and successful and make more money than them. He was one of several (all men) who waxed lyrical about the way his fantasy life fed his work (in terms strongly reminiscent of Sherman McCoy as Master of the Universe). The image in these fantasy projections of masculinity came from popular culture—Philip Marlowe, the Lone Roger, every role ever played by Humphrey Bogart, John Wayne, and Clint Eastwood—and were presented with considerable irony and postmodern self-consciousness as a kind of half-serious game that adds another dimension of pleasure and meaning to the job, but that also needed to be laughed at. The transcripts of many of these interviews read as if they were written jointly by John Cleese and Manuel Puig.

The postmoderns of all political colors had a clear sense of the need to keep their private lives under review. I received an impression of considerable volatility in the sexual partnerships and personal relationships of people in this milieu. This kind of interview research cannot measure the extent of that volatility but can report the respondents' common view that the nature of the work puts the "private world" of relationships under continuous strain. Some made a sharp distinction between work and their private *time* with family or friends, yet in the work itself saw no boundary between the private and professional *self*. Others simply merged private and work life to a remarkable extent. Most interviewees talked of *planning* their leisure time as a deliberately recuperative feature of life. They talked of golf, rugby, family life, playing the flute, and—frequently—regularly getting drunk as ways of attaining another state of consciousness that distanced them from work. Many of them referred to themselves or colleagues as people who needed two or three "real" vacations a year, often solitary "wilderness" experiences on boats, motor bikes, safari treks, or *empty* distant beaches. The "private" was self-consciously *constructed* as a counterweight to the gregarious and omnivorous life of work that "eats you up and spits you out."

Nobody wanted to be still doing the job at forty-five. Most wanted to be able to retire or to do something new by that age. They would be "out of touch," tired, perhaps even bored by then. The self-styled anarchist mused:

"I suppose it's a fantasy, a sort of—well if you were a woman you might have a baby. I can't do that. But if I thought I'd be working at this pace at forty.... So you sort of have a fantasy like 'I'll retire to a desert island,' or 'I'll be a novelist,' you probably won't do it but you need it as a dream just so you can get up in the morning and give out all that energy one more time." It *is* a young business and perhaps they will, some at least, be able to retire, or set up training consultancies as one of the most antibureaucratic types wanted to do. (Back-door routinization and professionalization of course.) Some of the women plan to work part-time when they have children; some do so already. The young woman who is creating an infrastructure of accounting, publicity, and field recruitment for a loose amalgam of self-employed freelance women may be on to a very profitable thing.

One ex-qualitative researcher who is now a very successful advertising executive was cynical about the future of the qualitative research business. He argued that the business had "blown it" by being unwilling to "build firms to a viable size." The pickings were too easy and it was tempting to settle for a high income in a small partnership rather than face the financial and organizational challenge of growth. He was just as committed to creativity, innovation, and egalitarian *practice* as were the qualitative researchers, but he differentiated between the requirements of the financial infrastructure and organizational techniques to optimize creativity. "You don't have to be a cottage industry in order to be innovative. In fact, if you stay a cottage industry you won't be able to afford to be creative in the long run." He felt that one root of the problem was the reluctance of "the old hippies in the business" (and the young ones too) to compromise one iota of their autonomy to shoulder serious *corporate* responsibilities. Those who have remained in the business do not see it quite this way. It remains to be seen whether the postmoderns of qualitative research manage to find a way of building their firms without being captured in Weber's dreaded iron cage. The indications are that if they don't, they are in danger of being taken over by advertising and design agencies who have far more capital to play with and who are less squeamish about the risk.

6

The New Class as Capitalist Class: The Rise of the Moral Entrepreneur in America

James Davison Hunter and Tracy Fessenden

Nowhere has there been more speculation about the changing place and the significance of the knowledge workers in the contemporary world than on the American scene. Out of this speculation, one hypothesis has emerged as predominant. In rough contours, the growth of the knowledge and information sector in the post-World War II economy has spawned a new and distinct social class whose collective political ideology is defined by a fundamental hostility toward capitalism. The antagonism is much more than a bookish quarrel over the principles of a morally just economy. To the contrary, because of its preferred access to the institutions and credentialling of higher education and its relative control over the various mass media, the "knowledge class" has established itself as an elite in competition with the interests of the traditional capitalist elite. As always, the spoils of such conflict are political power and social and economic privilege; the emergence of the New Class, therefore, represents nothing less than the beginnings of a New Class conflict—not between rich and poor, as the Marxist would have it, but rather between rival elites.

Some call it the invention of conservative intellectuals who are resentful of the increased standing of their more politically progressive colleagues, but the New Class hypothesis has grounding in empirical observation. It explains the proliferation of special interest organizations committed to curbing industrial pollution, monitoring the conditions of labor, regulating the practices and policies of trade, and controlling and redistributing and enlarging the sharing of corporate profits. It explains the university-based protest of commercial exploitation in the Third World and the university-organized opposition to corporate interests in South Africa. These are only the most obvious illustrations of the point. More systematic observations of the anticapitalist disposition of knowledge workers can be found in a wide variety of studies of elite opinion. The Lichter and Rothman studies of the American media elite conducted in the early 1980s, for example, demonstrated an overt prejudice against big business, particularly against the multinational oil companies.[34] The 1987 Religion and Power survey showed a similar hostility toward the workings of free enterprise on the part of university-based intellectuals, the national media, and the mainline religious clergy.[35] As this study and still another of regional elites in the Midwest have shown, this antagonism is particularly intense the further removed knowledge workers are from the mechanism of profit making.[36] Analysis of national election data and the General Social Surveys confirm this interpretation as well. However convincing the evidence, the New Class hypothesis is anything but a canon of accepted wisdom in American social science. Controversy centers mainly on the question of whether the New Class truly constitutes a "class." Opponents of this hypothesis concede that there is disaffection for the workings of the market among some knowledge workers, but claim that knowledge workers as a whole are too ideologically diverse to justify lumping them together into a single class. Philosophy professors and journalists of the underground press may loathe capitalism, but no evidence suggests that a much larger number of kindergarten teachers, copy editors, Xerox technicians, and the like— knowledge workers all—are equally antagonistic or antagonistic at all toward capitalism. Finding no empirical data to suggest that knowledge workers comprise either a "class-in-themselves" or a "class-for-themselves," skeptics of the hypothesis tend to dismiss the phenomenon as the embellishment of political rhetoric.

At present the debate about the New Class is at something of an impasse. Some continue to argue that it is a class; others insist it isn't. Some say it is socially and politically significant; others say it is neither. Intensifying the debate is the fact that opposing positions carry different political implications. Conservatives who seek an analytical device for scapegoating the range of contemporary social problems tend to embrace the idea; progressives, not anxious to see their own political agenda tied to collective interests, tend to reject it. As analytic assertions fly back and forth, so too do political accusations.

But this impasse is by no means the end of the story. Indeed, the impasse itself suggests that the entire issue may be conceptualized incorrectly, in which case the reality of the New Class phenomenon on the American scene could be far more complicated than anyone has yet allowed. This is our position precisely. We would propose that the evidence from the American context suggests that the New Class is not so much a distinct class opposed to capitalism, but a sector of the economy that is part and parcel of the evolution of American capitalism. In this sense, the growth of the so-called New Class represents not the undermining of capitalism, but its expansion and transformation. Thus, what has been seen as class competition between one class that defends the interests of capitalism and another that assaults it may in fact be a dispute between two different kinds of capitalists, each of whom operates with different conceptions of what capitalism should be.

The Evolution of Capitalism

The history of capitalism has always been the story of its expansion and transformation rather than its decline. There is no good reason we should assume it to be different now.

If the constants of capitalism are the legitimacy of private property and a spirit of acquisition and competition, it is also marked by two other fundamental traits: one, reliance upon ever-improving technologies of production, and two, the institutionalization of rational forms of economic organization. In the last centuries both the technology upon which capitalism has depended and its institutional form of organization have evolved dramatically. In the period of early capitalism (from roughly the thirteenth to the mid-eighteenth century), capitalist enterprise depended primarily upon handicraft production and was organized through the home and local guilds. A system of finance and trade was also developing at the international level at this time, but until the rise of the modern nation-state mercantilism was by no means a fully rationalized method of exchange. In the period of "full capitalism" (from about the middle of the eighteenth century to the end of the First World War), profit-making activity depended upon the production of goods by machines, machine technology depended in turn upon an increasingly rationalized factory system, and family-owned business establishments were gradually replaced by more impersonal but more rationally efficient corporate structures. In late or postindustrial capitalism, a period running roughly from mid-century to the present, capitalism continues to be organized within a bureaucratic setting, but the mode of production has shifted to dependence upon what Daniel Bell has called "intellectual technology." This is an economic system whose chief problem is the organization and application of science and whose paradigmatic (but by no means exclusive) institution is the university or research institute. The heart of this stage of capitalist development is no longer the industrial production of material goods, but the development and the distribution of the new ideas, information, and knowledge.

To characterize this latter stage, as Ralf Dahrendorf has, as "post-capitalist," is to miss the point. Dahrendorf called this period postcapitalist because of the changing nature of political and social authority he observed within it. But while capitalism has undeniable political preconditions and consequences, its organizing principles are economic, not political. All the features of free market activity continue to be present. The only real difference between earlier and later expressions of capitalism is in the resources being produced, distributed, and exchanged. In this later context, knowledge and information become the principal form of property; technological expertise and cultural credentials become the primary forms of capital. It is in this that the so-called New Class has its institutional basis and relationship to the market. On the face of it, then, there is a good reason to conceptualize knowledge workers as actors *within* capitalism, not apart from it.

But there is more to recommend our viewing the knowledge sector (or at least significant parts of it) as part and parcel of the evolution and transformation of capitalism rather than an instrument of its demise. Making this case is the principal theme of this chapter.

As with any phase of economic development, the present epoch is marked not by stasis but by the continued expansion and modification. Our empirical focus is a new niche of profit-making activity that has emerged within the context of postindustrial capitalism. This new niche represents the expansion of profit-making activity from information markets geared toward utilitarian ends to the realm of "moral markets." At the vanguard of this development are knowledge workers who combine the skills and the activities of the classical industrial entrepreneur (who produces and distributes new material goods) as well as the more recent entrepreneur (who markets new symbols, meanings, interpretations, and images). These are moral entrepreneurs, who derive their livelihood from the production and distribution of new ways of thinking and acting morally. This empirical concern may seem relatively narrow in light of the claims we put forward about the knowledge sector as a whole, but the existence and activity of moral entrepreneurs as a group within that sector have far-reaching implications for establishing our argument.

Morality as Market: Economic and Cultural Considerations

We use the term "moral entrepreneur" not simply as a rhetorical device—a metaphor to describe political or moral ideologues who make money by trading on sympathy or guilt. We use it to identify a new kind of economic actor whose trade constitutes a new sector of the postindustrial economy. But in what way is any of this genuinely new? One need not be a social historian to recognize that there have long been people who have derived their livelihood from moral enterprising. Leaders in the international temperance movement in the first half of the nineteenth century, for example, managed an adequate living from their efforts to persuade people of the evils of alcohol. Protestant revivalists, from Jonathan Edwards to Charles Finney, Billy

Sunday to Jimmy Swaggart, have carved out an acceptable middle-class living (or better) from riding the gospel circuit. Reformers in the Sunday school and later common school movements, domestic science, abolitionist, and women's suffrage movements were also compensated for their social reform efforts. These historical cases, however, only point up the novelty of moral reform on the present scene.

In the past, moral advocacy tended to support the institutions and ethos of bourgeois society, never questioning (though often calling into visibility) its Protestant, theistic foundations. These efforts sought to foster moral asceticism by encouraging thrift, hard work, and moderation or abstinence in drink; to promote church attendance and develop biblical literacy; and to protect the traditional family structure by honoring the authority of the father and husband, elevating the role of mother and wife, preserving children and families from the hardships of forced labor, and enshrining the home as a haven. By contrast, moral enterprising on the present scene reflects the dissolution of bourgeois society—often endorsing its demise, sometimes struggling valiantly to preserve it from change.

The historical and institutional momentum, however, favors the former. Some activists and organizations given to progressive moral change, such as the American Humanist Association and the Council for Secular and Democratic Humanism, are openly hostile to traditional theism of whatever brand—Protestant, Catholic, or Jewish. Many others oppose the interests and institutions of theism only indirectly, by denying traditional religion as a basis for political order and social change. The American Civil Liberties Union and the People for the American Way would be counted among the more prominent of these. Several of the newer moral enterprises work to erode the ethos of bourgeois society by either repudiating or altering traditional forms of ascetic practice. Gone are the prohibitions that would inhibit how, when, or where one spends one's leisure time or sexual energy. Prohibitions do remain over tobacco, alcohol, and drug use—in some cases they have even intensified—but what drives these enterprises are secular moral considerations of health and longevity rather than the pietistic requirement of worldly mortification. Still other moral enterprises work toward legitimating alternatives to the bourgeois family structure. Women's rights organizations (such as the National

Organization for Women), reproductive rights organizations (such as Planned Parenthood and the National Abortion Rights Action League), and gay rights organizations are the most conspicuous enterprises laboring toward this end.

As important as these qualitative differences is a quantitative shift in the amount of moral enterprising taking place in America in recent decades. Moral entrepreneurship may have existed in the past, but only in the last half of the twentieth century can one speak of it as a measurable sector of the information economy. This is perhaps best seen in the remarkable growth of voluntary associations committed to social change. Take the number of church-based, ideologically identified public affairs organizations as an illustration. In the mid-nineteenth century there were no more than a few dozen in existence. At the end of World War II their number had grown to around 400 and at present there are over 900. That is, more of these groups have been founded in the last four decades than had been founded in the entire previous century. The figures are even more dramatic outside the religious realm. Of the hundreds of secular organizations currently involved in public affairs in America, 80 percent were founded after 1960. In actual numbers, over 1,500 ideologically identified public affairs associations were established in this period.[37]

The texture of this change can be appreciated a little better by considering the organizational growth within different sectors of the moral marketplace. In 1989 there were twenty-three reproductive rights organizations compared to eight in 1972; seventy-five animal rights organizations compared to eighteen in 1972; eleven antismoking organizations compared to three in 1972; sixty-seven gay rights organizations in 1989 compared to six in 1972; fifty-eight women's rights organizations compared to ten in 1965; sixty-one disarmament organizations compared to eighteen in 1970; and three right-to-die organizations, up from two in 1972. As new as many of these enterprises are, they are by no means shoestring operations. One-fourth of the animal rights organizations, for example, have annual budgets of over one million dollars and a staff of over thirty people. One of them has an annual budget of 16 million dollars. Likewise, one-fourth of all gay rights organizations have annual budgets of over $100,000. Half of these had annual budgets over the one million dollar mark, and one had a budget of 90 million dollars. So too, nearly two-thirds (62 percent) of all abortion rights groups reported annual budgets of over one million dollars in 1989. The largest of these reported a budget of 299 million dollars. One-third of these groups reported having staff of over thirty people. Much the same story can be told of other sectors of the moral marketplace.

A third difference between past and present forms of moral entrepreneurship concerns the role of the state. In the past, knowledge production, and specifically moral entrepreneurship, typically operated independently of government approval or subsidy. By contrast, the major part of the knowledge industry at present is only possible with government assistance. It is the state, after all, that has paid for the phenomenal expansion of higher education and for public- and private-sector research and development. So too the creation of moral markets has only been possible with government patronage. Insofar as these moral enterprises are defined as philanthropic organizations, they are organized under a different tax code (typically 501 c3) and thus receive financial subsidizing from the government. In addition, they very often work with, pressure, and receive the endorsement of such government agencies as the U.S. Surgeon General's Office, the Environmental Protection Agency, the Food and Drug Administration, and the like. It is the active partnership of the state in these enterprises that guarantees not only the stability and growth of the moral marketplace but the expansion of its power as well.

The establishment of new moral markets within the postindustrial market economy provides both the context and the opportunities for new forms of profit making. But what is the nature of that activity? In almost every way it follows the model of classical capitalist entrepreneurship.

Moral Entrepreneurs: A Profile of Background and Commitment

Deborah Slicer, a 35-year-old philosophy professor at the University of Montana, founded the animal rights group, Students for Animals, while completing her doctorate at the University of Virginia. Asked whether most such groups are university-based, she said that there is within the animal rights movement "a really diverse range in terms of education, in terms of background. At one end of the spectrum, we have a former career Air Force pilot. On the other end of the spectrum, we have folks like me, and then a lot of people who are housewives. So on education and work background, there's diversity, but we do tend to be middle class, and white."[38]

What Slicer says of the demographic composition of the animal rights movement is largely true of each of the moral enterprises we observed. Most of the leading activists fit this profile such as it is: white, middle class, and typically well educated. Animal rights activist Henry Spira, for example, is a self-educated Manhattan high school teacher and former merchant marine with a background in union reform, civil rights, and Vietnam war protest. Alice Mehling, for the last fifteen years the executive director of the New York based, proeuthanasia Society for the Right to Die, is a wife and a mother in her mid-sixties, a former reference librarian and one time journalist at *Time* and *Vogue*. Before coming to America and co-founding the Washington-based People for the Ethical Treatment of Animals (PETA), Ingrid Newkirk was educated in England and India, the daughter of a well-to-do British family. Berkeley, California activist Mark Pertchuk, at thirty-three the executive director of the nation's largest antismoking organization, Americans for Non-Smoker's Rights, is a former public interest lawyer and lobbyist. University of Pennsylvania professor Gary Francione made a name for himself as a successful lawyer before becoming involved in animal welfare, for which he is a frequent litigator. Much rarer are people like Norma McCorvey, who was a high school dropout when, pregnant for the second time at twenty-two, she agreed to be "Jane Roe" in the celebrated Supreme Court case that legalized abortion on demand. With the politicization of the abortion issue in subsequent years, McCorvey has gone public, appearing on the college lecture circuit, on talk shows, at rallies, and on the front pages of Washington and New York newspapers. But McCorvey would seem to be an exception to the rule, an exception created by opportunity rather than social predisposition. The typical case tends to be found among the highly educated, urban and suburban middle class.

As there tend to be similarities in background, there is a corresponding commitment to middle-class idealism, very much comparable to the idealism that impassions the more traditional kind of entrepreneur. Whether pursued as an avocation or a full-time job, moral enterprising is marked by commitment to an ideal and a passion to realize it. Ingrid Newkirk, for example, expressed this well in describing her "life's work" with PETA:

> There's always been a sense of personal urgency, as if animals are speaking to me, and I know I've talked to social workers in other areas who have exactly the same feeling, that the children or the elderly are speaking to them, or whatever. I know that I always had something inside of me that bonded me to nonhuman beings, even ones that I might be afraid of, or find particularly unattractive. I have something inside me that makes me feel very sick, worried, and responsible about the abuse of nonhuman beings. This is my life's work, this is why I exist, and there is not a thought that it could ever be different.[39]

For "Ramona," an active member of the Animal Liberation Front, a vigilante group committed to freeing animals from research labs, the sense of mission was just as clear and intense. "I think I was born to do this," she said. "I really do. I can't imagine a more satisfying extracurricular activity [than being on a raid]."[40] The late Washington, D.C. activist Mitch Snyder's commitment to the homeless left his wife and children alone and on welfare. "I just was not and am not capable of being a traditional father and husband," he explained. "Who I am does not allow me to do things that other people do. I can't distinguish between my kids and other peoples'. I understand the biological relationship, but I feel as deep a sense of responsibility for kids I've never known as I do for them. I don't have the time and energy to give much one-on-one, and so I'm very hard on the people around me. I give to the people in the shelter, I give to the people in the streets, I give to people who are suffering, but that has little to do with people who are around me."[41]

For others, their "calling" and their idealism is more diffuse. Which issue they champion has less to so with moral constitution than it does with opportunity—the right job becoming available to them at the right time. For example, Alice Mehling said of her position as executive director of the Society for the Right to Die: "I didn't exactly seek this out as a particular thing but it fascinated me. It was one of those accidental things where it coincided: me looking for something I wanted to do. Them looking for someone to do it."[42] Similarly, Mark Pertchuk claimed that his commitment to nonsmokers' rights derives partly from intrinsic zeal but largely from professional "fit":

> I knew for a long time—probably ten or twelve years—that I wanted to be a public interest lobbyist and it was for that reason that I went to law school. While I was in

school, I worked with Ralph Nader as an associate in his lobbying organization. So, what specifically got me into this organization was not that I was involved in this issue, or the issue of tobacco or nonsmokers' rights particularly, but that this is what was available to me at that stage of my career. It was available. I wanted to do this kind of advocacy and it fit directly. I consider myself to be a public interest professional. Volunteers who do this on the side tend to be motivated purely by passion. For me this is something about which I am passionate—in that I feel that what I'm doing is the right thing to be done for society—but it's also something which I enjoy doing professionally as a professional public interest advocate.[43]

The Element of Risk

The entrepreneurial venture requires impassioned commitment to an idea or an ideal in large part because of the great risk involved for those who give their lives to it. This is as true for the moral entrepreneur as it is for the traditional entrepreneur. There is always a sacrifice of time and money, and perhaps even more importantly, the risk of a ruined reputation and damaged respectability. Animal rights advocate Deborah Slicer expressed the sense of personal risk of reputation that comes with "talking to the press ... and then appearing foolish"; or of talking to people and having them "disagree very vociferously or even violently with you." The important thing, she emphasized, is to "just to do it anyway." The point is well taken, according to Ingrid Newkirk. Such risks, she maintained, can really be reviewed as occasions for pressing home her perspective on animal rights. "I sincerely believe in the end that by taking these risks you are going to catch the majority of the people—catch their imagination, morality, and conscience—and eventually, when the message is repeated enough times, when the facts are repeated enough times, there will be a change in society. But I'll admit, it's a long painful road to get there."

The hope in the end, of course, is that risk-taking will eventually generate growing social acceptance of the position being advocated. A striking example of this kind of "pay-off" can be seen in the euthanasia movement. For example, an observer who heard the first president of the Society for the Right to Die speak in support of euthanasia in 1939 recalled that "those Saturday night Jordan Hall meetings were wild. Every kook in Boston went. Tomatoes were not actually thrown at the clergyman, but he was bombarded verbally." The first patients' rights bill presented by the society to the legislature in 1947 was characterized by opponents as "anti-God, un-American, and a menace." No legislative sponsor was found. As recently as August 1976, *The New England Journal of Medicine* observed that euthanasia was only then "coming out of the closet." Today thirty-eight states have enacted Living Will Laws, which protect the rights of patients or their families to forego or end life-sustaining treatment in cases of terminal illness. A brochure put out by the Society for the Right to Die states that "in the five decades since its founding, the society ... has evolved from what was viewed by many as a small group of extremists with dangerous ideas into a mainstream movements responding to humankind's most deeply felt hopes and fears about illness and death."[44]

Another illustration of risks taken and opportunities found can be seen in the antismoking movement. Mark Pertchuk observed that when

> People first started up standing up for their rights as nonsmokers maybe twenty years ago, they were really considered jerks. For example, if someone said at a cocktail party in 1975, "you know, your tobacco smoke is really making me sick, would you mind not smoking or would you mind smoking outside"—it would have been considered bad etiquette. Or if someone said during the middle of the dinner, "Would you please not smoke, I can't really eat my salad," it would have been considered very nerdy. Besides, individual protests did not really have much of an impact. But then we and other groups began successfully promoting local [anti] smoking ordinances—and now there are hundreds of them. Now it's as though the smoker is nerd.

In some cases, however, the risk assumed by moral activists goes far beyond the loss of respectability. Members of the underground, quasi-terrorist Animal Liberation Front, for example, have risked heavy prison sentences for bombing animal research facilities, destroying equipment, and stealing laboratory animals. "M," a member of this group, reflected on his participation in a recent laboratory raid this way:

> It's weird. Before I was involved with this, life was really pretty comfortable. I mean, I'm taking risks now that do not need to be taken. I have a wife, some kids, some cars. I've worked hard to get where I am. I'm a business man, for chrissakes. What do I have to gain from this? It's not like I am robbing a bank and spending the money. Up to this point, I've had a pretty enjoyable life, and compared to those animals, it's been a pretty damn nice life. I may be caught, I may have to spend a lot of time in jail. But it would balance out in the end. It would be okay. Looking at the costs and the benefits, it's worth it."[45]

From the prospective of the ALF's organizational strategy, it has also been worth it. Thanks to the publicity generated by their break-ins at the Universities of Pennsylvania and California, NIH funds to projects in those laboratories were suspended, and regulations for animal experimentation conducted elsewhere have become increasingly strict.

A similar story can be told within the reproductive rights campaign. Long-standing activist Bill Baird was convicted and jailed in 1965 for exhibiting contraceptives in prohibition of New Jersey law, and again in 1967 for presenting a lecture about birth control at the Boston University campus, where he gave a can of contraceptive foam to an unmarried nineteen-year-old woman in the audience. (At that time only doctors could legally dispense birth control devices or information, and then only to married couples.) Of the thirty-six days he spent in Boston's Charles Street jail, Baird said: "It was as if they had hung me from my thumbs. The cell was cold. The mattress was thin. There were mice in the cell, and rats. I picked bugs out of the food. I went from 175 lbs to 146." But the Supreme Court's 1972 decision in *Baird v. Eisenstadt* overturned both convictions, along with restrictive birth control laws in twenty-six states. The case was cited six times in the majority opinion for *Roe v. Wade*.[46]

The moral would seem to be that with patience, sacrifice will be rewarded; with perseverance, risk will be vindicated. Yet as with traditional form of entrepreneurship, perseverance is never enough by itself.

The Marketing of a Moral Product

The success or failure of traditional entrepreneurial ventures almost always hinges upon an effective sales pitch. This is no less true for the moral entrepreneur. "There are times," conceded Ingrid Newkirk,

when people are like poor animals in the circus; you have to bash the cymbals to pay attention. You have to introduce gimmicks. It should be enough to be able to convince people with the facts. It's sad, but the facts aren't enough, so you find yourself yourself trying to think creatively about how to get attention to your message. Unlike the industries that oppose us, we don't have millions of dollars at our disposal to take out ads in the papers, so we have to make sure we're thinking about ways to get free advertising for the idea. And that can be very simple things, but newspapers won't come out to cover you simply telling the truth every day, without having something "photographable," something extraordinary, so we routinely brainstorm about ideas, and it can be any thing from having a man climb up a flagpole outside of a fur store and perch up there, to having a "cruel cosmetics" dump in an oversized wastebasket outside the capitol, to erecting scaffolding and building a sculpture about animals, to engaging in acts of civil disobedience.

Such "gimmicks" abound in virtually all moral enterprises. To dramatize the demands of the Community for Creative Non-Violence on behalf of the homeless, activist Mitch Snyder and other members of the group have let cockroaches loose in the White House, lived for weeks in cardboard boxes on Mayor Marion Barry's front steps, created a national monument to the homeless—a sculpture of a family sleeping on a steam grate—and marched down Pennsylvania Avenue behind a horse drawn cortege bearing the body of a homeless person who had recently frozen to death.

Often the most effective way for an organization to sway public opinion in it's favor is to enlist the help of celebrities and other elites who have already been converted to the cause. The Society for the Right to Die, for example, routinely lists in its publications the names of prominent supporters who have, over the years, included Dr. Harry Emerson Fosdick, Dr. William Sloane Coffin, W. Somerset Maugham, Sherwood Anderson, Margret Sanger, Robert Frost, Abigail Van Buren (Dear Abby), and Gloria Steinem. Mark Pertchuk says that organization's drive to prohibit smoking in public spaces gained impetus when "celebrities like Bruce Springsteen began to say, 'You know, I really don't like tobacco smoke around me,' or when Larry Hagman carried around a fan to blow smoke away from himself." The 1986 spokesman for the American Lung Association's antismoking campaign was Patrick Reynolds, grandson of R.J. Reynolds of the eponymous tobacco company, the second largest in the United States. (Reynolds insisted that his antismoking views are rooted in "personal concerns," but admitted that the publicity hasn't hurt his nascent acting career.)[47] Various abortion rights groups who participated in the 9 April 1989 March on Washington each claimed the support of an ad-hoc "Hollywood Women's Political Committee" who sent as its representatives Anne Archer, Morgan Fairchild, Veronica Hamel, Polly Bergen, Cybill Shepherd (the 1990 spokeswoman for Voters for Choice), Susan Sarandon, and Marlo Thomas. Honorary "Hollywood men" who participated in the March included Leonard Nimoy and Phil Donahue. Lynn Cutler, Democratic National Committee vice-chairman, admitted that her group would "give anything to have the kind of impact [the pro-choice celebrities] have. If they are willing to help the foot-soldiers, that's great. The Republicans have boring celebrities. I mean who do they have—Greg Louganis?"[48]

Another publicity generating tactic is the staging of David-and-Goliath scenarios in which an individual or small group publicly takes on a well-known and well-funded institution as an adversary. When high-school science teacher Henry Spira's investigation of sex experiments on cats at the American Museum of Natural History generated such headlines in New York tabloids as "Congress pays for Sex sadism at Museum," the resulting public outcry caused 121 congressmen to ask the NIH for an explanation, and subsequently to demand that it's guidelines for animal care be revised. Newkirk's People for the Ethical Treatment of Animals has mounted protests against animal testing of cosmetics, winning concessions from cosmetics giants like Avon, Revlon, Faberg, Mary Kay, Benetton, Noxell, and Amway. Newkirk, the editors of Fortune magazine said by way of praising her tactics, "has imposed PETA's ethics on companies … the same way trains impose themselves on stalled sedans."[49] In a case that received international publicity, gay rights advocate Andrew Exler sued Disneyland for violating his civil rights by prohibiting dancing by same-sex couples, and Disneyland quietly dropped its twenty-year ban. "When you take on somebody like Disneyland," Exler said, "when the little guy takes on a powerful corporation and wins—I think that's fantastic."[50]

While these groups have sought to mobilize public opinion to the end of changing laws, others have favored the alternative strategy of using the law to manipulate public opinion. John Banzhaf, founder and director of the Washington-based Action on Smoking and Health, described his group's strategy as:

> A general philosophy of what we call legal activism, which is a generic term for using the law as a means of changing social policy. We pretty much start out with the axioms in legal activism that we are outgunned and outclassed. That we are almost always facing a bigger, stronger opponent with more money, more clout, and more words. Therefore, one of the key axioms is that we want to go into proceedings where we have what we call the maximum amount of legal leverage. Where we have to put in the least to get the most out. So we tend to avoid those

issues where the other side is going to have the advantage by way of its size, or its clout, or its political connections. What we like to do, therefore, is to pick very carefully areas where they [tobacco interests] cannot use their muscle, more precisely where the outcome doesn't depend solely on muscle. Where we have the law, some kind of particular advantage.[51]

Like Banzhaf, Mark Pertchuk attributes the success of his antismoking organization to its strategy of capitalizing on perceived advantages:

Our goal is to see the tobacco industry go out of business. I think what may distinguish our success is that we've been able to capitalize skillfully on events as they occur. We're extremely responsive. We are constantly taking advantage of circumstances as they occur. For example, if the tobacco industry does something really repulsive, which they happen to do fairly frequently, we will immediately drop what we are doing and respond to events as they occur, take advantage and exploit them for the purpose of changing public policy in a progressive way. The example I'm most proud of is the success we had in getting Federal legislation banning smoking on short airline flights. It was really a political miracle and if you look at that success and perhaps contrast it with the legislative campaign of Handgun Control Inc. Vs. The National Rifle Association it may shed some light. I feel we skillfully managed a strategy of taking advantage of circumstances as they came about.

More often than not a variety of strategies is adopted. In anticipation and then immediately in the wake of the Supreme Court's Webster decision in the spring of 1989, for instance, abortion rights leaders advocated a combination of tactics. As examples of "creative organization" that doesn't "wait for money or convenience" pro-choice activist Rachel Burd suggested bringing supportive elites ("politicians, labor leaders, clergy") into the movement; "turning the tables" on pro-life by adopting their tactics of picketing, leafleting, and generally "raising hell"; encouraging "spontaneous and planned guerrilla responses" to opposition groups, and creating "audacious public policy" by pressuring lawmakers to submit "amendments, laws, and new funding regulations that favor abortion."[52]

Because what is at issue are deeply held beliefs about right and wrong, it is not surprising to witness extremism at this level as well. While most groups prefer to create a marketing strategy well within the law, the Animal Liberation Front is unique in pursuing one that openly flouts it. In a single year the group has claimed responsibility for $3.5 million in damages to a farm animal diagnostic laboratory under construction at the University of California-Davis, bomb threats and attempted break-ins at the Yerkes regional primate center in

Atlanta that necessitated the installation of $200,000 in new security equipment, and the destruction of $600,000 in research equipment at the University of California, Riverside. Dr. Thomas Hamm, head of Stanford's research animal facility, said that his life has repeatedly been threatened by the group. A New York scientist studying Parkinson's disease in monkeys found an ax smashed through his door. However extreme such actions are, they do draw attention to the debate, punctuate the seriousness of the claims being made, and can even sway the larger public to sympathy, if not support.

The point is that programs for moral and social change have become commodities, and that the activists themselves implicitly recognize this in the way they promote their agenda. The recent *Social Marketing: Strategies for Changing Public Behavior* (1989) makes this recognition explicit, encouraging activists to be systematic in applying moral marketing techniques to "map the social marketing environment," "analyze the behavior of target adopters and the diffusion of social products," carefully "design the social product," assess the "distribution channels," and finally "develop a social marketing plan."[53] According to the authors, only by being this overt and methodical about what they are doing—marketing a commodity—will social activists be effective in their efforts.

The Spirit of Capitalism

Perhaps the most convincing evidence that this sector of the knowledge industry has aligned itself with rather than against capitalism is in their use of the language of free enterprise to talk about their own activity. When describing their objectives, strategies, and motivations, for example, moral entrepreneurs frequently employed such expressions as "taking on a rival industry and winning," "weighing costs and benefits," and having "to put the least in to get the most out." These locutions do more than suggest that moral entrepreneurship proceeds according to an economic model, although the suggestion is certainly there. As significant from our perspective is the hint they give of the monetary interests at stake in moral entrepreneurship.

Though many of the groups we investigated operate with budgets totaling well into the millions, the competition for these dollars is often stiff. This is well illustrated in the animal rights enterprise. Deborah Slicer, of the grass-roots, self-funded organization Students for Animals, complained that the rifts in the animal rights movement as a whole are not strategic but financial.

> A lot of these organizations are becoming really wealthy. PETA [Newkirk's People for the Ethical Treatment of Animals] is a multimillion dollar fund now. They do things like run full-page ads in Harper's, or in the Washington Post. They sponsor concerts, they do a lot of mailing to members, lobbying, and they're also paying their employees pretty well. Before they did that, they had working for them a lot of young and transient people, who would work really hard for a while and then burn out and move on. And now they have people working for them who can actually live in [Washington] D.C. on the salary they are making, and live fairly comfortably, and do this for an extended period of time, and do it well. But in terms of funding grass-roots organizations like ours, PETA has just been really stingy.

In response, the executive director of PETA invoked the rhetoric of the marketplace to defend her organization's wealth:

> Well, we were once a small group, and I well understand that if you don't have money, if you haven't been able to generate it yourself, that you could be a bit jealous of other groups who have. I think it's a mistake, but I do understand how people think that way, for there to be a blanket condemnation of groups who acquire money to fuel their own work, not acting simply as fundraising arms for the now hundreds and hundreds of small groups across the country.

"We do provide support to the Charlottesville group," Newkirk protested, but then qualified that statement with a flattering comparison to her own organization:

> It's sort of like, if a movie star sends you a hundred dollars, there's a tendency to think, "Well, they have, you know, X millions of dollars; how could they do this?" What is not realized is, a lot of people who fall into that category are also giving money to an incredibly large number of charities, and probably every charity is saying, "How disgusting. They only gave us a hundred dollars." So we have helped to support the Charlottesville group, and many other groups across the country. However, what we do primarily, with the money we raise—we work our money. We're like a small group gone big.

Newkirk concluded by defending the values of industriousness, thrift, and perseverance:

> When people ask me how you make money, my advice is very simple. You do things, and money comes to you. You prove yourself. If you have to give your time, you do it. This organization had no outside money for a long time, and

certainly not enough to pay salaries for a couple of years, and everything at the start, we paid for by ourselves. We were working out of a very cold and damp basement flat in Tacoma Park; that's where we acquired volunteers. They complained bitterly, and we'd bring portable heaters to work in the winter. And we worked every waking moment—this was our passion. We had full-time jobs, we worked evenings and weekends, we cut corners—but we're not special in any way.

Moneymaking initiatives have emerged as by-products of other moral entrepreneurial activities as well. The most visible example in Anita Roddick's worldwide enterprise of "Body Shops," which market cosmetics to socially and environmentally conscious consumers. To produce the all-natural, "cruelty-free" (that is, not tested on animals) products she sells in biodegradable containers in 300 shops around the world, Roddick builds factories in high-unemployment areas, buys her ingredients from Third World agricultural communities, and always pays First World wages to their workers. The paper bags she uses in her stores are not only recyclable but made from banana plants, generating a cash crop for impoverished Nepalese farmers. The foot massage rollers she sells are made at training schools for homeless children in south India, which the Body Shop funds. Proprietors of her United States shops must pledge to devote two hours a week to community service in order to secure the franchise. "We educate, educate, all the time," Roddick says.

There's training in the shops, a training school in London, and one in New York. Not for sales. We have courses on body care, but also on topics like drugs and in urban survival. For courses on aging we bring anthropologists and elderly women. We have AIDS sufferers come in to talk. We have a video company and send out a video once a month for all staff, including franchise staff, to show the community projects we're involved in. It's understood when you come in as a franchise that you should be involved in community projects—a battered women's shelter, an AIDS program, whatever—and that your staff should participate during working hours. If a franchisee didn't, she wouldn't get anymore franchises—which would be death to her, since owning a Body Shop is a license to print money.[54]

Together, Roddick and her franchise "print money" at the rate of over $120 million in sales every year.

The ascendancy of the antismoking movement has also spurred the success of several businesses that market stop-smoking strategies for profit. Smokeenders, for example, charges its clients $295 for a six week program of supervised cutting down and "behavior-modification." For $595 the Schick Centers offer would-be nonsmokers a two-week crash course in quitting, consisting of mild electrical shock treatment and group support. A Solomon Brothers survey reported that $100 million was spent on stop-smoking programs in 1987, and predicted that amount would grow to $250 million by 1991.[55] The antismoking crusade has also generated profits for Lyndon W. Sanders, president of Kandue International, which owns and operates the Non-Smokers Inn in Dallas, Texas. Sanders, who has no trouble keeping the Inn's 135 rooms filled, has hosted such staunch tobacco haters as Surgeon General C. Everett Koop and the star of *Dallas*, Larry Hagman. Moreover, pressured by threats of litigation, corporations have found it economically advantageous to hang "No Smoking" signs in the workplace. John Finney of the Institute for the Study of Smoking Behavior and Policy at Harvard's Kennedy School pointed out that the Surgeon General's report establishing the dangers of sidestream smoke "added enormous impact" to the nonsmokers' rights movement "because it established the rationale for corporate liability. Tobacco is a dangerous substance, and an employer who doesn't do anything about it is likely to be sued."[56] An added incentive for corporations to prohibit smoking is increased worker productivity. Management consultants have suggested that companies can save $300 to $1000 annually per smoker by insisting they quit. A 1985 article in *Health Care Strategic Management* entitled "Increasing Productivity through On-Site Smoking Control," claims that "approximately 92 non-smokers can accomplish the same work as 100 smokers."

Remarking on this report, the Marxist newspaper *Workers Vanguard* observed with chagrin "There are powerful interests at work here. Behind Big Brother is Big Business, rubbing its hands in anticipation of a profitable speedup—particularly for the nation's 33 million office workers—encouraged by the U.S. Surgeon General, the Meese Police, and yuppie power prudes. The bosses' concern is not for our health but for their balance sheets. Profit, not health, is the bottom line of the antismoking crusade."[57]

Profit may also be the bottom line for the health care industry as hospitals create guidelines on withholding or granting medical care to the terminally ill. Dr. Russell E. Butler, the attending physician to Paul Brophy, whose family went to court to have his feeding tube removed, insisted that:

The last thing anybody wants is for the Brophy decision to become a model for economic decision making. That's why a lot of people testified against it. They feared the economic and social domino effect. If you put "persistent vegetative state" on a diagnosis, there's going to be a DRG that says 22.1 days and there'll be no economic reimbursement after that because of the diagnosis. That's abominable. To have insurance and economic interests come in and say, "You will limit care because of the diagnostic code," is going to be the opposite of what anyone intended.[58]

Yet there are signs that hefty lawsuits and unfavorable reimbursement policies may in fact be pressuring hospitals to cede to the views of euthanasia supporters more readily than they otherwise might. At a panel discussion of the Seventh Biennial Conference of the World Federation of Right to Die Societies entitled "Making Law in the United States," Julienne Delio testified that Blue Cross/Blue Shield would no longer pay for her husband's hospitalization because, while terminally ill, he was no longer considered in need of acute care. "I owe the hospital over $157,000 so far," Delio said, "and they have made it clear that they would hold me directly responsible for it and would press me for payment. I told them I would not pay them for care that neither Danny nor I consented to."[59] Recently, some families have successfully brought charges of battery (unconsented-to-touching) against hospitals that refused to honor their requests to terminate treatment for a family member. In *Strachen v. JFK Memorial Hospital*, $140,000 was awarded to the parents of a 20-year-old man for emotional distress caused by a hospital's failure to remove their son from a respirator after he had shot himself in the head. In a related case, *Franson v. Raditch*, an Oregon right-to-life group agreed to pay $217,000 in an out-of-court settlement to the parents of a baby born with birth defects, in reparation for having obtained a mandatory court order requiring life-sustaining treatment in opposition to the parents' wishes.

Economic actions have not been overlooked by strategists within the abortion rights movement. In a special issue entitled "Abortion without Apology," timed to coincide with the Supreme Court's *Webster* decision in the spring of 1989, the *Village Voice* advocated in a headline that abortion rights supporters should "Begin the Campaign for RU486." "Drug company executives," the paper editorialized, "should be forced to trot out their free-enterprise rhetoric and proclaim their right to produce a safe, effective oral abortifacient. Perhaps they could form a consortium: antiabortionists can't boycott *all* the aspirin makers."[60]

The Fruits of Entrepreneurial Labor

From our perspective, the rewards of moral entrepreneurship would seem rather meager, the most visible compensation being years of public unpopularity if not ridicule. A closer look, however, reveals that moral entrepreneurship yields many of the same rewards as traditional entrepreneurship.

Fortune is certainly one of these rewards: rarely fabulous wealth, but often enough a comfortable, middle- to upper middle-class, professional salary. Documenting this is not easy since most of these entrepreneurs are reluctant to disclose the particulars of their salary. Even so, the evidence can be inferred from the location of the overwhelming majority of these enterprises in the high-priced cities of Washington and New York, (and also Boston, Chicago, San Francisco, and Los Angeles). Most indications suggest that the captains of these moral industries do quite well financially, and that some may even be getting rich. Take reproductive rights advocate and media maven Bill Baird. Though he grew up poor in New York City and started out by driving a van through poor neighborhoods distributing birth control information door-to-door, he eventually came to operate several abortion clinics bearing his name and to draw a salary he refused to divulge. "When the Pope tells you his salary," he demurred, "I'll tell you mine."[61] Undoubtedly there are other moral entrepreneurs like him. Faye Wattleton draws a six-figure salary from her position as president of Planned Parenthood. Anita Roddick's Body Shops have given her a net worth of $200 million, making her the third wealthiest woman in Britain. Mitch Snyder demanded—and got—$150,000 from the producers of a television movie made about his life. The money, he said, went to helping the homeless.

Fame is another one of the rewards. The move from obscurity to public attention is built into the kind of work that moral entrepreneurs do: because of their willingness to take a public stand on behalf of their cause, they invariably find themselves thrust into the spotlight of the local, regional, and national media. *Fortune* magazine recently named Ingrid Newkirk one of the "Twenty-five most Fascinating

Business People of the Year." The movie deal Mitch Snyder made was prompted by previous celebrity involvement and an appearance on CBS's *60 Minutes* during which Mike Wallace compared him to Martin Luther King. Planned Parenthood's Faye Wattleton is featured as frequently in beauty and fashion magazines as in the literature of the abortion debate. Fame also comes by the virtue of rubbing shoulders with celebrity advocates. Anita Roddick says that her favorite Body Shop clients are Britain's Royal Family: "They are incredibly supportive. They tend to go in and buy little gift packets for their evening guests—in particular the Princess of Wales, because the shop is right near Kensington Palace. Prince Charles understands our philosophy more than anybody. He lives and breathes what we are doing."[62]

One can infer that fame and relative prosperity clearly figure in as important benefits of moral entrepreneurial labor. Yet when asked directly about the kinds of rewards that motivated them to continue pressing their agenda, few of the activists we spoke to mentioned either factor. Instead, virtually all responded, in one way or another, that it was the belief and hope of "having made a difference"—in the quality of a few peoples lives, in canons of moral acceptability, even in the course of social and cultural history. Fame and fortune aside, the most meaningful compensation for the moral entrepreneur would appear to be, in a word, power. Homeless activist Mitch Snyder, who first staged a hunger strike to protest overcrowding in the prison where he was serving time for car theft, said its success was "very empowering, because then you realize that you can move them [prison officials], what about the rest of things? ... You could make things change if you were willing to stick by what you believed in."[63]

The results of the moral entrepreneurs' efforts to "make things change" were articulated in a wide variety of ways.

Sometimes the change was relatively trifling. Deborah Slicer, for instance, spoke of defeating a bounty law for Virginia coyotes and, more gratifyingly, of converting a class of ethics students to vegetarianism. "These are small things, on the cosmic scale," she said. "But you have got to pat yourself on the back, even for the little things, in order to go on." At the opposite extreme were those who enjoyed a rather exaggerated sense of their own accomplishments. Bill Baird, for example: "I've researched it through the years," he said.

"There is nobody who has done as much to change the laws on contraception and abortion as I have. Nobody. I personally have saved the lives of thousands of women who would have died at the hands of quacks if the law had not changed."[64] Animal rights lawyer Gary Francione projected a similar sense of power into the future. "Rights for blacks and women were *the* constitutional issues of the 19th and 20th centuries," he claimed, yet "[a]nimal rights, once more people understand the issue, will emerge as *the* civil rights movement of the 21st century."[65] Still others, such as Ingrid Newkirk, had a more tempered sense of accomplishment. Mindful as anyone that social change often comes in tiny increments and at heavy cost, she still averred that since she had become involved in the animal rights movement, its success has surpassed even her most imprudent expectations: "Our goal when we started was to be radical, to promote fearless positions on animal rights, to challenge all the 'givens' about society's treatment of animals, and then hope that out of that, there would be a shift, that what was seen as radical in 1980 would be commonly accepted by 1990. But we never hoped really to achieve as much as we have."

Though perceptions of their own accomplishments varied, virtually all spoke of how the possibility of making a difference motivated them in their work. For antismoking activist Mark Pertchuk, the goal of a "smoke-free America" and the importance of his own role in bringing it within reach were what kept him involved in the antismoking movement:

> No one died last year from nuclear war. No one died ten years ago from nuclear war. But 35,000 Americans die each year from smoking. So when you create a smoke-free society, which is what we are doing, you are actually making a radical change in the quality of life for America. If I didn't feel I was needed in the nonsmokers' rights movement, I would not be nearly as motivated to do what I do, but I actually feel the work that I personally am doing is critical. I feel as if my contributions are important.

More candidly, Pertchuk admitted, "I like winning. I like beating the tobacco industry, which controls so many of the state legislatures in the U.S. And it gives me great satisfaction to fight the tobacco industry, even if we sometimes lose, because I think if we *don't* fight them, then they have a real capacity for evil." Ingrid Newkirk set less lofty goals, but the message was essentially the same: "If you change one person's opinion on anything we deal with, that's reason enough to continue. And I know that you don't see the results of a lot that you do, in many movements. You can give someone a new idea, and they don't say, usually, "Thanks I'll change my life." But if they don't change their lives then, when they see that idea next, it won't be the first time, so you've softened it up for them. We lay the gravel so someone else can come along and pave the road."

Alice Mehling of the Society for the Right to Die was less willing to wait around to see change happen. "It's a frustration I feel. I would like to be at a point in my life where I do things because I feel strongly about the issue, whether or not I make a difference. But I don't have that dedication. I've been frustrated in working for things I have cared about and not seeing change happen. I guess I don't have it in me any more to do that. I'd rather stay with something where I feel I can make a difference. It's not enough to care." Mehling described the differences she had made in programmatic terms—that is, the sale and distribution of publication, videotapes, and sample "living wills"—but suggested that the larger achievement these activities pointed to was the growing acceptance of euthanasia in American society.

Ambivalence, notwithstanding, the power to define the socially acceptable is power indeed.

Ideological Tensions

The legitimate ideology of traditional entrepreneurship has always been the unassailability of personal freedom: Mainly freedom from government interference, but also the freedom to risk failure and chance success. The entrepreneur is nothing if not the "free-spirit," the one who "marches to a different drummer," the one whose spirit and will is both unpredictable and unflagging. The moral entrepreneurs we investigated both follow and depart from this model. There is, on the one hand, a clear antistatist credo implicit within these circles. Yet for them, freedom from government interference is not just freedom for unhindered economic activity. It also tends to mean freedom on behalf of moral action and moral decision-making. The vast majority adheres to the libertarian dogma that the state should stay out of the private lives of private individuals. The problem is that their public and political objective, more often than not, is the creation of *more* law:

tighter regulations, increased legislation, more stringent public policy, all geared toward safeguarding or promoting an individual's enjoyment of only recently defined "moral freedoms." Between their philosophical commitment to moral freedom and their practical and political commitment to more law, there is at least a constant tension. In some cases these commitments exist in open contradiction.

Rhetoric that allies libertarian ideals with the force of law has long been the province of the reproductive rights movements. Norma McCorvey, alias Jane Roe, explained that when she told her twelve-year-old daughter of her participation in the Supreme Court decision that legalized abortion, her daughter:

> looked up the word "abortion" in the dictionary and came back and said, "But Mom, are you a baby killer?" I said "This law is so a lady who doesn't want a baby, she can go to a clinic where there's doctors and nurses and go home and lie down two or three days and go on with her life, and later she can choose to have a baby." She's proud of me, that I'm Jane Roe.... She's got her choice to do whatever they [sic] want with their own bodies. I didn't benefit from my own law, but my sisters who came after me benefited and that makes me very happy.

Roe v. Wade, McCorvey said, "means freedom."[66] The somewhat uneasy coexistence of radical individualism with claims to the protection of law within the pro-choice movement is made apparent in the remarks of an activist who requested anonymity in deference to the wishes of her family. When asked by a male questioner to respond to the proposition that "we need to develop a new ethic of abortion that expresses the viewpoint of everyone involved," she had this to say: "*We* need? *We?* My friend, the day you get pregnant is the day *we* develop an ethic of abortion. Why use my body as the field for your moral battle? Make your ethics for your own body. I have my own life and my own principles and it's been tough enough already.... So I can do without the enforced guidance of God/law on this issue." In the same breath she then insisted, "Give me *more* options—better birth control, subsidized child care, paternal child support—not fewer."[67]

Analogous tensions pervade the rhetoric and organizational strategies for other moral entrepreneurial movements as well. Committed to eradicating the "speciesism" that licenses human beings to subordinate the individual rights of sheep, cows, and laboratory rats to their own interests in being clothed, fed, and possibly armed against disease, Ingrid Newkirk has no qualms about imposing her own beliefs upon others, and enlisting the law in that effort. "Because of humankind's lack of moral imagination," she said, *"We activists have to tell people exactly what they should do.* People have to be pushed, society has to be pushed. Those who care deeply about a particular wrong have to pressure the general population ... [and] eventually a law is passed. Great changes often begin with the law."[68] Strangely, none of the animal rights activists we spoke to considered the illegal tactics of the underground Animal Liberation Front—bombing laboratories, stealing research, threatening scientists—antithetical to the quest for protective legislation. On the possible reluctance of some legislatures to support a movement that condones or openly advocates such activities,Deborah Slicer remarked, "But you have to work through those channels, you do. There are some sympathetic legislators. It's important to write those letters to your congressman, to go into her or his office and tell them what you think, it does have an impact. And I don't really see any inconsistency between advocating using those channels and being supportive of the ALF—that's maybe another channel, too." When asked if she thought the actions of the ALF trample on the rights of researchers and of those their work benefits, Slicer responded, "There are some grey areas for me in the research issue. And I do try to read both sides of the break-in issue, their [the ALF's] side, and also the researchers' [side]. I guess I just question the validity of research because it's research. I'm probably being somewhat pretentious, but some of us have to be, some of it to me seems clearly not morally justifiable."

Less ambivalent on the question of his opponent's rights was Mark Pertchuk, who insisted that smokers had *no* rights that his organization needed to be mindful of or upon which it could conceivably infringe. In one interview he revealed that he regretted the name of his own organization, Americans for Non-Smokers' Rights.

> It's misguided to think that [the nonsmoking movement] is about rights at all. When you call it nonsmokers' rights there is an implication, which is unintended, that it is in contrast to the smokers' rights. There is no such contrast. We are not interested in telling smokers not to smoke. We are interested in preserving clean air to protect nonsmokers. Its a situation that does not impinge on any conceivable, reasonable right that a smoker may have. In other words, no one in their right mind other than the tobacco industry would argue that a smoker has the right to blow smoke into a child's face at dinner. Right, in any legal sense of the word, right doesn't exist there.

Their conviction of the nonexistence of their opponents' rights is perhaps what makes those in the antismoking movement the most litigious of any of the groups we investigated. The past few years have seen a wave of lawsuits brought against the tobacco industry, often by former smokers or their families suing for injuries allegedly caused by smoking. The law, as John Banzhaf explained, is the movement's favored sphere of activity and the one in which it has been most successful.

The right-to-die movement has also shown a good deal of legal savvy in promoting legislation to protect the rights of patients to forego life-sustaining treatment. Fenella Rouse, director of legal services for the Society for the Right to Die, explained that "In the American legal system, the right to refuse treatment—the right, in other words, to be 'let alone'—is an important aspect of autonomy and individuality. [In cases of terminal illness,] it is the patient who determines what constitutes a benefit and, whenever possible, defines his or her own well being subjectively. The patient is permitted to ask, 'What do I want?' and the question for the physician is 'What does this patient want, regardless of what others, even a majority, would choose?'"[69] Alice Mehling articulated the challenge faced by the right-to-die movement as "the new medical technology vs. Patient autonomy": "I've got a body; you've got a body, everybody's got a right, and the right to die with dignity is therefore kind of a universal right that everybody should have. The key thing is to be in control of decision making throughout your entire life. Why should you turn yourself over to strangers to make decisions for you? You've got to protect yourself against the bureaucratic approach to this kind of thing, which means that you've got to stand up for your rights." For all its advocacy of patients' rights, however, the right-to-die movement reflects a tension between individual freedoms and the unilateral actions of agencies solicited to promote them. When the legal or medical establishment adopts policies to safeguard the patients' right to terminate their treatment, the result can occasionally be seen as the curtailing of freedom for the very group the policy ostensibly protects. For example, the Society for the Right to Die recently published a position paper adopted unanimously by the American Academy of Neurology, which states both that "the moral and ethical views of health care providers are secondary to the patient's and family's continuing right to grant or refuse consent for life-sustaining treatment" *and* that "patients in a persistent vegetative state do not have the capacity to experience pain or suffering," therefore "medical treatment in general provides no benefit to these patients."[70]

The Moral Entrepreneur as Metaphor

The premise of our inquiry has been to take the concept of moral entrepreneurship at face value. The term is not merely a metaphor, but corresponds to an objective, empirically verifiable development in the market system of advanced capitalism. It refers to individuals whose activity resembles in nearly every way that of the classical product-oriented entrepreneur but whose commodity and trade is a particular kind of moral judgment. Even those whom we readily think of as paragons of anticapitalist activity take entrepreneurial risks, market their symbolic wares, compete with each other for scarce resources, and draw financial remuneration and other compensation for their efforts.

Let us be absolutely clear about our argument. Moral entrepreneurs are not coterminous with the generic class of knowledge workers in advanced society. This is not another label for the New Class. Moral entrepreneurs constitute a small but growing sector of the postindustrial knowledge industry. But however small, it cannot be ignored or wished away in the interest of theoretical neatness. The moral entrepreneur is a curious, albeit undeniable, presence in the marketplace of advanced capitalism.

The phenomenon of moral entrepreneurship, therefore, has sociological significance in and of itself. But here we must contradict ourselves somewhat. Though moral entrepreneurs exist as a reality, sui generis, their primary sociological significance is as a metaphor for the larger knowledge sector. Their existence and their activity illuminate the dialectical relationship between the knowledge sector as a whole and the dynamics of advanced capitalism. How is this?

Clearly, very few knowledge workers are movement activists like the ones described here. Yet in America, there is a strong entrepreneurial character to much of the knowledge work that takes place in the larger knowledge sector. There is something very entrepreneurial in the work of therapists, for example, who are attempting either to establish a practice or to maintain a full roster of clients. They advertise in the telephone book and depend upon referrals from satisfied former patients. There is something manifestly entrepreneurial about the work of the expanding armies of consultants who provide contractual services on behalf of business, the agencies of government, schools, families, and individuals. Whether they work alone or as members of a firm, these knowledge workers operate their professional lives first and foremost as businesses, out to satisfy the needs of their clients. There is something undeniably entrepreneurial about the work of attorneys—even public interest attorneys—who are attempting to establish either a lucrative practice or else a sterling reputation. They do not exist without clients to represent. And as in the other cases, clients are nothing more than customers who must be brought in and whose needs must be attended to. Much the same can be said of journalists, computer technicians, research scientists, and on and on down the list of new knowledge-based occupations. One need not elaborate further. True, one can well imagine that there are some knowledge-based occupations that are virtually removed from the demands and logic of the marketplace, (those controlled by and serving the needs of the state) but in America (perhaps unlike Europe) they are relatively few. The point is that if the demands and logic of the market shape the activities of the movement activists we have observed here—those who intuitively seem so distant from our image of "capitalist man"—then the demands and the logic of the market must also shape the activities of a wide range of other knowledge workers.

If it is fair, then, to characterize knowledge workers as economic actors, as willing and even eager participants in free market activity, then a dialectic is at play. On the one hand, the knowledge sector is shaped by realities of capitalism, but by virtue of the distinct cultural ethos it has produced, the knowledge sector is playing a decisive role in the transformation of capitalism. This is seen in the transformation of management styles and practices, in employee work patterns, in sources of employee motivation and discipline, and so on.

Our argument, then, is that the conventional ways of thinking about the status and role of knowledge workers in advanced capitalism have been misconceived. As we argued at the start of this chapter, the New

Class is not so much a distinct class opposed to capitalism, but a sector of the economy that is part and parcel of the evolution of American capitalism. It is true that there are knowledge workers who are genuinely anticapitalist. They disdain economic competition, profit making, and the concentration of private wealth to the disadvantage of the poor, and they would just as soon see the total destruction of the capitalist system. Their number, however, is fairly small, and they are almost exclusively found far removed from any economic activity.[71] Certainly this ideological posture is not a defining characteristic of the knowledge sector in America.

Yet while their moral and political outlook is not anticapitalist, it is fair to say (if the survey evidence is to be believed) that their moral and political outlook tends to be antibourgeois. A disproportionate number of elite knowledge workers reject the nineteenth-century bourgeois family as normative. A disproportionate number reject the epistemological and moral underpinnings of traditional asceticism. A disproportionate number reject the bourgeois concept of public justice. And so on. One can make political judgments about whether this is good or bad, but sociologically, it points to an important conclusion. Bourgeois culture is in decline not because we now know that it was inherently "chauvinistic," "oppressive," or even "religiously obscurantist," nor because, in the end, truth and justice always prevail. Rather, bourgeois culture is in decline because it is no longer an adequate stimulus to contemporary capitalism. That is to say, the moral order that sustained nineteenth- and early twentieth-century capitalism no longer provides the cultural "tool kits" to make capitalism work smoothly. The conflict between the so-called New Class and the old moneyed class rests not on the former's rejection of capitalism per se but on its rejection of the moral order that sustained capitalism at a particular stage in its development. If this is correct, then it is to the knowledge sector, and to the category of people we have called moral entrepreneurs in particular, that we must look to see how a newer moral order—one that greases the wheels of postmodern capitalism—takes shape.

7

The New Class on the Periphery: Modernization, Professionalism, and Clientelism in Southern Italy

Paolo Jedlowski

Although the so-called New Class hypothesis has never really been taken up in discussion of the rise of the middle classes in Italy, the picture here is not unlike that of other industrialized countries. Southern Italy, however, presents a special situation that can best be expressed as "the jumping of a phase." Its socioeconomic structure appears to be that of a "postindustrial" society, but no proper industrial phase ever occurred. Thirty years ago the majority of the working population were farmers; today most work in the service sector. There was never a period when the majority held jobs in industry. This is not to say that southern Italy is undeveloped. In the last thirty years individual and general wealth have increased enormously. While there remains a strong discrepancy between the northern and southern regions of Italy, the standard of living in the south today is very near the European median. This development, however, is primarily the result not of an endogenous growth of the local economy, but of a series of national policy decisions that have transferred large sums of government money to the south. This "assisted development," financed by the state is steered by local political elites, who handle the flow of resources and mediate between the state and the requests of the local society.

These conditions mean that we must characterize the New Class somewhat differently here than in other chapters of this volume. In the absence of significant industrialization, the new middle class of education, health, and communications professionals has no "old" and consolidated middle class of merchants, bankers, technicians, and so on with whom to compare itself. As it happens, many of these professions are also just beginning to establish themselves in the region. The real opposition to the New Class is represented by the middle-class, white-collar bureaucrats who administer the government assistance programs. My argument in the following pages is that the professional logic of the New Class, in effect, opposes itself to the logic of the established public bureaucracies. Having grown up in a period when employment in the public sector was the highest aspiration of a population in exodus from agriculture, these bureaucratic classes are themselves strongly dependent on the favors of the local political system, to which they stand in a relationship of client to patron. The fulfillment of their duties is marked by a strongly personalistic logic, which implies that these are seen not as obligations given in the definition of the job of public servant but as *favors* one does for *particular* citizens. The development of a "legal-rational" type of bureaucracy, in accordance with the well-known Weberian formulation, has affirmed itself here in a more formal than substantial way. What looks like the standard legal-rational framework is in reality a complex system of particularistic exchanges and of personalized relationships between functionaries, politicians, and clients.

This attitude of the bureaucratic middle classes has roots as much in peasant culture as in the modernization process. In fact, even in the post-World War II period, wide sectors of economic life in southern Italy were dominated by the logic not of the *market* (which has penetrated very slowly and only in certain sections) but of *reciprocity*.

In the absence of strong industrial development economic life centered on personalistic relations rather than the anonymous exchanges typical of modern market societies. When government money was funneled to this area of the country, the patron-client relationship—which in modern societies guaranteed social integration in a context of generalized mistrust of the state—reproduced itself in the local political system, giving rise to new forms of clientelism in the administration of public resources.

Made up largely of the highly educated middle classes, the New Class in southern Italy opposes this system, in which administrators subordinate the needs of communities and individuals to the interests of their client networks. Outfitted with the "cultural capital" of their university education, members of the New Class want to maximize the value of this capital to the detriment not only (and not so much, in this context) of economic capital, but of the kind of "capital" that comes with membership in a particular political family or social clan. In a social world that has bypassed industrialization on its way to modernity, the New Class bears the burden of the "modernization of consciousness" that elsewhere comes about as a gradual result of market and other forces.

Southern Italy is not a totally homogeneous area. Because our research was based for the most part on long narrative interviews and case studies, it was necessary to concentrate on a certain representative area: the urban zone of Cosenza, in the Calabrian region.[72] Thirty years ago, Cosenza was the agricultural and commercial center of a rather enclosed region with few channels of communication with the rest of the country. Today it is the chief town in a relatively wealthy province crossed by important commercial routes, the seat of a number of administrative centers and all types of services.

The physical changes in the urban development—houses, offices, roads, shops—are extraordinary, but no more so than the changes in the social structure. As one of our interviewees said, "When I was a schoolboy the world here was completely different. Cosenza was a place where all people knew each other, where a strict distinction of classes was the rule.... I was brought up in an agrarian culture, where a ruling class clearly existed and a ruled class did too. Nowadays Cosenza is nearly a metropolis.... There is a middle class everywhere; it is the leading class by now." It is doubtful that the middle class is in fact the "leading class"; however, it is true that the most powerful are now the new political and bureaucratic classes who have very little in common with the old landed aristocracy, and whose culture and way of life are not easily distinguished from those of the middle classes in Italy as a whole. These new urban middle classes are always populated less by artisans and tradesman than by service sector employees, most of them public employees.[73]

Within the public services, certain occupations are becoming more prestigious and others less. For example, teachers, who years ago held a position of authority, are now much less revered because there are so many of them, and so many well-educated people. Other professions are becoming internally stratified. Doctors and engineers, for example, distinguish members of their own professions according to who practices independently and who works for others. We have chosen to focus on those emerging occupations that produce and use symbolic knowledge, and are therefore part of our hypothetical definition of the New Class. As representatives we have chosen psychologists, advertising agents, and television journalists.

The psychologists' relevance to the New Class discussion is evident: they represent a professional group of recent formation whose function is the production of universes of signification where actions and feelings find expression. As we shall see, the social function of the psychologists extends beyond the particular "therapy" they offer. The work of the advertisers and journalists also concerns the production and use of symbolic knowledge. We can think of them in this context as the private sector counterparts of the psychologists, nearly all of whom, in Cosenza, are employed by the state. Our interviews with bureaucratic functionaries have essentially comparative value, and we will not linger on their work except as it helps us to understand the originality of the New Class and the meaning of its action in the given social context.

In Cosenza, each of these groups is relatively privileged. In a situation of widespread unemployment (19.2 percent in 1987), simply having a regular job is an objective privilege. But the members of the New Class have *chosen* their jobs. Work for them is not just a source of income; it is also, or ought to be, an avenue of personal fulfillment (or, as they express it themselves, of "self-realization"). Many of our interviewees reported having abandoned a secure career—for example, in a bank or a school—in order to seek riskier but more "gratifying" jobs that accorded better with their personal aspirations.

When we began our research we expected that most of the members of the New Class—modern intellectuals, innovative elites—would be children of middle-class parents, often themselves intellectuals. This proved to be only partly true. The bureaucratic functionaries are, for the most part, descendants of middle-class families (probably thanks to the importance of being in the "right" family to get these jobs in the first place), but the social origins of the New Class professionals are much less uniform. Some are children of teachers or of professionals, but most (more than half of our interviewees) had parents who were poor and poorly educated: miners, housemaids, and so on. The New Class seems thus to be an upwardly mobile one.

Generally, Cosenza's New Class is more left-leaning than the other layers of the middle class, confirming the hypothesis of most of the international literature on the phenomenon. It is difficult, however, to know exactly how to account for this political orientation. We prefer to think of a sort of "elective affinity" between the typical New Class professionals and those who, during the 1960s and 1970s, were the protagonists of Italy's student-protest movements.[74] As we will see, most of our interviewees had participated in these movements, and many of them had remained faithful to the ideals they pursued then by putting their skills as social critics (literally) to work. If the early 1970s were the years of protest and politics, the 1980s have been the years of professionalizing and institutionalizing their abilities in legitimate bodies of knowledge, and in some cases of consolidating power thanks to their self-appointed status as "experts" on social issues.

In putting together the profiles that follow, we tried to draw out the connection between the interviewees' present jobs and their former experiences, and to give special attention to the concept of "professionalism" of which they are the bearers. The remainder of the chapter assesses the significance of their work in the larger social context. After pointing out the ambiguity of the concept of "the public" in southern Italy, we compare the (public) logic of "professionalism" with the (private) logic of "clientelism." Finally, we return to some general considerations concerning the hypothetical New Class in this context.

Psychologists: The Goal of Professionalism and the Modernization of Consciousness

In Italy, the profession of psychologist is relatively new. The first chair of psychology in an Italian university was established in 1945, and the first degree courses were offered only in 1971 at Padua and Rome. Our interviewees in Cosenza are almost all degreed in Rome and are a part of the first real generation of Italian psychologists. The fact of their having studied outside Cosenza and of having gone to university in the 1970s (the years of highest student unrest in Italy) featured prominently in the stories of our interviewees. Most of them had been active in these movements and had belonged to left-wing organizations. They constitute a generation not only in a demographic sense, but also in a political and cultural sense.

Their participation in the social movements of the 1960s and 1970s seems to have been especially influential in the first phase of their work as psychologists. Simply by returning to Cosenza they were introducing the contents of cultural flaws into a social structure that had remained largely untouched by them. In order to understand how this was so, we need to recall the extent to which the development of the welfare state in the 1970s contributed to the social movements of those years. It was at that time that Italy passed laws that radically modified existing social and health-care policies. These laws sought to establish, at least formally, a modern welfare system that would safeguard the well-being of everyone, regardless of their social or political standing. The new services thus put into effect strongly influenced the trade union movement as well as the protest movements of students, workers, and women. The influence, moreover, was reciprocal: not fortuitously, in the absence of strong social movements today, these laws are now being scaled back and reformulated.

The psychologists we interviewed found work in the services put into effect by these laws. Back in Calabria, degrees in hand, they were looking for their first jobs just when public mental health services were being established for the first time. To both their local administrators and their prospective clients, the psychologists had to justify their fitness for an only recently created task. Not only was the job of public mental health practitioner unheard of, it was also largely superfluous, since the state had provided these services without the community's ever having asked for them. So when the psychologists talk about their first years on the job, they frequently portray themselves as having been pioneers. They were the first to deal with clients who had to be "taught" to use the services of the *consultorio familiare* or the territorial mental health clinics.[75] But they were pioneers also in dealing with the administrators of the local public health units, who were unprepared to think of the new services as anything besides interesting instruments for creating new job appointments and managing new resources in a clientelistic way.

By practicing the job for which they had been trained, the psychologists gradually created a social demand for their services. In fact, a considerable amount of their time is devoted to the "education of users," as some some of our interviewees described it. Psychologists are the bearers of a new language, new words for naming external, social relations and internal feelings, desires, and needs. The borders of "what can be said" are pushed back, above all in the sexual sphere, but also in every kind of matter relating to human relationships and intimacy.

In the first phase of their practice the principal elements of the psychologists' work are advertising their services, establishing relationships with administrators, setting up their offices, and finding out as much as they can about their client population. In this phase, they tend to capitalize on what they define as patterns of social, as much as properly psychological, "dysfunction," and here the influence of their participation in the social movements of the 1970s is evident. Later, when their practices are established, they tend to enter a period of reflection on their proper role. For a few of our interviewees, this means offering psychotherapy on the (admittedly very small) private market. If the first phase is that of the "militant-operator," the second is that of "professional."

The interviewees, however, had different ideas about what constitutes a "professional." For some, the character of mental health services remains political. This type of operator is fully aware that his or her interpretation of other people's needs is a political act. Transforming those needs into questions and supplying adequate replies is a process of reality-defining that requires the taking up of a moral-political position, not the "scientific" application of professional knowledge. He or she sees the move toward "professionalization" of service sector employees as a strategy for establishing corporate privileges. While these operators are interested in defining the theoretical basis of their activity and of keeping up with the literature in their field, they nevertheless remain critical of the corporate tendencies inherent in the idea of professionalism.

This type of operator remains interested in problems and needs that are social and relational rather than purely mental; they prefer to work in the *consultori*, for example, or in the services for children or the elderly. By contrast, those who are in closer contact with mental illness are more apt to welcome professionalization. For this second type of operator, being a professional means two things. On one hand, it means keeping up with research in the field, and so of having recourse to postuniversity "refresher" training. On the other, it means comparing themselves to doctors (that is, psychiatrists) on the level of credentials and intellectual status. They have pursued, on a local level, a strategy of professionalization that has been the national norm for many years. The ad hoc institutionalization of formative routes, the founding of associations, and, most recently, the establishment of professional registers have been the steps toward the professionalization of intellectual occupations, in Italy as elsewhere.[76] Psychologists face a great opposition here, however, when they claim that their professional status confers a legal right to practice psychotherapy. The opposition comes largely from psychiatrists, who, understandably have no wish to surrender their monopoly on patients' psyches.

Most of the psychologists we spoke to who work alongside psychiatrists admitted that the relationship between them was problematic. Generally, the psychologists saw the psychiatrists as hostile toward them and overly concerned with defending their own privileges. The major problems, however, are really on the side of the psychologists, who suffer from professional insecurity, an inability to define their own role with precision, a sense of the inadequacy of their own university training in psychotherapy, and, finally, a difficulty in explaining what they do in terms as "scientific" and socially legitimate as those used by doctors. The latter point seems to be particularly keenly felt. In the largely traditional culture of Cosenza, where mental or emotional disturbances have usually been resolved with the help of family, neighbors, or the church, or else necessitated medical treatment, psychologists must struggle continuously for social legitimacy.

In reality, the psychologists' and psychiatrists' jobs are very different. The psychologist's principal tool is the *conversation*. When one sees a psychiatrist, by contrast, the meeting is usually called a visit or an examination. For the psychiatrist, the patient is constituted as an object to be considered in a certain measure apart from his subjective disposition. Psychology, while its task is also to cure, must focus attention on the relation between the patient and the operator. The cure cannot be achieved without the participation of the patient, who must adopt the logic of the cure as his own.

Thus psychotherapy is, an encounter, a communication. It is a therapy expressed as an exchange of words. The aim of the encounter is to reply to a request for help in such a way that the petitioner learns to solve his problem for himself. Unlike the psychiatrist, the psychologist actually renounces responsibility for the patient's health. One of our interviewees said that the psychologist "does not change the behavior of the patient ... he creates conditions for nurturing the energies, the resources that the person already has within himself." As an "encounter," therefore, psychotherapy is certainly peculiar. As another of our interviewees said, it is "a sonata for piano duet."

The psychologists we interviewed were reluctant to explain their activity in "scientific" terms. The metaphors they used were drawn from an impressive range of theories, indicating a mistrust of an excessively consolidated and statistical language. The psychologist— especially when practicing as a psychotherapist—works on *relations* between human beings, in the first place on that relation which is established between himself and his patient. Unlike the psychiatrist, the psychologist cannot constitute the patient's body, or his mind, as an *object* to study in an impersonal way. The "interpretation" of the symptoms cannot be fixed once and forever: the psychotherapeutical discussion is a perpetual self-criticism.

This seems to be the principal obstacle to the "professionalization" of the psychologists. On the one hand there is a desire to acquire the status already belonging to other intellectual professions, and on the other hand, the absence of an objective corpus of knowledge. The professional activity of the psychologists obeys a "rationality" that hardly recognizes itself in the forms of rationalization that were the basis for institutionalizing the first great bourgeois professions.

But in another sense the social effects of the psychologists' work are congruent with the processes of rationalization that have characterized the great season of Western modernity. Here the formation of the *modern* conscience must be looked at two different ways. On one side, it tends toward abstraction, to the formalization of social relations in a universe of standardized and anonymous rules. On the other, it privileges the processes of individuation, the development of each person's idiosyncratic "personality" and ability to make autonomous choices. Both of these aspects of modern consciousness are cultivated by the psychologists' work.

Psychologists try to formalize, in a professional way, "helping-relationships" that, traditionally, have been entered into by close friends, relatives, or parishioners and priests. Psychologists professionalize these relationships by setting them in the context of at least relatively formalized theories. In the private market, the service is ruled by the exchange of money. In a situation where private demand is scarce, and where psychologists mainly work in the public service (as in Cosenza), the cash-nexus is replaced by rules imposed indiscriminately by the psychologists themselves. These rules determine where and when the meeting will take place, the duration of the therapy, and so on. All of this obliges the patient to represent himself as an anonymous client who receives help not because he has "connections" but simply because he is a citizen of a welfare state.

The desire or the occasion to make oneself anonymous is typically absent in the traditional culture of the south, and so psychologists contribute an element of "modernization" to this social context. But in doing so, paradoxically, they also contribute to the subject's constitution of his individuality. This process is a fundamental feature of modern culture. Being an individual means having a personal biography and placing a premium on one's own uniqueness. This enables the individual to make choices: without the individuation process, the passage from "a world of destiny to a world of choice"—in Max Weber's formulation—would make no sense. The psychologists' emphasis on the individual's responsibility for his own decisions and his own well-being is a part of the construction of this process. Elsewhere it might be taken for granted, but in southern Italy, where the individual can extricate himself from the traditional cultural networks (family, church) only with great effort, the passage from *destiny* to *choice* has quite far-reaching implications.

Communications Professionals: Market and Creativity on the Periphery

As we have seen, the professional world of the psychologists is more or less homogeneous: almost all of them have the same university background; almost all of them work exclusively or at least mainly in the public services. The professional world of the communications industry is much more varied. Our interviews with people in this sector focused on advertisers and television journalists. Locally, at least, both of these professions are quite new. Though television journalists might claim to be the heirs of newspaper reporters, the differences between print and electronic media are sufficiently great to have made one of our interviewees remark that his profession is "without a history." Somewhat like the psychologists, the television journalists feel themselves to be "pioneers," charged with the social task of "modernization."

In this context, modernization means first of all managing modern information technology and gaining widespread acceptance for its use. But, at least for the advertisers, who work in the private sector, modernization also means establishing the presence of the *market* in the local social structure. Finally, for everyone, modernization means *communicating*: getting the news out, integrating the local reality with what is going on nationally and internationally, and so "opening" Calabrian culture to extraregional influences.

We have seen that the psychologists' work concerns the private sphere: in many ways, it actually produces it, by developing a new consciousness of intimacy and interiority. However, it also has implications for the public sphere, since it creates new languages, identifies new social needs, and cultivates new attitudes toward public service. By contrast, the work of communication specialists is directed toward the public sphere, but it also subtly enters into the private. This is true in two ways. On the one hand, communications professionals (journalists in particular) shape the realm of *public opinion*, whose existence is one of the strongholds of the liberal bourgeois organization. But in a situation of diffused clientelism, where every "public" affair is in reality an encounter of private-interest pressure groups, influencing public opinion actually means garnering support for *private* interests. Jürgen Habermas described this as the "refeudalization of the public sphere" in mass society. In this context, however, it does not happen as a "perversion" of the opinions of an existing bourgeois-liberal type (which has never really been present here anyway), but as the creation and colonization of the public sphere on behalf of groups of clients. On the other hand, the communications industry (especially advertising) involves the elaboration and the diffusion of a series of messages that, while they occupy *public* spaces, are explicitly designed to reorient the imaginary "private" world of individuals in favor of one desire or another. (Habermas 1962, 1974).

All of this makes for a complicated situation. It is only partly under the control of the local operators, however; even given the many local newspapers and private radio and television stations, most of the news that arrives at the periphery flows out from the center.[77] This explains why the expansion of this sector in Cosenza has been slow, but it does not mean that it is without interest. Even here, the 1970s introduced innovations: new laws have favored the establishment of small radio broadcasting companies and private television stations that, in turn, supply new fora for local political pressure groups, as well as for the advertising ventures of small producers and tradesmen in the local market. The advertising agencies where our interviewees work were all founded in the late 1970s as a result of this development. Even journalism has seen some important innovations: the establishment (again in the 1970s) of a local seat of the RAI (the state broadcasting corporation) has created a demand for qualified professionals in this part of the country. Even the various private broadcasters have created a need for certain occupations—journalists in particular—and so contributed to the growth of this sector.

What impresses us in the communications field is therefore the novelty, but also the variety, of the occupations. The professionalization—that is, the formal institutionalization—of these occupations is less advanced than we have seen among the psychologists. Jobs in this sector are fluidly defined, allowing easy passage from one occupation to another. In fact, one of the most interesting things about this business is the frequency with which people change jobs. Almost all of our interviewees have changed their occupation many times, and even now most of them do more than one job. For communications professionals more than for anyone else, it seems, work must be a source not only of income but also of personal gratification and "self-realization." In order to achieve this "self-realization" they are willing to take risks, and job security here becomes less and less of a priority.

We will not describe this professional universe in detail, but we would like to indicate certain characteristics of its members. For now we will concentrate on the advertisers, and will return to the others in the next section.

The advertisers we interviewed can be divided into two types. (As always in these cases, this does not mean that we have identified two distinct *groups*, but rather a polarity of attitudes.) The first type is represented above all by the permanent employees of the advertising agencies. These people use a very technical jargon, sprinkled with marketing terms, as though what they were best at advertising was themselves. For them, "professionalism" implies not only the ability to do their job but also to impose their own social function on the market; in effect, to sell themselves. Their professionalism, they imply, distinguishes them from local radio and television operators who have not yet differentiated their advertising activity from the direct management of the broadcasting station. Identifying themselves as professionals also impresses potential clients.

Usually the proprietors of small to average-sized stores and restaurants, these clients have few resources to invest in advertising. When they do invest, they want immediate, tangible results, and are often wary of delegating the management of their business to others. Therefore, as our interviewees say, clients must be "educated": in what they can expect from the advertising agency, in a sense of long range planning, and in the commercial function of an "image."

The advertisers' major problem, therefore, is the poverty of the productive and commercial system. As representatives of the logic of advanced capitalism, their thinking often clashes violently with that of potential clients in a poorly developed market, who tend to be suspicious and risk-averse. And in some ways they encounter a "market" that is, in reality, politically protected.[78] The entrepreneurs in Calabria are obliged to come to terms with a political system that holds the reins of public resources and manages the contracts and the production orders. In the same way, the advertisers have found that even in their profession it is necessary to have "patrons." This is particularly evident when they compete among each other to manage information campaigns or to promote the conventions of public institutions. The common experience is that the advertiser who "knows someone" or, even better, "belongs" to a certain political figure gets the job. For work in the private sector the situation is often the same; the Calabrian economic system tends to divide itself into bands, with each establishment doing most of its business with others in the same political "friendship" area. The "free market" exists in appearance only, since the mechanism of the "favor bank" of preferential links, frequently counts for more than the efficiency of services or the quality and economy of products. The "free market" is, in effect, the advertisers' utopia. Only in a market that prized the ability to supply good products and services over the ability to keep good company could their standard of professionalism prevail. For this type of operator, work is the source of personal gratification, but the ability to bring in money, the economic gratification, is also very important. It is interesting to see that, as in the case of the psychologists, the majority of those in the communication industry come from the lines of militants and sympathizers of the protest movement of the 1960s and 1970s. Participation in those movements taught them much of what they use in their work—such as the ability to make up slogans, or to "read" society and its tendencies. That aside, however, there is little trace of their having taken part in these movements, unless it be the premium they place on autonomy and the pleasure they take in being "in the vanguard." For a second type of operator, however, the 1970s are still very much alive in the present. If the first group are the pure (or at least aspiring) professionals, the second are the "critics," or, as one of the representatives of this type identified them, the "creative-marginals." This group generally works part-time in advertising, and relies on another job, usually also in the communications area, for a steady income. It is advertising, however, rather than the second job, that fulfills their creative aspirations and need for "self-realization."

Many of these operators directly connect their advertising activity with their experience of the protest movements. As one of them explained, "Advertising is the continuation in our era of—how can I say?—of discussions that do not exist anymore, of cultural clubs that do not exist anymore ... that atmosphere in which we feel a little bit like orphans." For this group, advertising has become a privileged place of cultural action that has no way of expressing itself elsewhere. In the 1970s, many of them were the ones responsible for the "cultural happenings" in Cosenza that repeated, on a reduced scale, events that were taking place in other Italian cities. Today, advertising gives them a forum for autonomous and above all, *creative* activity, something almost approaching "art." According to one of our interviewees, one of the forces behind the events of the late 1960s and 1970s was the fantasy of liberating the "artistic expression" of the people. The historical defeat of the movement of those years is seen by this group as more than political: it was the defeat of a universal artistic utopia. For our interviewees, modified historical conditioning leaves open only the possibility of carving out a creative niche *within* the "system." Since the market has developed a growing interest in creativity as a function of the need to commercialize its products, it has, paradoxically, become a haven for these disenchanted heirs of the late 1960s. These astute "children of the century," as they like to define themselves, put their creativity in the service of production in exchange for a sort of liberty. Their desires coincide with those of the first group in one respect: the utopia, the dream, is the market. (And certainly they would add that the market is a market of dreams; as all of them know, when you buy a brand of cigarettes, it's not the tobacco you buy, it's the image.)

The language of this type of operator is brilliant, refined, very often ironical and self-ironizing, but it is also marked by an acute perception of being on the periphery. Calabria's provincialness, which shows itself in its whole culture, frustrates them. Here on the periphery, unappreciated and underutilized, they miss the chance to express their full creative potential. As one of them characteristically lamented, "I should not have been born in Cosenza. Whoever wrote that script made a mistake." It is noteworthy how often our interviewees connected the concept of the "periphery" or "margin" with the events of the late 1960s and 1970s. In the words of one of them, "If nineteen-sixty-eight had any meaning at all, it wasn't only political. It was a kind of tribal tom-tom that was heard throughout the world and to which every area of the world replied.... The drama of Calabria and

Cosenza is that the utopia, the dreams, the needs, the rhythms, are the same as elsewhere, because we know what is happening, but we are not able to reply. The sound of the tom-tom reaches us, but we haven't got a tom-tom, we cannot reply."

The events of 1968 are seen as the great moment of the unification of consciousness, of the "tribal" diffusion of utopian dreams, attitudes, and desires. But this agitation reveals the marginality of Calabria: "We hear the tom-tom, but we cannot reply." In what sense? If it is true that in 1968 certain sectors of Calabrian society started dreaming the same wishful dreams dreamt in many other parts of the world, it is also true that Calabria also opposed this way of thinking with the harsh reality of its traditional order. Our interviewees also suggested that, in the "Global Village" created by telecommunications, knowing how to "reply to the tom-tom" means having access to the media. The media of national importance, however, are concentrated in Rome or in the urban centers of the north, and the message sent out by remote provinces like Calabria often go unheard. The "Global Village" has centers and peripheries.

Our interviewees' awareness of this problem comes from their place in the information market. The market helps to define the periphery as an area exposed to the cultural products coming from the center but having no access, or little access, to the means of producing and distributing these products.

The Ambiguity of the Public Sphere in Italy

The work of Cosenza's psychologists and advertisers brings elements of what we used to consider "modernity" into a world largely characterized by a traditional culture. However, these elements have not been readily assimilated, and the conflict between the new professions and the local culture goes very deep. Its roots may lie, in fact, in the conception these people have of themselves as "professionals." Even though, as we have seen, they approach the question of formal professionalization differently, none of them doubts his own qualifications and abilities, and thus his right to possession of the "cultural capital" that ought to bring income and prestige. In the strongly traditional local society, however, income and prestige accrue to one by virtue not of professional credentials but of one's position within preferential social networks. We are drawing a contrast here between a *logic of professionalism* and a *logic of clientelism*, that reverberates with another, perhaps more fundamental contrast between *abstract* and *personalistic* relations. Both are well illustrated in an anecdote told by a young professor in Cosenza. This professor keeps his accounts at an important local bank and usually carries his transactions at the local head office. The office is frequently very crowded, and the professor always queues up at the counter to wait his turn with the others. Invariably someone jumps the queue, greets the clerks by their first names, and is served before the others waiting in the line. Annoyed by this behavior, the professor finally decides to write a letter of complaint to the director of the bank. The director sends a speedy reply, addressed not to the professor, but to his father. Surprised and offended, the director tells the professor's father, of whom he is an old friend, that he cannot understand why his son has complained. The director's argument is that the professor knows that he is well-known at the bank, and that the director is an old family friend. That being the case, why then doesn't the professor also jump the queue and announce himself when he comes into the bank? Out of the respect due to him and his family, the director promises, the professor will certainly be served immediately.

Few examples demonstrate the two mentalities so well. The young professor maintains that the service given at a bank counter is a *public* service; therefore all customers ought to be treated in the same way, according to standard procedures. He is indignant that this is not the case. Appearing not to understand the injury, the bank director replies with a claim of loyalty: your family knows that I know you; therefore I wouldn't think of treating you like everybody else. You need only make yourself seen." It needn't be pointed out to the director that the service at his bank is personalistic and that customers are not being treated equally. For him, the customers who present themselves simply as anonymous "users" are naturally to be served *after* those who are known to him. This elderly bank director is something of a throwback since today, even in Cosenza, banks treat their clients in more or less the same way, at least in the routine services. But in any case, most Calabrians are of the opinion that "being recognized" by the employees of whatever establishment is useful; it helps to speed up the paperwork and usually guarantees good service. This is true not only in banks; it counts for any type of service ostensibly offered to the "public."

What we're meeting here is the diffusion of a *clientelistic* mentality. The common characteristic of any type of clientelism is the element of *direct exchange*: the patron-client relationship is an exchange of benefits between two subjects who are usually, at least traditionally, endowed with unequal powers. In its strictly personal character and in the indeterminacy—at least in principle—of the benefits exchanged, the clientelistic exchange is radically different from the *contract*. In the latter, the contracting parties rely on impersonal and abstract rules—market rules—in carrying out a predetermined exchange. The clientelistic exchange is based instead on personal trust and the expectation of an ongoing relationship of reciprocity. In this way this is different also from the relationship between the individual and the modern state: it does not define the contracting parties' rights and obligations once and for all, but demands that the links that bind them be continually reextended and renewed. As others have pointed out, the clientelistic relationship neither depends on nor contributes to trust in superpersonal entities (e.g., the market and the state). Rather, it has traditionally arisen within societies that lack such trust, and tend to reproduce this lack, for which it compensates by constructing networks of personalized and particularistic relations.

Recently, some sociologists have focused on the transformation of traditional clientelism, which is based on relationships between prominent and common persons, into political clientelism, in which the "patron" tends to be a party organization that defends particularistic interests in exchange for votes and political loyalty. What we have been encountering is neither traditional nor political clientelism but rather a kind of "diffused clientelism," an attitude that privileges personal relations and tends to understand every public transaction as a relationship between individuals who exchange resources in a personalistic way. One way of explaining this ambiguity is to say that in Calabria the "public sphere" exists only formally, as the apparatus or institutions of the government, perhaps, but not as the consciousness that what affects one, affects others also.

The ambiguity of the public sphere corresponds to the absence of any concept of the "common good." The manipulation of public interests in the service of particularistic interests has long been the practice of local political elites, who derive their power from distributing public resources according to personalistic criteria. But this behavior is also diffused through the subordinate layers of governmental and paragovernmental bodies (banks, hospitals) whose employees do the same to claim their own slice of power. As Judith Chubb (1982) has demonstrated, these employees typically regard their duties as "favors" they give out at their own discretion. Often the "favor" simply consists in offering service more rapidly and cutting through red tape, though in rare cases it means actual corruption. Since the power of these employees derives from the shared willingness of other sectors of society to see duties as favors, they have no interest in changing the status quo. Able to do favors for others, they can in turn ask for and receive favors. Nothing antagonizes them more than the idea of a truly *public* service, one that functions according to universalistic criteria.

Our research demonstrates, however, that this attitude toward the public sphere is not without opponents. People who conceive of the public sphere as a place of meetings and exchanges between citizens with equal rights, who truly believe in the idea of a common good, and who think of the public services as services delivered in the same way to everyone—people who share the view of the Calabrian professor in our story—can be found in the ranks of the professionalized middle classes, particularly the so-called New Class.

The disastrous condition of the public services—a function of their being administered in a clientelistic way—generates in fact a clashing contradiction. In southern Italy, where individual incomes approach those of the north, the inefficiency of the public services—a variety of income "in kind"—truly handicaps the economy. Poor public hospitals, transportation, and schools pose few problems for the wealthy, who have recourse to private services as well as clientelistic connections. For the rest, lack of access to efficient services poses a genuine hardship.

The members of the New Class seem to be the most conscious of this contradiction. This is so because these people are in many ways the products of the "modern" culture that has developed in other regions of Italy. Moreover, many of them—the psychologists, for example—adhere, in their work, to the universalistic principles on which the welfare state is ostensibly based. The political and bureaucratic classes understand the services of the welfare state as one more service to be used in a clientelistic way—jobs to be distributed, users to be selected, contracts to be awarded. For the new professionals, by contrast, these are services that ought to be administered according to the needs of citizens, regardless of their standing in the community.

This antagonism between the old and the new middle class is not a quarrel about whether the welfare state should or should not exist. Both depend financially on its existence and happily endorse its expansion. Their argument, rather, hinges on the meaning of *welfare*: the common good (the New Class), or particular goods (the old bureaucratic classes). The members of the New Class see themselves as *citizens*, and the work they do concerns other citizens. To be a citizen means to refuse to define oneself primarily in terms of one's family or social standing, and to consider oneself as the bearer of largely impersonal functions. Citizens are equal regardless of birth, education, or wealth. Obviously the notion of citizenship appeals to abstraction: because of this, it has been slow to take root in a community where strongly personalistic relationships have been historically reproduced.

Hence there is friction between the New Class and the old bureaucratic and political classes. Where, for many reasons, the development of a bureaucracy has not coincided with the emergence of the idea of the *anonymity* of clients and functionaries so typical of modernity, the members of the New Class have had to promote that idea in order to secure their own professional status. While the old middle-class functionaries hold the power of dispensing "favors" to certain individuals, the New Class professionals can only claim power by winning recognition for their expertise; specifically, for their ability to discern and to provide for the common good.

Clientelism and Being Professional

The logic of professionalism stands in direct opposition to the personalistic-clientelistic system. In the measures to which it controls their careers, public service employees tend to reproduce that system by favoring the more well placed among their clients. For their part, the New Class professionals balk at demands for preferential treatment from this or that client. Theoretically, the more professionalized a group, the more hostile it is to a clientelistic system. In reality, obviously, the situation is less clear-cut, since professionals tend to rely on their own networks even while opposing clientelism. This emerged from our interviews with some of the journalists at the local RAI (state broadcasting) agency.

As a matter of official policy, RAI jobs are divided among members of different political parties. The exact numerical division of jobs at each regional agency is determined in centralized party negotiations. The parties' interest in controlling the nation's principal channel of mass communication is evident; the division of jobs among those who handle the information flow is, all things considered, a guarantee of relative pluralism (although it obviously excludes those who are not politically powerful enough to make themselves represented). As such it is substantially accepted as the least of the possible evils. Interestingly, however, this allotment of jobs, decided at the national level, extends and legitimates the clientelistic methods typical of the south. In both cases, jobs are awarded according to who knows whom rather than who knows best.

Journalists have different opinions of this situation. One of the directors of the local agency, given the opportunity to apply for the job of journalist, flatly refused on the basis of his opposition to the job division policy and resigned his position. Once a part-time advertiser, he now works in advertising full-time and freelances as a journalist on the side. More willing to compromise was a woman we interviewed who reluctantly accepted a "sponsorship" from the Communist Party because she knew that her credentials and experience alone were not enough to get her the job. Even during our interview she appeared not to have fully resigned herself to being the Party's "share" of the journalists in the Calabrian agency: "I am a *share* of the Party, do you understand? I am not Mrs. So-and-so, who knows how to do this and that, who has had this and that experience.... I am a share of the Party!" That the Party in question seems, until now, to have behaved correctly and not asked for anything from her "in exchange" for her position does not change the substance of her complaint: for her there is a radical disjunction between the way she conceives her own profession—experience, ability, accomplishment—and the criteria for job distribution that, as a rule, overlooks these qualifications.

Another journalist didn't see this as a problem. A member of the Christian Democratic Party since he entered journalism by way of politics, he gratefully remembered the help he received from prominent members of the party at different stages in his career. This help, in his words, was the "disinterested" support paternally offered by people of age and experience to a promising young talent. In this way he minimized his debt to a specific patronage group: he believed he had earned whatever help he received. For this journalist, clientelism and professionalism need not be antagonists: on the contrary, "good" clientelism actually rewards professionalism. "If I did not have the stuff for this job," he said, "they [the Party] probably would have stopped me from doing it—I say probably, I don't know." It is difficult not to think of this as an *ex post facto* rationalization, however, since his real acknowledgement of the role played by clientelistic networks in the advancements of his career would crack the veneer of the "professional" that he, like others, is concerned to preserve. His relationship to clientelism is above all instrumental—a means to the achievement of professional goals. While we would hesitate to call this journalist representative, there are enough like him to suggest that however much the members of the new professional middle class set themselves in opposition to clientelism, their behavior is frequently characterized, pragmatically, by compromise.

The New Class in Southern Italy

The action of the New Class in southern Italy can only be understood in relation to the historical transformation of the region. As Gramsci knew, the intellectuals' role in society can not be deduced from the content of their activity, but only discerned from the network of social relationships and circumstances in which they find themselves.

New Class professionals are among the actual heirs of a middle class of intellectual professionals in the south who until recently had a slice of power thanks to their monopoly over specialized intellectual functions. Expanded university education, the creation of a huge public and private services industry, and other factors have eroded the power of this class while at the same time contributing to the rise of a New Class of professionals, specialists in what we have been calling "symbolic knowledge." These are the "heirs" of the old doctors, lawyers, and engineers in only a limited sense. While remaining members of the older group within the local culture, our interviewees tend to lean strongly to the left and see themselves as members of an intellectual community whose borders extend far beyond Calabria. They are often at odds with the local culture, and present themselves to the community as the ideal facilitators of a process of "renewal" and integration into a wider cultural world. In some ways they are a new *generation* of the middle class: new due to the novelty of their professions, but also due to the particular features of their socialization. The meaning of their activities is not understandable outside the context of their social milieu. In this milieu—peripheral and, in most ways, traditional—they are the agents of a modernization process.

The "modernization" of which this New Class is the bearer finds expression in different ways. In all cases its members see themselves as "educators" as well as "pioneers." The culture they embody and diffuse is a secularized culture, pluralist in the field of knowledge, left-leaning on moral issues, open to self-criticism. It is indeed part of the "New Class culture" whose rise in Western societies Gouldner predicted. Here, however, the main feature of this culture is the promotion and diffusion of the principle of professionalism and, with it, of a logic of abstract relationships among citizens in the public sphere. In this sense the social function of the New Class in southern Italy is somewhat different from that described in other chapters of this volume. Rather than slipping the rationalization process into particular spheres of life that have not yet been touched by it—as for example in the "life-style engineering" described by Heuberger, Kellner, and Berger—the New Class in southern Italy is burdened with the task of *introducing* the rationalization process into an entire society that remains on many counts determined to reject it.

In general, what we have seen in southern Italy is the formation, since the Second World War, of a class of public employees who do not control the means of production but who otherwise handle the public resources of a society whose economy greatly depends on them. This class, the "state bourgeoisie," is made up of elites who ally themselves with the parties in power and act according to a clientelistic logic, and of subordinate layers of white-collar workers who administer the bureaucratic sectors of the public services according to a logic of "favors." This class has an explicit interest in the expansion of the welfare state, but it denies, in substance, the universalistic logic at the heart of the welfare system, since acceptance of the idea of the "common good" would oblige this class to make nonparticularistic, nonprivatistic use of the resources at its disposal.

Opposing the interests of this class are the New Classes who want to make their *professionalism* a bankable resource. The claim that credentials and expertise ought to confer substantial privileges—namely, money and power—is commonly made today by major sectors of the middle class in all of Italy. Their commitment to the idea of the common good, together with their claim to economic power, implies a curiously mixed allegiance to *both* the welfare state and the free market. Perhaps the commitment of the New Class to the public good enhances their status as professionals simply by distancing them from dependence on cultivating relationships with "patrons" and "friends."

Our research points to a vertical separation between two *types* of middle classes, but not, however, between a *symbolic knowledge* class and a *business* class. Thanks to the area's weak industrialization, an autonomous business class has never had the chance to develop. In Cosenza—and probably in the entire south—the members of the knowledge class are allied with at least those sectors of the business class who want to free the market from the stronghold of clientelism and to promote their own professional abilities. While the old bureaucratic classes benefit from the absence of a *public* sphere that functions as such, these members of the middle class are developing a concept of the public sphere that is unprecedented in the southern Italian context: a truly *public* sphere that operates according to legal-rational rules, in such a way that the universal rights the welfare state ostensibly came into being to secure will finally be realized.

At least in the cases we have analyzed, however, the new middle class seems disinclined to mobilize itself politically. While some time ago its members were the protagonists of an important phase of mobilization—the late 1960s and all that followed—today they prefer to pursue political objectives related to day-to-day life, or, more frequently, to join professional associations rather than political movements. In many ways they manifest the political ambivalence or indeterminacy that has always been a salient characteristic of the middle classes in modern societies, to whom the possibility of finding a relatively privileged niche in the social system is more attractive than taking sides in political conflicts. For its part, the patron-client system—which relies on and enforces personal, mutually beneficial relationships between members of different status groups—is hostile, in substance, to the formation of class consciousness and class conflicts.[79] But in the present-day south—where immigration no longer creates tensions, where income and the expectation of well-being have grown enormously, where local and national culture are becoming more and more integrated—the clientelistic system meets growing opposition from marginal social groups who see themselves excluded from the selective criteria by which privileges are distributed. On the side of these groups are members of the new middle class who are no longer willing to pay the social costs of clientelism and who hope to reap new privileges on the basis of their professional status.

Returning to the New Class, we can conclude by saying that its development in the south remains in the embryonic stage. We have identified occupational groups with an important role to play in the modernization process, but who, at least for now, lack the social and political legitimacy required to become real agents of cultural change. In this context it would be out of place to hypothesize, as others have, that the New Class is antagonistic toward capitalism, since the capitalism of southern Italy is a rather particular institution. Moreover, the members of the professions we have considered can hardly be called a "class": they do not see themselves as such, nor can we point yet to a functional difference between the knowledge class and the business class. It is true, however, that these groups are guiding the process of rationalization and secularization in the south, and that, politically, they hardly qualify as conservatives. For the most part, however, the collective identity of these new middle classes is yet to be determined.

Notes

Chapter Two

1   A very good discussion and resume of the development of the New Class, from which I learned a lot, is given by Ch. Joppke, *Zur Theorie der New Class*, manuscript, Frankfurt am Main 1985, 79-165.

2   Harrington's attempt to classify in a personal fashion theorists according to their "attitudes toward the New Class(es)" seems in many respects to be extremely unconvincing, particularly also since his definition of the New Class remains rather vague.

3   A number of neoconservative critics of the New Class see themselves, following Schumpeter's view, as part of this class. Thus one could prolong the subtitle of Bruce-Briggs' New Class reader "America's Educated Elite Examined By ... America's Educated Elite."

4   The term New Class has a long and varied history that goes back to Michael Bakunin. Bakunin did not believe in the emergence of a power position in the form of a "dictatorship of the proletariat" but rather in a "new class, a hierarchy of real and pretended scientists and scholars," who would rule the country after a Socialist revolution (cit. in Bruce-Briggs 1979, 11). The Yugoslav dissident Milovan Djilas contributed a new meaning to the term New Class when he spoke of the political bureaucrats and party ideologists who only want to build an economic order that is dependent on them and that would serve as the basis for their power over the whole of society (see Djilas 1957). The contemporary version, which came up in the debate of the seventies, was originally coined by Daniel Patrick Moynihan and David Bazelon. In the course of this debate it experienced shifts in meaning and reorganizations with respect to the influence and power aims of the New Class. Whereas Moynihan saw the main characteristic of New Class experts as their "enthusiasm for human welfare," Bazelon saw it manifested more generally in their interest in planning, similar to the hallmark of professionals in the technical sector. (For more details on the

215

origin and use of the term New Class see Bruce-Briggs 1979, 1-18, and Bazelon 1966, 48-53).

5   Bell speaks, using a metaphor by Warren Weaver, of the problems of "organized complexity," that is, how to deal with large organizations and systems of variables that have to be taken into consideration when rational decisions are to be made. In this way, every solution and every recipe represents a reduction in complexity. See also J.T. Barry, who directly speaks about the New Class being hired solely to manage the complexity of big organizations. J.T. Barry, "Welcome to the New Class," in *Commonweal*, 16 February 1979, 73-77.

6   For other analytically interesting theses on the new middle-class strata which are coming from a structuralist and neo-Marxist point of view, cf. N. Poulantzas, *Klassen im Kapitalismus—Heute*, Berlin-West 1975; "On Social Classes," in *New Left Review* 78, March-April 1973; S. Mallet, *Die neue Arbeiterklasse*, Neuwied/Berlin 1972; A. Gorz, *Strategy for Labor*, Boston 1967; "Technical Intelligence and the Capitalist Division of Labor," in *Telos* 12, Summer 1972. A good historical review of the new middle-class strata, with special emphasis on the German discussion of the reasons for the rise of fascism is given in Burris 1986.

7   It is unfortunate that an author like John McAdams in his otherwise excellent analysis did not heed the character of New Class knowledge. In his study he only deals with one wing of the "knowledge elite," namely that whose objective class interest is the "expansion of government's role in the economy." In this way he automatically presupposes for the New Class a hostility towards capitalism, business, and the market economy per se. See John McAdams, "Testing the Theory of the New Class," *The Sociological Quarterly* 28, 1, 23-49.

8   The authors of this volume use neither strict neoconservative nor neo-Marxist perspectives of defining the New Class phenomenon as background characterization. Instead they concentrate on the origin and actual empirical behavior of certain new professions and their relations to their clients, the state, political parties, and other power groups in order to identify their significance. This may help to provide empirical rather than theoretical insights into the internal relationship between New Class membership and concrete practical behavior. This is a crucial issue, raised in Irving Louis Horowitz 1979.

9   For an interesting discussion on the formation of the service class and its presumed political behavior see Goldthorpe 1982.

10 After the completion of this manuscript, Christopher Lasch's new book, *The True and Only Heaven*, was published. In the final chapter, Lasch discusses the New Class phenomenon along the same lines I have drawn. His assessment, however, is considerably different in that his major objective is to question the idea of progress in general. Even though he agrees with Gouldner's characterization of the New Class as the most progressive force in modern society, Lasch doubts whether this stratum can play a significant role in the "society of hope" he envisages.

Chapter Three

11 Quotation marks used in the text are generally reserved for key terms, slogans, and expressions which are regularly and significantly found in the empirical field

we have studied. We have italicized those terms which are significant from our point of view.

12   For a general discussion of the expansion of consulting services in all spheres of life cf.: H. Schelsky, *Der selbständige und der betreute Mensch*, Frankfurt am Main/Berlin/Wien 1976; I. Illich, *Entmündigung durch Experten. Zur Kritik der Dienstleistungsberufe*, Hamburg 1979; M. Schmiel, *Das Beraten*, Köln 1972.

13   From the vast literature on this subject, the following were particularly helpful: E. Heinen et al., *Unternehmenskultur, Perspektiven für Wissenschaft und Praxis*, München/Wien 1987; W.H. Staehle, *Management, Eine verhaltenswissenschaftliche Perspektive*, München 1989 (4. Aufl.); Th. J. Peters and R. H. Waterman, *In Search of Excellence*, New York 1982; E. Dülfer (Hrsg.), *Organisationskultur. Phänomen—Philosophie—Technologie*, Wiesbaden 1988; T. Deal and A. Kennedy, *Unternehmenserfolg durch Unternehmenskultur*, Bonn 1987; E. Schein, *Organizational Culture and Leadership: A Dynamic View*, San Francisco/Washington/London 1985; O. Neuberger and A. Kompa, *Wir, Die Firma*, Weinheim und Basel 1987.

14   Our study on business consulting has been carried out since 1986. It is still not totally complete; the full explanation of all the data from our study will be published in a later book. Our study does not claim representativity in the statistical sense, nor is it quantitative in its outlook. We have carried out qualitative research based on more than forty extensive open interviews with highly qualified people in the field of consulting and their clients. They are also based on extensive qualitative content analysis of various materials in this field and in various professional journals. Our qualitative method is oriented at an "understanding sociology" as defined so fruitfully by Max Weber. As an understanding sociology it is very much an interpretive approach, observing all the criteria of validity, which are of utter importance here.

15   An interesting discussion of forms of consulting can be found in the excellent empirical study by K.-D. Hohr, *Alltag der Organisationsberatung*, Diss. Frankfurt am Main 1988.

16   To what degree competence in the fields of the social sciences and psychology are demanded in contemporary forms of management and business is mirrored in the major scientific work on management in Germany: W.H. Staehle, op cit.

17   On the dubiousness of this method compare the critical account in *Management Wissen*, vol. 7, 1986.

18   For an account cf.: *Management Wissen*, vol. 2, 1988.

19   For a critical discussion of the NLP method cf.: *Psychology Heute*, Mai 1987.

20   On the closeness of pseudoscientific models to charlatanism cf.: *Management Wissen*, vol. 2, 1988.

21   For a general account of the various methods used by consultants cf.: G. Comelli, *Training als Beitrag zur Organisationsentwicklung, Handbuch der Weiterbildung für die Praxis in Wirtschaft und Verwaltung*, München 1985; W. H. Staehle, op. cit.; K.-D. Hohr, op. cit.

22   For the relevance of creativity training in organizations and techniques of creativity training compare: R. Höhn, *Die Technik der geistigen Arbeit—Bewältigung der Routine—Steigerung der Kreativität*, Bad Harzburg 1979; H. Schlicksupp, *Innovation, Kreativität und Ideenfindung*, Würzburg 1981; K.-D. Hohr, Op.Cit.

23   For a general presentation of qualitative dimensions in the consulting market cf.: "Berater und Dienstleister," *Sonderbeilagen der Frankfurter Allgemeine Zeitung* from 10 June 1986 and 3 May 1988; R. Berger und Partner GmbH, *Jahresbericht 1988* und *Geschäftsentwicklung 1989*, München 1989-90.

24   For the general discussion of the imperatives for the humanization of the world of work cf.: E. Ulich, et al., *Neue Formen der Arbeitsgestaltung—Möglichkeiten und Probleme einer Verbesserung der Qualität des Arbeitslebens*, Frankfurt am Main 1973; W. S. Neff, *Work and Human Behavior*, New York 1985; F. Herzberg, *The Managerial Choice: To be Efficient and To be Human*, Salt Lake City 1982.

25   For a critical position of the unions on business consulting cf.: J. Reindl, *Unternehmensberatung und Rationalisierung: Anleitung zur betrieblichen Gegenwehr durch Betriebsräte und Belegschaften*, Saarbrücken 1986.

26   For a general overview of the history and the types of organizational development cf.: A. v. Deym, *Organisationsplanung. Planung durch Kooperation*, Berlin/München 1979; W.H. Staehle, op. cit; R.-W. Scheuss, *Strategische Anpassung der Unternehmung*, Zürich 1984.

27   For an overview and variants on the changing structures in organizations and management compare: W. H. Staehle, op. cit; Th. J. Peters and R. H. Waterman, op. cit; R.-W. Scheuss, op. cit; H. Hinterhuber (ed.), *Zukunftsorientierte Unternehmenspolitik*, Freiburg 1984; B. Madauss, *Projektmanagement: Ein Handbuch für Industriebetriebe, Unternehmensberater und Behörden*, Stuttgart 1984.

28   On the significance of teamwork in industry cf.: H. K. Wahren, *Zwischenmenschliche Kommunikation und Interaktion im Unternehmen*, Berlin/New York 1987.

29   For a general discussion and presentation of moderation techniques cf.: D. Ibielski and N. Küster, *Handbuch der Unternehmensberatung*, Berlin 1976; E. Schnelle (ed.), *Neue Wege der Kommunikation. Spielregeln, Arbeitstechniken und Anwendungsfälle der MetaPlan-Methode*, Königstein/Ts. 1978; G. Comelli, op. cit.

30   For a general discussion of quality circles in industry and its limits cf.: D. Hutchins, *Quality Circles Handbook*, London/New York 1985; P.Beriger, *Quality Circles und Kreativität: Das Quality-circle-Konzept im Rahmen der Qualitätsförderung in der Unternehmung*, Bern/Stuttgart 1986.

Chapter Four

31   From the Ministrie van Welzijn Volksgezondheid en cultuur's "Brief over het cultuurbeleid, toegezonden aan de Tweede Kamer," 15 May 1985.

Chapter Five

32   The author was assisted in a proportion of the interviews and with background research and with translation from the German of Kellner and Heuberger's writing by Dr. Camillia Fawzi El Solh, to whom grateful thanks are offered.

33   *Code of Conduct*, Market Research Society and Industrial Marketing Association, Twentieth Century Press, London, January, 1990. The section on Basic Principles set out on P7 begins: "Research is founded upon the willing co-operation of the public and business organizations. It depends upon public and business confidence that it is conducted honestly, objectively, *without unwelcome intrusion and without harm to informants*" (my italics). A later paragraph includes the phrase "They must also be assure that ... they will in no way be *adversely affected or embarrassed* as a direct result of their participation in a research project" (my italics). There follow 20 rules designed to ensure this protection to informants. The rules are not, however, formulated in such a way as to preclude skillful use of the "disruptive techniques discussed above.

Chapter Six

34   See S. Robert Lichter, Stanley Rothman and Linda Lichter, *The Media Elite*. Bethesda: Adler and Adler, 1986.

35   This data was collected and summarized in Hunter, J. D., John Herrmann, and John Jarvis, "Cultural Elites and Political Values: A Cross-National Comparison," Under review, *Sociology: The Journal of the British Sociological Association*, 1989.

36   See Michele LaMont, "New Middle Class Liberalism and Autonomy from Profit-Making: The case of Quebec," unpublished manuscript, Princeton University, 1989.

37   These figures are derived from Robert Wuthnow, *The Restructuring of American Religion*. Princeton: Princeton University Press, 1988. See also David Knoke, *Organizing for Collective Action: The Political Economy of Associations*. New York: Aldine, 1990.

38   From a personal conversation with the authors, October 1988.

39   From a personal conversation with the authors, October 1988. Subsequent statements attributed to Newkirk are from this interview unless otherwise noted.

40   As quoted by Mike Sager, "Inhuman Bondage," *Rolling Stone* (24 March 1988): 178.

41   As quoted by Laura Smith, "Aiding the Homeless His Own Way," *The Declaration*, Charlottesville, Va. (5 October 1989): 5-6; and by Gwenda Blair, "Saint Mitch," *Esquire* (December, 1986): 226-228.

42   From a personal conversation with the authors, October 1988.

43   From a telephonic conversation with the authors, October 1988.

44   As reported in the *Society for the Right to Die: The First 50 Years 1938-1988*, privately printed.

45   As quoted by Mike Sager, "Inhuman Bondage," 178.

46   As reported by Andy Merton, "Bill Baird's Holy War," *Esquire* (February 1981): 25-31.

47   As reported in "Biting the Hand: A Reynolds Battles Smoking," *Newsweek* (28 July 1986): 45.

48   As reported in "Hollywood's Activists, Taking up the Banner," *Washington Post* (10 April 1989): B 1-2.

49   "Do Not Hop Gently into That Good Night," *Fortune* (1 January 1990): 64.

50   As reported by Frank Clancy in "Heroes from Hard Times," *Mother Jones* (July-August 1986): 22.

51   From an interview reported in Ronald J. Troyer and Gerald E. Markel, *Cigarettes: The Battle Over Smoking*. New Brunswick: Rutgers, 1982, 85-86.

52   Rachel Burd, "Pro-Abortion Strategies," *Village Voice* (11 April 1989): 35.

53   Philip Kotler and Eduardo L. Roberto, *Social Marketing: Strategies for Changing Public Behavior*. New York: Free Press, 1989.

54   As quoted by Jon Steinberg, "The Body Biz," *Ms.* (September 1988): 52.

55   As reported by Joan O'C. Hamilton, Emily T. Smith, et al., "'No Smoking' Sweeps America: Smokers Are Fast Becoming Outcasts—Both Socially and Legally," *Business Week* (27 July 1987): 40-46.

56   As reported by Otto Friedrich, Robert Ajemiam, et al., "Where There's Smoke," *Time* (23 February 1987): 22-23.

57   "Warning: Anti-Smoking Crusade Dangerous to Your Rights," *Workers Vanguard* (20 May 1988), Excerpted in Harper's (September 1988): 20-21.

58   Quoted by Lawrence J. Lebowitz, "Brophy Revisited," *Massachusetts Medicine* (January-February 1987): 14.

59   Society for the Rights to Die Newsletter, September 1988, 3.

60   "Pro-Abortion Strategies," *Village Voice* (11 April 1989): 35.

61   As quoted by Merton in "Bill Baird's Holy War."

62   Quoted by Lisa Distelheim, "The Entrepreneur," *Life* (September 1988): 28.

63   As quoted by Blair, "Saint Mitch."

64   As quoted by Merton, "Bill Baird's Holy War."

65   Gary Francione, in a roundtable discussion published in *Harper's* (August 1988): 44-52.

66   As quoted by Debbie Nathan in "Jane Roe Speaks Out," *Village Voice* (11 April 1989): 44.

67   Anonymous, "Real Corpses," *Village Voice* (11 April 1989): 31.

68   Ingrid Newkirk in a roundtable discussion published in *Harper's* (August 1988): 44-52. Emphasis ours.

69   Fenella Rouse, "Legal and Ethical Guidelines for Physicians in Geriatric Personal Care," *Geriatrics* 43 (August 1988): 69.

70   Position paper, "Position of the American Academy of Neurology on Certain Aspects of the Care and Management of the Persistent-Vegetative-State-Patient," adopted by the Executive Board of the American Academy of Neurology, (21 April 1988).

71   See LaMont in the work cited.

Chapter Seven

72   What follows is based on forty long interviews with bureaucrats and New Class professionals, as well as on materials made available to us by the interviewees (brochures, policy statements, etc.). Cosimo Conte, Sonia Floriani, and Catia Zumpano assisted the author in conducting the interviews.

73   Sylos Labini pointed out these shifts in 1974. What is interesting is that, in the north, the new white-collar workers are about equally distributed over the public and private sectors while in the south, the majority work for the state. A. Pizzorno "*I Ceti medi nei meccanismi del consenso*," (in Cavazza and Graubard)

suggests a political reason for this: the conservative middle class functions as a "consent machine" in favoring the alliance between the great industrialists of the north and the upper state bourgeoisie of the south. To us this theory is no longer entirely satisfying. As we'll see in this chapter, the new middle classes are less willing to consent to such an alliance, a reluctance in keeping with their anticonservative political tendencies.

74 The idea of such an "elective affinity" was first put forward by Frank Parkin. It is neither practical nor desirable here to give a detailed account of the student protest movements. What should be remembered, however, is that the Italian student movements were somewhat different from those in America or other parts of Europe. First of all, the period of mobilization began in 1968, here as elsewhere, but here it continued for a good ten years, and largely cut across class and educational boundaries. In fact, the student movements were very closely linked with the protests of certain strata of the working class.

75 The *consultorio familiare* are probably the Italian equivalent of what are called "family-planning" clinics in America, where users, mostly women, are given advice and assistance in contraception, prenatal care, "parenting," and family life. They were established in the 1970s when laws on abortion and divorce were radically revised, largely in response to the feminist movement. Territorial mental health services were set up when large numbers of the mentally ill were deinstitutionalized in 1978. In general, these new health services are oriented toward prevention rather than cure, and combine medical treatment with social intervention. The latter point implies the sociological disease paradigm that gained adherents in the 1970s but is now the subject of widespread criticism. The extent to which this criticism has taken root is suggested by the fact that social and health-care services are almost always administered separately under new government policies.

76 See Jackson and Larson.

77 Most areas have local newspapers, but nearly every other Italian periodical is published in Rome or Lombardy. Book publishing is more diffused, but remains concentrated in the north and central regions. And Milan is fast becoming the headquarters for most of the television networks.

78 A further constraint on the development of a free market here is the "long shadow" of the Mafia. Those who run small businesses don't advertise if they're hiding from the mob.

79 On the obstacles that clientelism puts in the way of collective action in general and class action in particular see L. Roniger, "Social Stratification in Southern Europe," in Eisenstadt et al (1984).

Bibliography

Achterhuis, H. *De markt van welzijn en geluk*. Baarn, 1980.

Adriaansens, H.P.M. en A. C. Zijderveld. *Vrijwillig initiatief en de verzorgingsstaat*. Deventer, 1981.

Anonymous, "Real Corpses." *Village Voice* (11 April 1989): 35.

Archer, Margret S. and Salvador Giner, editors. *Contemporary Europe: Class, Status, and Power*. London: Weidenfeld and Nicolson, 1980.

Bagnasco, A. *Le tre Italie*. Bologna: Il Mulino, 1977.

Baldissera, A. *La svolta dei quarantamila*. Torino: Comunita, 1988.

Barca, L. *Le classi intermedie*. Rome: Editori Riuniti, 1989.

Barry, J.T., "Welcome to the New Class." *Commonweal* (16 February 1979): 73-77.

Baudrillard, Jean. *Selected Writings*. Edited by Mark Poster. Stanford: Stanford University Press, 1988.

Bazelon, David T. "The New Class." *Commentary* (August 1966): 48-53.

Becker, H.S. *Art Worlds*. Berkeley: University of California Press, 1982.

van Beetz, F. "Cultuur en Steden." *Rijks Planologische Dienst*. Jaarverslag 1988. s-Gravenhage, 1989.

Bell, Daniel. *The Coming of Post-Industrial Society*. London: Heinemann, 1974.

Bell, Daniel. *The Cultural Contradictions of Capitalism*. London: Heinemann, 1976.

Bell, D. "The New Class: A Muddled Concept." B. Bruce-Briggs, ed., *The New Class?* 169-90.

Bell, Donald. "Up from Patriarchy." Robert A. Lewis editor. *Men in Difficult Times*. Englewood Cliffs, N.J.: Prentice Hall 1985.

Berger, Peter L. *The Capitalist Revolution*. New York: Basic Books, 1986.

Berger, Peter L. "The Worldview of the New Class: Secularity and its Discontents." B. Bruce-Briggs, ed., *The New Class?* 49-55.

Berger, R. und Partner GmbH. *Jahresbericht 1988 und Geschäftsentwicklung 1989*. Munich, 1989, 1990.

Beriger, P. *Quality Circles und Kreativität: Das Quality-circle-Konzept in Rahmen der Qualitätsförderung in der Unternehmung*. Bern/Stuttgart, 1986.

van Berkel, K. *Renaissance van de cultuurwetenschap*. Amsterdam, 1986.

Berman, Marshall. *All that is Solid Melts into Air*. New York: Simon and Schuster, 1982.

Bevers, A. M. "Cultuurspreiding en publieksbereik. Van volksverheffing tot marktstrategie." A.M. Bevers, editor. *Ons diaconale land. Opstellen over cultuurspreiding*. Amsterdam, 1988. 64-99.

Bevers, A.M. "Particulier initiatief en cultuur. Over de roi van burgers en overheid bij de opriching en consolidering van kunstinstellingen." *Sociologisch Tijdschrift* jrg. 14, 2, 1987. 255-90.

"Biting the Hand: A Reynolds Battles Smoking." *Newsweek* (28 July 1986): 45.

Blair, Gwenda. "Saint Mitch." *Esquire* (December 1986): 226-28.

Boissevain, J. "Patronage in Sicily." *Man* 1, 1966.

Bourdieu, Pierre. *Reproduction*. London: Sage, 1977.

Bourdieu, Pierre. *Distinctions*. Translated by R. Nice. London: Routledge and Kegan Paul, 1984.

Brint, Steven. "'New Class' and Cumulative Trend Explanations of the Liberal Political Attitudes of Professionals." *American Journal of Sociology* 90, 1 (July 1984): 30-71.

Bruce-Briggs, Barry, editor. *The New Class?* New Brunswick, N.J.: Transaction Books, 1979.

Brugman, H. and M. Vernoy. "Ware vriendschap is wederzijds." *Onderzoek van de Nederlanse Federatie van Vrienden van Musea.* Laren, 1989.

Burd, Rachel. "Pro-Abortion Strategies." *Village Voice* (11 April 1989): 35.

Burnham, James. *The Managerial Revolution.* Bloomington: Indiana University Press, 1957.

Burris, Val. "The Discovery of the New Middle Class." *Theory and Society* 15 (1986): 317-49.

CBS, *1899-1984. Vijfentachtig jaren statistiek in tijdreeksen.* Den Haag: Staatsuitgeverij, 1984.

CBS, *Sociale en Culturele Verkenningen 1988.* Statistiek van het vrijwilligerswerk.

Carboni, C. editor. *I ceti medi in Italia.* Bari: Laterza, 1981.

Carboni, C. editor. *Classi e movimenti in Italia, 1970-1985.* Bari: Laterza, 1986.

Carboni, C. editor. *Appropriazione statale del tessuto sociale e nuovi movimenti collettivi.* Milan: Angeli, 1986.

Catanzaro, R. *L'imprenditore assistito.* Bologna: Il Mulino, 1979.

Catanzaro, R. "Struttura sociale, sistema politico e azione collettiva nel Mezzogiorno." *Stato e Mercato* 8, 1983.

Catanzaro, R. editor. *Società, politica e cultura nel Mezzogiorno.* Milan: Angeli, 1989.

Cavazza, Fabio Luca and Stephen R. Grabaud, editors. *Il caso italiano.* Milan: Garzanti, 1975.

Chandler, Jon, Angela Henry, and Mike Owen. *New Product Development and Paradigms.* Context Research, 103A Oxford Street, London W1R ITF, October 1988.

Chaney, David. "The Department Store as Cultural Form." *Theory, Culture, and Society* 1, 3, 1983.

Chubb, Judith. *Patronage, Power, and Poverty in Southern Italy.* Cambridge: Cambridge University Press, 1982.

Clancy, Frank. "Heroes from Hard Times." *Mother Jones* (July-August 1986): 22.

Collins, R. *The Credential Society. An Historical Sociology of Education and Stratification.* New York: Academic Press, 1979.

Comelli, G. "Training als Beitrag zur Organisationsentwicklung." *Handbuch der Weiterbildung für die Praxis in Wirtschaft und Verwaltung.* Munich, 1985.

Congi, G. *Imprenditori e impresa in Calabria.* Cosenza: Marra, 1986.

Dahrendorf, Ralf. *Class and Class Conflict in Industrial Society.* Palo Alto, Cal.: Stanford University Press, 1959.

Dalla Chiesa, N. *Il Giano bifronte.* Milan: Etas Libri, 1987.

Deal, T. and A. Kennedy. *Unternehmenserfolg durch Unternehmenskultur.* Bonn, 1987.

von Deym, A. *Organisationsplanung. Planung durch Kooperation.* Berlin/Munich, 1979.

DiMaggio, P. "Classification in Art." *American Sociological Review.* 1987. 52: 440-55.

Distelheim, Lisa. "The Entrepreneur," *Life* (September 1988): 28.

Djilas, Milovan. *The New Class.* New York: Praeger, 1967.

"Do Not Hop Gently into that Good Night," *Fortune* (1 January 1990): 64.

van Doorn, J.A.A. *Rede en Macht.* Den Haag, 1989.

Drion, H. "De rode draad in de burgerlijke cultuur." *Vrije Nederland.* 4 January 1986.

Dülfer, E. (Hrsg.) *Organisationskultur. Phänomen—Philosophie— Technologie.* Wiesbaden, 1988.

Eco, Umberto. "Interview." *The Independent Magazine.* London (23 September 1989).

Ehrenreich, Barbara and John Ehrenreich. "The Professional-Managerial Class." *Radical America* 11, 2 (March/April 1977).

Ehrenreich, Barbara and John Ehrenreich. "The New Left and the Professional-Managerial Class." *Radical America* 11, 3 (May/June 1977).

Eisenstadt, S.N. and R. Lemarchand. *Political Clientelism, Patronage, and Development.* London: Sage, 1981.

Eisenstadt, S.N. and L. Roniger. *Patrons, Clients and Friends.* Cambridge: Cambridge University Press, 1984.

Eisenstadt, S.N., L. Roniger, and A. Seligman. *Center-Formation, Protest Movements, and Class Structure in Europe and the United States.* New York: New York University Press, 1987.

Evaluatie van het Beleid van de Minister WVC op het gebied van de Beeldende kunsten, Bouwkunst en vormgeving in het tijdvak 1984-1987. Ministrie van Welzijn, Volksgezondheid en Cultuur. Rijswijk, 1988.

Fantozzi, P. "I sistemi di relazione." *Progetto* 23, 1984.

Featherstone, Mike. "Consumer Culture: An Introduction." *Theory Culture and Society* 1, 3, 1983.

Featherstone, Mike. "Lifestyle and Consumer Culture." *Theory, Culture and Society* 1, 1 (1987a).

Featherstone, Mike. "Towards a Sociology of Postmodern Culture." Paper prepared for the symposium "Social Structure and Culture," organized by the Sociological Theories Section of the German Sociological Association. University of Bremen, June 1987b.

Featherstone, Mike. "Consumer Culture, Postmodernism and Global Disorder." Paper presented at the Conference on Religion and the Quest for Global Order. St. Martin, West Indies: Mimeo, October 1987c.

Fischer, G. "Wiederaufbereitung im Bayerischen Wald." *Manager Magazin* (December 1986).

Francione, Gary. "Roundtable Discussion." *Harper's* (August 1988): 44-52.

Frankfurter Allgemeine Zeitung, major daily newspaper in Germany.

Freidson, E. *Professional Powers*. Chicago, London: University of Chicago Press, 1986.

Freidson, E. "Les professions artistiques comme defi a l'analyse sociologique." *Revue Francaise de Sociologie*. 1986. 431-443.

Friedrich, Otto, Robert Ajemiam, et al. "Where There's Smoke." *Time* (23 February 1987): 22-23.

Galbraith, John Kenneth. *The New Industrial State*. Boston: 1967.

Gambetta, D. *Trust: Making and Breaking Cooperative Relations*. Oxford: Basil Blackwell, 1988.

Gehlen, A. *Zeit-Bilder. Zur Soziologie und Ästhetik der modernen Malerei*. Frankfurt am Main, 1965.

Giddens, Anthony. *The Class Structure of Advanced Societies*. London: Hutchinson, 1973.

Glazer, N. "Lawyers and the New Class." B. Bruce-Briggs, ed. *The New Class?* 89-100.

Goldthorpe, J. "On the Service Class, Its Formation and Future." *Social Class and the Division of Labour*. A. Giddens and G. Mackenzie, editors. Cambridge, 1982: 162-85.

Goodyear, Mary, Market Behaviour Ltd. "The Writing on the Wall." *MRS Newsletter*, March 1989.

Gorz, A. *Strategy for Labor*. Boston, 1967.

Gorz A. "Technical Intelligence and the Capitalist Division of Labor." *Telos* 12 (Summer 1972).

Gouldner, Alvin W. *The Future of Intellectuals and the Rise of the New Class*. New York: Seabury, 1979.

Gramsci, Antonio. *Gli intellettuali e l'organizzazione della cultura*. Torino: Einaudi, 1949.

Graziani, A. and E. Pugliese. *Investimenti e disoccupazione nel Mezzogiorno*. Milan: Angeli, 1979.

Graziani, A. "Mezzogiorno oggi." *Meridiana* 1 (1987).

Graziano, L., editor. *Clientelismo e mutamento politico*. Milan: Angeli, 1974.

Gribaudi, G. *Mediatori*. Torino: Rosenberg & Sellier, 1980.

Haanstra, F., editor. *De Samenhang onderwijs-beroepspraktijk in de sector van de beeldende kunsten*. Beleidsgerichte studies van Hoger onderwijs en Wetenschappelijk onderzoek nr. 12. SCO. Amsterdam, 1987.

Habermas, Jürgen. "The Public Sphere." *New German Critique* 2 (1962).

Habermas, Jürgen. *Strukturwandel der Öffentlichkeit*. Neuwied: Hermann Luchterhand Verlag, 1974.

Hacker, A. "Two 'New Classes' or None?" B. Bruce-Briggs, ed., *The New Class?* 155-68.

Hamilton, Joan O'C., Emily T. Smith, et al. "'No Smoking' Sweeps America: Smokers are Fast Becoming Outcasts—Both Socially and Legally." *Business Week* (27 July 1987): 40-46.

Harrington, M. "The New Class and the Left." B. Bruce-Briggs, ed., *The New Class?* 123-138.

Heinen, E. et al. *Unternehmenskultur, Perspektiven für Wissenschaft und Praxis*. Munich/Vienna, 1987.

Herzberg, F. *The Managerial Choice: To be Efficient or to be Human*. Salt Lake City: Olympus, 1982.

Hinterhuber, H., editor. *Zukunftsorientierte Unternehmenspolitik.* Freiburg, 1984.

Hochschild, Arlie R. *The Managed Heart.* Berkeley/Los Angeles: University of California Press, 1983.

Hochschild, Arlie R. "Reply to Cas Wouters' Essay on *The Managed Heart.*" *Theory, Culture, and Society* 6, 3 (1989): 439-45.

Höhn, R. *Die Technik der geistigen Arbeit—Bewältigung der Routine—Steigerung der Kreativität,* Bad Harzburg, 1979.

Hohr, K.-D. *Alltag der Organisationsberatung.* Diss. Frankfurt am Main, 1988.

"Hollywood's Activists, Taking up the Banner." *Washington Post* (10 April 1989): B 1-2.

Hoogbergen, T. "Zorgen om een cultureel klimaat." *School* 1, 1-89.

Horowitz, Irving Louis. *Winners and Losers. Social and Political Polarities in America.* Durham, N.C.: Duke University Press, 1984. First published as "On the Expansion of New Theories and the Withering Away of Old Classes." *Society* 16, 2 (January/February 1979).

Hunter, J.D., John Herrmann, and John Jarvis. "Cultural Elites and Political Values: A Cross-National Comparison," under review, *Sociology: The Journal of the British Sociological Association,* 1989.

Hutchins, D. *Quality Circles Handbook.* London/New York: Pitman, 1985.

Ibielski D. and N. Küster. *Handbuch der Unternehmensberatung.* Berlin, 1976.

Illich, I. *Entmündigung durch Experten. Zur Kritik der Dienstleistungsberufe.* Hamburg, 1979

Jackson, J. A., editor. *Professions and Professionalization.* Cambridge: Cambridge University Press, 1970.

Jedlowski, P. "Il servizio informale." *Inchiesta* 74 (1986).

Joppke, Ch. "Zur Theorie der New Class." Manuscript, Frankfurt am Main, 1985.

Kellner, Hansfried, and Frank Heuberger, "Zur Rationalität der 'Postmoderne' und Ihrer Träger." *Soziale Welt* 8, Sonderband 6, *Kultur und Alltag* (1988).

Kellner, Hansfried, and Frank Heuberger. Working papers, "New Class Project: Check-list of Central Dimensions." 1987a.

Kellner, Hansfried, and Frank Heuberger. Working papers, "Modern Professionalism—Overt and Hidden Technocrats." 1987b.

Kempers, B. "De macht van de markt; aanbod, afname en bemiddeling van moderne kunst in Nederland." *Kunst en Beleid in Nederland* nr.3, Amsterdam, 1988. 13-66.

Kirkpatrick, J.K. "Politics and the New Class." B. Bruce-Briggs, ed., *The New Class?* 33-48.

Kleinman, Philip. *The Saatchi and Saatchi Story.* London: Weidenfeld and Nicholson, 1987.

Knoke, David. *Organizing for Collective Action: The Political Economy of Associations.* New York: Aldine, 1990.

Knulst, W.P. "Van vaudeville tot video." *Sociale en Culturele Studies-12.* Sociaal en Cultureel Planbureau. 's-Gravenhage, 1989.

Konrád, Gyorgi, and Iván Szelényi. *The Intellectuals on the Road to Class Power.* New York: Harcourt Brace Jovanovich, 1979.

Kotler, Philip and Eduardo L. Roberto, *Social Marketing: Strategies for Changing Public Behavior.* New York: Free Press, 1989.

Kreukels, A.M.J. en J.B.D. Simonis (red.). Publiek Domein. *De veranderende balans tussen staat en samenlevving.* Jaarboek Beleid en Maatschappij. Meppel, 1988.

Kriesi, Hanspeter. "The New Social Movements and the New Class in the Netherlands." *American Journal of Sociology* 94, 5 (March 1989): 1078-1116.

Kristol, Irving. *Two Cheers for Capitalism.* New York: Basic Books, 1978.

Kuhry, B. and R. Van Opstal. "De arbeidsmarkt naar opleidinscategorie 1975-2000." *Centraal Planbureau-Werkdocument.* nr. 17. 's-Gravenhage, 1987.

"Kunst te leen. Oorsprong, opkomst en bloei van de artotheek." *Vrij Nederland* (28 January 1989).

LaMont, Michele. "Commentary and Debate," *American Journal of Sociology* 92, 6 (May 1987): 1501-06.

LaMont, Michele. "New Middle Class Liberalism and Autonomy from Profit-Making: The Case of Quebec." Unpublished manuscript, Princeton University, 1989.

Larson, Magali. *The Rise of Professionalism.* Berkeley/Los Angeles: University of California Press, 1977.

Lasch, Christopher. *The True And Only Heaven. Progress and Its Critics.* New York, London: Norton, 1991.

Lash, Scott, and John Urry. *The End of Organized Capitalism.* Oxford: Polity Press, 1987.

Lebowitz, Lawrence J. "Brophy Revisited." *Massachusetts Medicine* (January-February 1987): 14.

Leiss, William. "The Icons of the Market Place." *Theory, Culture and Society* 1, 3, 1983.

Lichter, S. Robert, Stanley Rothman, and Linda Lichter. *The Media Elite.* Bethesda, Md.: Adler and Adler, 1986.

Lodge, David. *Nice Work.* London: Secker and Warburg, 1988.

McAdams, John. "Testing the Theory of the New Class." *Sociological Quarterly* 28, 1 (1987): 23-49.

Madauss, B. *Projektmanagement: Ein Handbuch für Industriebetriebe, Unternehmensberater und Behörden.* Stuttgart: 1984.

Mallet, S. *Die Neue Arbeiterklasse.* Neuwied/Berlin, 1972.

Management Wissen, monthly journal published in Germany.

Manfredi, John. *The Social Limits of Art.* Amherst: University of Massachusetts Press, 1982.

Market Research Society Newsletter, May 1989.

Market Research Society and Industrial Marketing Association. *Code of Conduct.* London: Twentieth Century Press, January 1990.

Martin, Bernice. *A Sociology of Contemporary Cultural Change.* Oxford: Blackwell, 1981.

Meer dan 1 miljard. De economische betekenis van de professionele kunsten in Amsterdam. SEO-rapport. Stichting voor Economisch Onderzoek, Universiteit van Amsterdam. Amsterdam, 1985.

Merton, Andy. "Bill Baird's Holy War." *Esquire* (February 1981): 25-31.

Mills, C. Wright. *White Collar.* New York: Oxford University Press, 1951.

Mooij, J.J.A. *De wereld der waarden. Essays over cultuur en samenleving.* Amsterdam, 1987. Zie: "De veerkracht van het burgerlijk cultuurideaal." 89-109.

Moulin, R. "De l'artisan au professionnel: l'artiste." *Sociologie du Travail* 4 (1983). 388-403.

"Museumbeleid in de jaren tachtig, een inventarisatie." *Metropolis M* nr. 5/6 1987. Themanummer over het beleid van directeuren van musea voor moderne en hedendaagse kunst.

Nathan, Debbie. "Jane Roe Speaks Out." *Village Voice* (11 April 1989): 44.

Neff, Walter Scott. *Work and Human Behavior.* New York: Aldine, 1985.

Neuberger O. and A. Kompa. *Wir, Die Firma.* Weinheim/Basel: 1987.

Newkirk, Ingrid. "Roundtable Discussion." *Harper's* (August 1988): 44-52.

van Noort, W. *Bevlogen Bewegingen. Een vergelijking van de anti-kernenergie-,kraak—en milieubeweging.* Nijmegen, 1988.

Oosterbaan Martinius, W. *Schoonheid Welzijn Kwaliteit.* Amsterdam, 1985.

Paci, M., editor. *Capitalismo e classi sociali in Italia.* Bologna: Il Mulino, 1978.

Parkin, Frank. *Class Inequality and Political Order: Social Stratification in Capitalist and Communist Societies.* London: Paladin, 1971.

Parkin, Frank. *Middle Class Radicalism.* Manchester: Manchester University Press, 1968.

Peters, T.J. and R.H. Waterman. *In Search of Excellence.* New York: 1982.

Pizzorno, A. "I ceti medi nei meccanismi del consenso." Cavazza, F.L. and S. Graubard. *Il caso italiano.* Milan: Garzanti, 1974.

Polanyi, K. *The Great Transformation.* New York: Holt, Rinehart & Winston, 1944.

Position Paper, "Position of the American Academy of Neurology on Certain Aspects of the Care and Management of the Persistent-Vegetative-State-Patient," adopted by the Executive Board of the American Academy of Neurology, 21 April 1988.

Poulantzas, N. *Klassen im Kapitalismus—Heute.* Berlin-West: VSA, 1975.

Poulantzas, N. "On Social Classes." *New Left Review* 78 (March/April 1973).

Prandstaller, P. *Forze sociali emergenti: quali, perché.* Milan: Angeli, 1988.

Prandstaller, P. *Le nuove professioni nel terziario.* Milan: Angeli, 1989.

Pryor, F. L. "The 'New Class': The Concept, the Hypothesis and the Idea as a Research Tool." *The American Journal of Economics and Sociology* 40, 4 (October 1981): 367-80.

Psychologie Heute, monthly journal published in Germany.

Reindl, J. *Unternehmensberatung und Rationalisierung: Anleitung zur betrieblichen Gegenwehr durch Betriebsräte und Belegschaften.* Saarbrücken, 1986.

Riesman, David. *The Lonely Crowd.* New Haven: Yale University Press, 1950.

Rouse, Fenella. "Legal and Ethical Guidelines for Physicians in Geriatric Personal Care." *Geriatrics* 43 (August 1988): 69.

Sager, Mike. "Inhuman Bondage." *Rolling Stone* (24 March 1988): 178.

Schein, Edgar H. *Organizational Culture and Leadership.* San Francisco: Jossey-Bass Publishers, 1985.

Schelsky, Helmut. *Die Arbeit tun die Anderen.* Opladen, 1975.

Schelsky, Helmut. *Der selbständige und der betreute Mensch.* Frankfurt am Main/Berlin/Vienna, 1976.

Scheuss, R.-W. *Strategische Anpassung der Uternehmung.* Zürich, 1984.

Schlicksupp, H. *Innovation, Kreativität und Ideenfindung.* Würzburg, 1981.

Schmiel, M. *Das Beraten.* Cologne, 1972.

Schnelle, E., editor. *Neue Wege der Kommunikation. Spielregeln, Arbeitstechniken und Anwendungsfälle der MetaPlan-Methode.* Königstein/Ts., 1978.

Schumpeter, Joseph. *Capitalism, Socialism, and Democracy.* New York: Harper Brothers, 1942.

SCP 1988. Sociaal en Cultureel Planbureau. Sociaal en Cultureel Rapport 1988. 's-Gravenhage, 1988.

Séguéla, J. *Ne dites pas á ma mère que je suis dans la publicité ... Elle me croit pianiste dans un bordel.* Paris: Flammarion, 1986.

Siebert, R. "Tra pubblico e privato, la famiglia." *Politica ed Economia* 6 (1986).

Smith, Laura. "Aiding the Homeless His Own Way." *The Declaration*, Charlottesville, Virginia (5 October 1989): 5-6.

Society for the Right to Die Newsletter, September 1988, 3.

Society for the Right to Die: The First 50 Years 1938-1988. Privately printed.

Staehle, W.H. *Management, Eine verhaltenswissenschaftliche Perspektive.* Munich, 1989 (4. Aufl.)

Stearns, Peter N. *Be a Man: Males in Modern Society.* New York and London: Holmes and Meier, 1979.

Steinberg, Jon. "The Body Biz." *Ms.* (September 1988): 52.

Steinfels, Peter. *The Neoconservatives.* New York: Simon and Schuster, 1979.

de Swann, A. *Kwaliteit is klasse.* Amsterdam, 1985.

de Swann, Abram. *In Care of the State: Health Care, Education, and Welfare in Europe and the USA in the Modern Era.* Cambridge: Polity Press; Oxford: In association with Basil Blackwell, 1988.

Sylos Labini, Paolo. *Saggio sulle classi sociali.* Rome: Laterza, 1975.

Toffler, Alvin. *The Culture Consumers.* New York: St. Martin's Press, 1964.

Touraine, Alain. *The Post-Industrial Society.* New York: Random House, 1971.

Tousijn, W. *Le libere professioni in Italia.* Bologna: Il Mulino, 1987.

Troyer, Ronald J. and Gerald E. Markel. *Cigarettes: The Battle over Smoking.* New Brunswick, N.J.: Rutgers University Press, 1982, 85-86.

Ulich, E. et al. *Neue Formen der Arbeitsgestaltung—Möglichkeiten und Probleme einer Verbesserung der Qualität des Arbeitslebens.* Frankfurt, 1973.

Vaessen, J.A.M.F. *Musea in een museale cultuur.* Zeist, 1986.

Veblen, Thorstein. *The Engineers and the Price System.* New York: B.W. Huebsch, 1921.

WVC 1985. Ministrie van Welzijn Volksgezondheid en Cultuur. Brief over het cultuurbeleid, toegezonden aan de Tweede Kamer. 15 May 1985.

Wahren, H.K. *Zwischenmenschliche Kommunikation und Interaktion im Unternehmen.* Berlin/New York, 1987.

"Warning: Anti-Smoking Crusade Dangerous to Your Rights." *Workers Vanguard* (20 May 1988), Excerpted in *Harper's* (September 1988): 20-21.

Weaver, Paul. "Regulation, Social Policy, and Class Conflict." *The Public Interest.* 50 (Winter 1978).

Weber, Max. *Economy and Society*. Edited by Guenther Roth and
   Claus Wittich. Translated by Ephraim Fischoff et al. New York:
   Bedminster Press, 1968.
Wiener, Martin J. *English Culture and the Decline of the Industrial
   Spirit 1850-1980*. Cambridge: Cambridge University Press, 1981.
Wijmans, L.L. *Beeld en betekenis van het maatschappelijk midden.
   Oude en nieuwe middengroepen 185 to heden*. Amsterdam, 1987.
Wilterdink, N. "Gouldner's Nieuw Klasse." *Amsterdams Sociologisch
   Tijdschrift* 7 (December 1980): 316-38.
Wolfe, Tom. *The Bonfire of the Vanities*. New York and London:
   Bantam Books, 1987.
Wolfe, Tom. "Money Fever: A Look at American Society." Southern
   Methodist University, Distinguished Lecture Series, April 17, 1990
   (unpublished).
Wright, Robin. *The Day the Pigs Refused to be Driven to Market*.
   London: Hart Davis and McGibbon, 1972.
Wuthnow, Robert. *The Restructuring of American Religion*. Princeton:
   Princeton University Press, 1988.
Ziegler, J.W. "Leadership and the Individual Artist." *Management for
   the Arts* (1986) 1,3.
Zijderveld, A.C. *Steden zonder stedelijkheid*. Deventer, 1983.
Zijderveld, A.C. *Bedrijfscultuur. Fantoom en feit*. SMO-Informatief
   88-5. 's-Gravenhage, 1988.

Contributors

PETER L. BERGER is University Professor of Religion and Sociology and director of the Institute for the Study of Economic Culture at Boston University. His many books include *Invitation to Sociology* (Doubleday, New York), *The Social Construction of Reality* (with Thomas Luckmann; Doubleday, New York), and *The Capitalist Revolution* (Basic Books, New York).

ANTON M. BEVERS spent 1979 to 1986 in the civil service at the Department of Cultural Affairs, The Hague. From 1986 to 1990 he was associate professor of sociology at Tilburg University, and is at present professor of sociology of art at Erasmus University in Rotterdam. He has published in the fields of sociology of culture and art.

TRACY FESSENDEN is a Ph.D. candidate in theology, ethics, and culture at the University of Virginia. Her dissertation is on biological essentialism and national identity in Anglo-American social fiction.

FRANK W. HEUBERGER is research associate at the Institute for the Study of Economic Culture and assistant professor of sociology at Boston University. He has published on modernity and sociological methodology. Forthcoming is his book *Problemlösendes Handeln* (Campus, Frankfurt/New York).

JAMES DAVISON HUNTER is professor of sociology and religious studies at the University of Virginia. He has published six books, including the forthcoming *Culture Wars: The Struggle to Define America* (Basic Books, New York) and *Evangelicalism: The Coming Generation* (Chicago).

PAOLO JEDLOWSKI teaches sociology at the University of Calabria (Italy) and has researched and published in the fields of sociology of knowledge and theories of modernity. His publications include *Il tempo dell' esperienza* (Angeli, Milano), and *Memoria, esperienza e modernitá* (Angeli, Milano).

HANSFRIED KELLNER is professor of sociology at the Johann Wolfgang Goethe University in Frankfurt. His publications include *The Homeless Mind* (with Peter L. Berger and Brigitte Berger; Random House, New York) and *Sociology Reinterpreted* (with Peter L. Berger; Doubleday, New York).

BERNICE MARTIN is emeritus reader in sociology in the University of London. Her main publications have been in the fields of the sociology of religion and the sociology of culture, notably *A Sociology of Contemporary Cultural Change* (Blackwell, Oxford, 1981).

ANTON C. ZIJDERVELD has taught at Wagner College in New York, Concordia University in Montreal, Tilburg University, and, at present, Erasmus University Rotterdam, where he is professor of sociology. His publications include *The Abstract Society* (Doubleday, New York) and *On Clichés: The Supersedure of Meaning by Function in Modernity* (Routledge & Kegan Paul, London).

Index